英訳付

仏像鑑賞ガイド

A Guide to Japanese Buddhist Sculpture

監修
副島　弘道
Supervisor
Hiromichi Soejima

英訳版監修
フェリス・フィッシャー
English language editorial supervisor
Felice Fischer

池田書店

はじめに
Foreword

仏像が好きですか?

仏像が好きですか? そう聞かれて、「いいえ」と答える人は少ないものです。誰もが仏像の魅力に気づいています。

日本中、どこに旅しても、時を経た古い仏像があります。そのどれもが、歴史や文化の大切な証人であるばかりか、なかには高い芸術性を持つものもあります。

仏像の魅力はつきることがありません。よく知っている仏像にも、新しい見方や、気づかなかったエピソードがあるものです。まして、これまで会ったことのない仏像を訪ねることは、心が躍るような体験です。

この本には、仏像に親しむためのいくつかの背景と、今回新たに選んだ訪ねたい日本の仏像トップ30を、たくさんの写真や役に立つ情報や新鮮な見方とともに紹介しました。ここには国宝の仏像の約四分の一を収めています。

手にとって、開いたページの仏像にひきつけられたら、この本を手にして、ぜひ、その仏像に会いに行ってください。仏像、人々、そして自分との、新しい出会いがきっと始まることでしょう。

監修者　副島弘道
(大正大学文学部教授)

Do you like Buddhist sculpture?

Do you like Buddhist sculpture? When asked this question, few people would answer "no."

Everyone is aware of the fascination of Buddhist sculpture. Wherever one travels in Japan, there are the eternal, ancient Buddhist sculptures. Each one of them is an important witness to Japan's history and culture, and among them are some of high artistic quality.

The fascination of Buddhist sculpture is never-ending. There are new viewpoints and undiscovered episodes relating even to statues that one knows well. Moreover, encountering sculptures one has never seen before is an experience that can make one's heart dance for joy.

This guide includes some background knowledge to help to make Buddhist images more accessible, and features a new selection of Japan's top 30 sculptures with many photographs and illustrations, as well as useful information and new viewpoints. Nearly one quarter of the Buddhist sculptures designated National Treasures are included.

If you pick up this book and become fascinated by the Buddhist sculpture on the page open before you, by all means please take this guide with you and go visit the image in person. It will no doubt lead to new encounters with Buddhist sculptures, with other people, and then with yourself.

Hiromichi Soejima
Supervisor
Professor, Faculty of Literature, Taisho University.

The Buddhist Sculpture of Japan

The first-time visitor to Japan might not have Buddhist sculpture at the top of his "must see" list. But, to take a tour of the ancient temple sites where these statues are enshrined, is to take a tour through the history of Japanese art and culture. Usually their setting is in tree-lined compounds, away from the urban bustle, which offer a place where one can still imagine what it might have been like one hundred or even one thousand years before. If one takes some time to look carefully, the rewards of discovering some of the most ancient and beautiful statuary in the world will be great. From the naturalistic images of the eighth-century mourners of *Hōryū-ji* temple's pagoda in Nara, to the exquisite elegance of the eleventh-century Heian period Amida Buddha surrounded by a host of bodhisattvas riding on clouds at the Phoenix Hall of *Byōdō-in* by River Uji, to the fearsome realism of Unkei's South Gate Guardians of 1203 at *Tōdai-ji*, the panorama of creative possibilities explored by the master sculptors of Japan is open to view.

This guide to Buddhist sculpture includes thirty works that have been designated as National Treasures or Important Cultural Properties by the government of Japan. The materials the artisans used are many, from gilt bronze, to clay, to lacquer, and most frequently, the many fine woods available in Japan, such as camphor, nutmeg, and Japanese cypress. The craftsmanship is outstanding for its vitality and attention to detail. The Western visitor can admire these works for their esthetic qualities, but seeing them in their temple settings also conveys the deep religious awe and devotion of the sculptors and the worshippers.

We hope this volume will help to communicate the richness of Japan's Buddhist sculptural heritage.

Felice Fischer
English language editorial supervisor
Curator of East Asian Art, Philadelphia Museum of Art.

日本の仏像

はじめて日本を訪れる外国の旅行者にとって、仏像が観光リストのトップにあがることはないかもしれません。しかし、仏像が置かれた古い日本の寺院を訪れることは、日本の文化と美術の歴史を旅することと同じ意味を持っています。木々に囲まれた、都会の雑踏を離れた古寺を訪ねれば、そこでは、百年どころか千年以上も昔のようすを、今もなお想像することができます。よく見れば、世界でも有数の古代の美しい彫刻がそこに存在していることに気がつくでしょう。奈良時代8世紀の法隆寺五重塔塑像の哀しみにくれる僧形像の自然な表現から、雲中供養菩薩像に囲まれた平安時代11世紀の宇治平等院鳳凰堂の阿弥陀如来像の優雅な上品さ、そして鎌倉時代1203年の運慶作東大寺南大門仁王像のもつ怖いほどの写実にいたるまで、日本の名匠たちの創造力が生んだ光景が眼の前に広がっています。

本書には国宝・重要文化財に指定された仏像が数多く収められています。日本の仏像の材質は、金銅仏、塑像、乾漆像、木彫像と多岐におよんでいますが、クス、カヤ、ヒノキなどの良質の木材で作られた木彫像が中心です。生命力にみちた細部にまでわたる日本の仏像の彫刻技術の優秀さは特筆されます。欧米からの訪問者は日本の仏像の高い芸術性に驚くとともに、そこに示された仏師や信者の深い信仰心にも同時に気がつくことでしょう。

本書が日本の仏像の豊かさを伝える一助となれば幸いです。

英訳版監修者　フェリス・フィッシャー
（フィラデルフィア美術館東洋美術部部長）

もくじ Contents

はじめに ……… 2
本書の見方 ……… 6

第1章 仏像の背景

Background 1 仏塔から仏像へ ……… 8
Background 2 日本の仏像の発展 ……… 12
Background 3 如来、菩薩、明王、天 ……… 18
Background 4 仏像の特徴 ……… 22
Background 5 仏像の作り方 ……… 30
Background Extra 仏像拝観の作法 ……… 36

第2章 各地の仏像を訪ねる

Area 1 奈良の仏像 ……… 38
止利作釈迦三尊像 ……… 法隆寺 40
観音菩薩立像（救世観音） ……… 法隆寺 42
塔本四面具 ……… 法隆寺 44
薬師三尊像 ……… 薬師寺 46
阿修羅像（八部衆像） ……… 興福寺 48
康慶作不空羂索観音坐像 ……… 興福寺 50
運慶等作無著菩薩立像、世親菩薩立像 ……… 興福寺 52
不空羂索観音立像 ……… 東大寺 54
四天王立像（広目天） ……… 東大寺 56
盧舎那仏坐像（奈良の大仏） ……… 東大寺 58
運慶・快慶等作金剛力士立像 ……… 東大寺 60
盧舎那仏坐像 ……… 唐招提寺 62
千手観音立像 ……… 唐招提寺 64
十一面観音立像 ……… 法華寺 66
薬師如来坐像 ……… 新薬師寺 68
運慶作大日如来坐像 ……… 円成寺 70
十一面観音立像 ……… 奈良国立博物館 72
■寺院ガイド／奈良 ……… 74

Area 2 京都の仏像 ……… 78
弥勒菩薩半跏像（宝冠弥勒） ……… 広隆寺 80
降三世明王立像（五大明王像） ……… 東寺 82
薬師三尊像 ……… 醍醐寺 84
定朝作阿弥陀如来坐像 ……… 平等院 86
雲中供養菩薩像 ……… 平等院 88
九体阿弥陀如来坐像 ……… 浄瑠璃寺 90
■寺院ガイド／京都 ……… 92

Area 3 関東その他の仏像 ……… 94
摩耶夫人及び天人像 ……… 東京国立博物館 96
普賢菩薩騎象像 ……… 大倉集古館 98
阿弥陀如来坐像（鎌倉大仏） ……… 高徳院 100
金色堂諸尊像 ……… 中尊寺 102
運慶作毘沙門天立像 ……… 願成就院 104
快慶作阿弥陀三尊立像 ……… 浄土寺 106
馬頭観音立像 ……… 観世音寺 108
■寺院ガイド／関東その他 ……… 110

Foreword 2
How to use this Guide 6

Chapter 1 The Background of Buddhist Sculpture

Background 1 From Pagoda to Buddhist images 8
Background 2 Development of Japanese Buddhist sculpture 12
Background 3 Nyorai, Bosatsu, Myō-ō, Ten 18
Background 4 The Characteristics of Buddhist images 22
Background 5 Making Buddhist statues 30
Background Extra Etiquette when visiting Buddhist sculptures 36

Chapter 2 Visit to Japanese Buddhist Sculptures

Area 1 Nara

Buddhist sculpture in Nara 38
Shaka Triad 40
Standing Guze Kannon 42
Four Walls of a Pagoda 44
Yakushi Triad 46
Ashura 48
Seated Fukūkensaku Kannon 50
Mujaku and Seshin 52
Standing Fukūkensaku Kannon 54
Four Heavenly Kings 56
Seated Vairocana (the Great Buddha of Nara) 58
Two Guardian Kings (Vajrapani) 60
Seated Vairocana 62
Standing Thousand-armed Kannon 64
Standing Eleven-headed Kannon 66
Seated Yakushi Nyorai 68
Seated Dainichi Nyorai 70
Standing Eleven-headed Kannon 72
Temple Guide in Nara 74

Area 2 Kyoto

Buddhist sculpture in Kyoto 78
Seated Bodhisattva Maitreya 80
Standing Gōzanze Myō-ō 82
Yakushi Triad 84
Seated Amida Nyorai 86
Bodhisattva Riding on Clouds 88
Nine Seated Amida Nyorai 90
Temple Guide in Kyoto 92

Area 3 Kanto and other areas

Buddhist sculpture in Kanto and other areas 94
Lady Maya and Attendants 96
The Bodhisattva Fugen Riding on an Elephant 98
Seated Amida Nyorai (the Great Buddha of Kamakura) 100
Golden Hall and Buddhist Sculpture 102
Bishamon-ten (Vaisravana) 104
Standing Amida Triad 106
Standing Horse-headed Kannon 108
Temple Guide in Kanto and other areas 110

本　書　の　見　方

How to use this Guide

作られた年代　Period / date of production (of the sculpture)

像の名称　Title

仏像の解説　Commentary

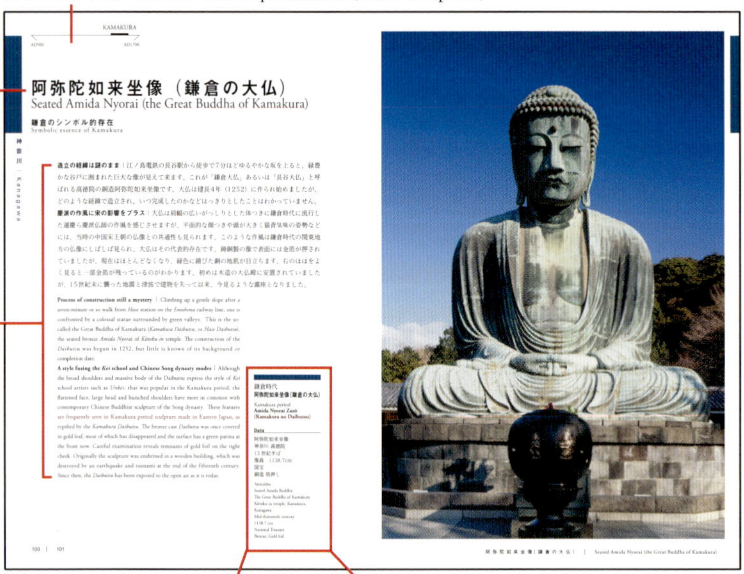

仏像のデータ　Database

日本語	データ例	English
作られた時代・名称 ローマ字表記	鎌倉時代 **阿弥陀如来坐像（鎌倉の大仏）** Kamakura period **Amida Nyorai Zazō (Kamakura no Daibutsu)**	Period of Production Title in Japanese
指定名称 所蔵者と安置場所 制作時期 像高 文化財指定 製作法、素材、技法など	**Data** 阿弥陀如来坐像 神奈川 高徳院 13 世紀半ば 像高　1138.7cm 国宝 銅造 箔押し Amitabha Seated Amida Buddha The Great Buddha of Kamakura Kōtoku-in temple, Kamakura, Kanagawa Mid-thirteenth century 1138.7 cm National Treasure Bronze, Gold foil	Formal (Sanskrit) name Collection (temple or museum) Date of production Height Designation as cultural property Materials and technique of production

●仏像名は文化財登録名称に準じていますが、一部は慣例による通称や略称を用いることがあります。また所蔵元の呼称と異なる場合もありますのでご了承ください。

●制作年代などにおける時代分類は日本美術史独特の分類であり、一般的な時代分類とは異なる場合があります。

●像高、制作年代などのデータは右記参考資料などを参照しました。古い年代の遺品など諸説あるものは、監修者の判断でより有力とされる説を採用しました。

[参考資料]「奈良六大寺大観」、「大和古寺大観」（岩波書店）、「仏教美術事典」（東京書籍）、「和英対照日本美術用語辞典」（東京美術）、「日本の国宝」（朝日新聞社）、「日本美術全集」（講談社）、「日本美術全集」（学習研究社）、「運慶　その人と芸術」副島弘道著（吉川弘文館）、「仏像に会いに行こう一美術の見かた・感じかた」副島弘道著（東京美術）

[写真提供]（登場順、敬称略、略称）奈良国立博物館（薬師寺観音菩薩立像、中宮寺菩薩半跏像、東大寺伝日光菩薩像、東京国立博物館蔵摩耶夫人及天人像、円成寺大日如来坐像、奈良国立博物館十一面観音立像）、amanaimages（第 1 ストゥーパ：©Adam Woolfit / Robert Harding World Imagery / Corbis / amanaimages、同：©WEST SIDE / SEBUN PHOTO / amanamages、高徳院阿弥陀如来坐像：©HIROSHI HARADA / SEBUN PHOTO / amanaimages、同：©MINORU KIZAKI / SEBUN PHOTO / amanaimages）、飛鳥園（法隆寺五重塔、飛鳥寺釈迦如来坐像、薬師寺日光菩薩像、東大寺金剛力士立像、東大寺広目天立像、興福寺八部衆立像、法隆寺釈迦三尊像、法隆寺金堂及び五重塔、東大寺大仏殿、興福寺北円堂、法隆寺救世観音立像、薬師寺薬師三尊像、興福寺不空羂索観音坐像、興福寺無著菩薩立像、興福寺世親菩薩立像、東大寺不空羂索観音立像、東大寺盧舎那仏坐像、唐招提寺盧舎那仏坐像、唐招提寺千手観音立像）、新薬師寺（本堂内部）、便利堂（東寺講堂内部、東寺持国天立像、法界寺阿弥陀如来坐像、法隆寺塔本四面具、平等院、東寺講堂、広隆寺弥勒菩薩半跏像、東寺降三世明王立像、醍醐寺薬師三尊像、浄土寺阿弥陀三尊立像、観世音寺馬頭観音立像）、鹿鳴荘（法華寺十一面観音立像）、中敦志（浄瑠璃寺九体阿弥陀如来坐像）、大倉集古館（普賢菩薩騎象像）、中尊寺、副島弘道（願成就院毘沙門天立像）

第 1 章
仏像の背景

Chapter 1
The Background of Buddhist Sculpture

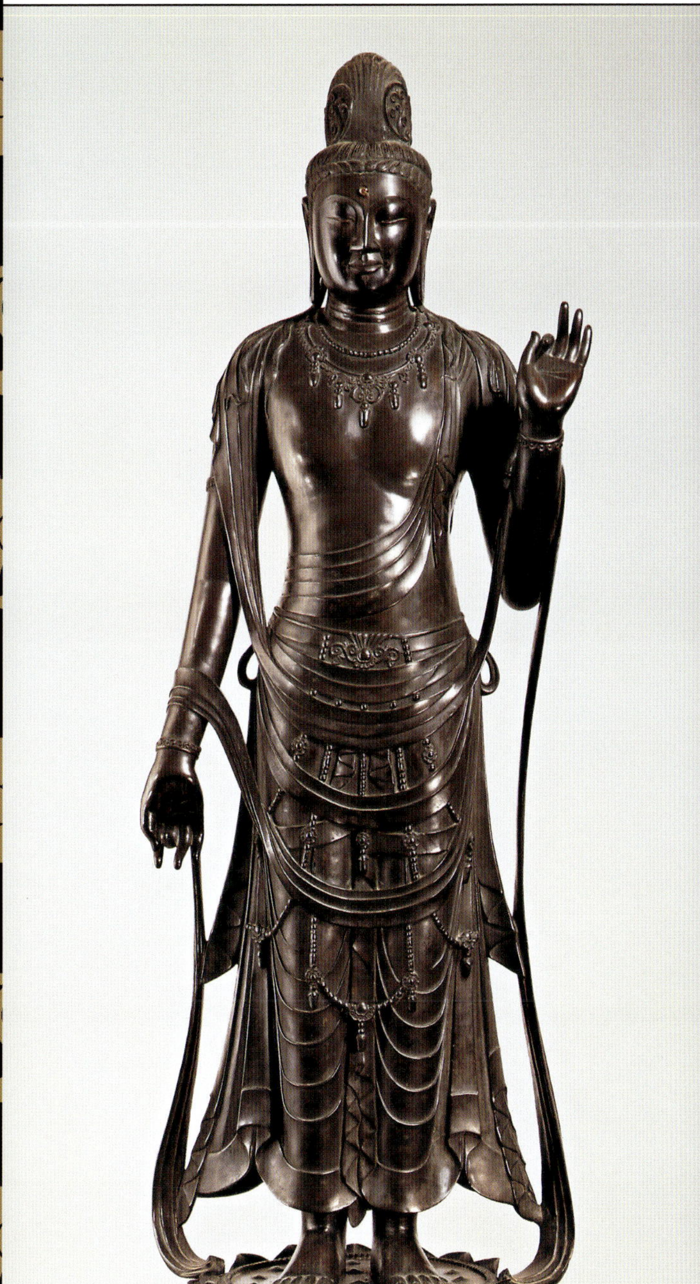

観音菩薩立像（聖観音）奈良 薬師寺
Standing Kannon (Shō Kannon), Yakushi-ji temple, Nara

※写真は本体のみ

Background　From Pagoda to Buddhist images

1　仏塔から仏像へ

仏像誕生以前の崇拝対象

仏教は紀元前5世紀頃、インドとネパールの国境近くにあった小国カピラヴァストゥで生を受けたゴータマ・シッダールタ（釈迦）によって開かれました。その後、紀元前3世紀には仏教はインド全域に広まりましたが、ふしぎなことに釈迦の死後数百年のあいだは仏像が作られることはありませんでした。それは悟りを開いてのち仏陀となった釈迦を、目に見える偶像としてあらわすことが不謹慎だと考えられたことが背景にあるようです。

当時の仏教徒たちは、迷いを倒すといわれる円盤形の武器である法輪や、釈迦がその樹下で悟りを開いたとされる菩提樹、釈迦の足跡を刻んだ仏足石などを釈迦のシンボルとして礼拝しました。

また、仏舎利（釈迦の遺骨）を釈迦の分身として信仰し、それを納めた塔であるストゥーパ（卒塔婆）がインド各地に建てられるようになりました。中国や日本の仏教寺院の塔も、もともと仏舎利を納めるための施設です。ちなみに、奈良県法隆寺などの五重塔の塔内には、仏舎利が納められています。

しかし、信仰の広まりとともに、より具体的でわかりやすい釈迦の姿が求められるようになりました。紀元1世紀末頃になると、西北インド（現在のパキスタン北西部）のガンダーラと、北インドのマツラーの地で仏像が作られ始めました。ここから仏像の歴史が始まったのです。

アショーカ王の第1ストゥーパ　インド
The first stupa of the king Ashoka, India

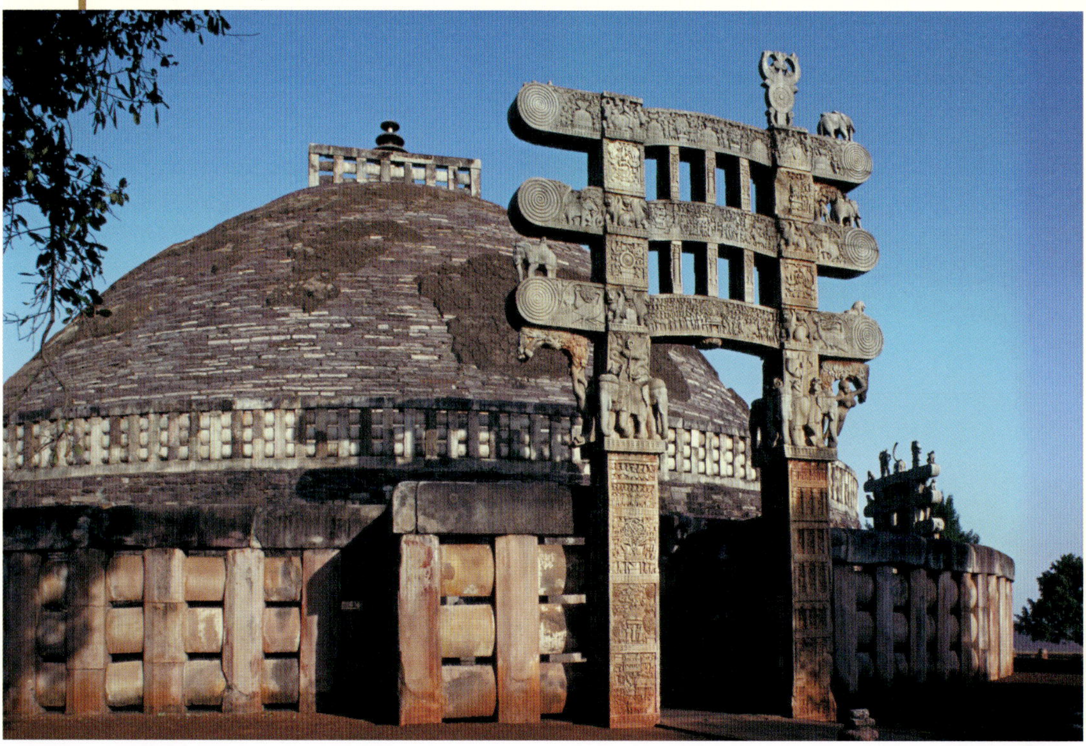

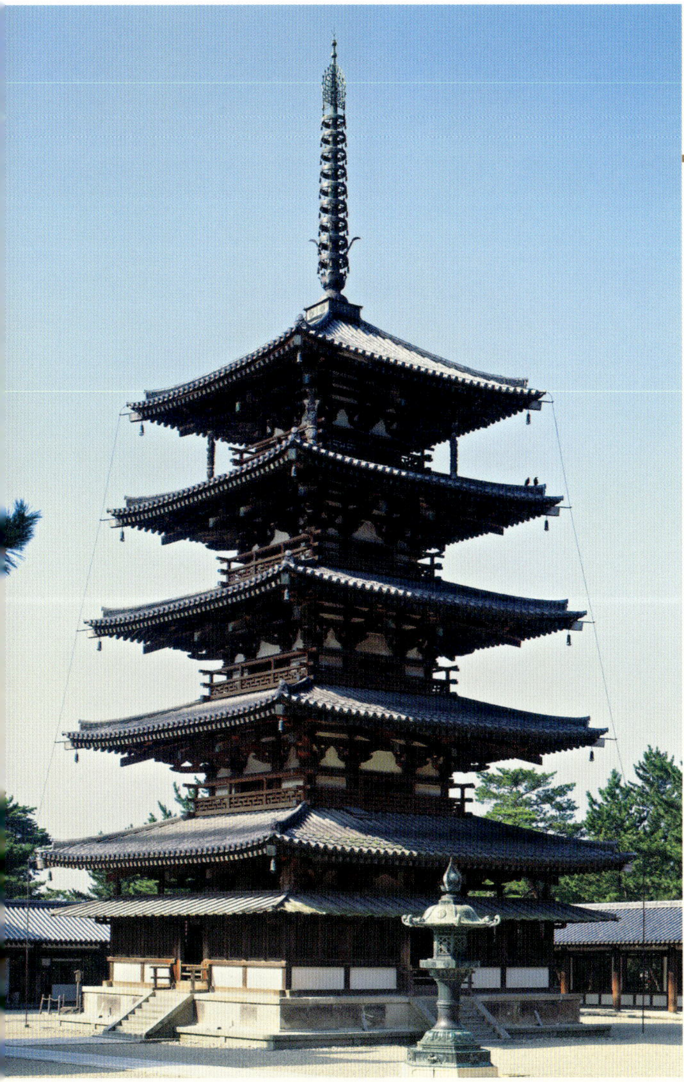

五重塔 奈良 法隆寺
Five-story Pagoda (Gojū no tō), Hōryū-ji temple, Nara

第1ストゥーパのレリーフ
The relief of the first stupa

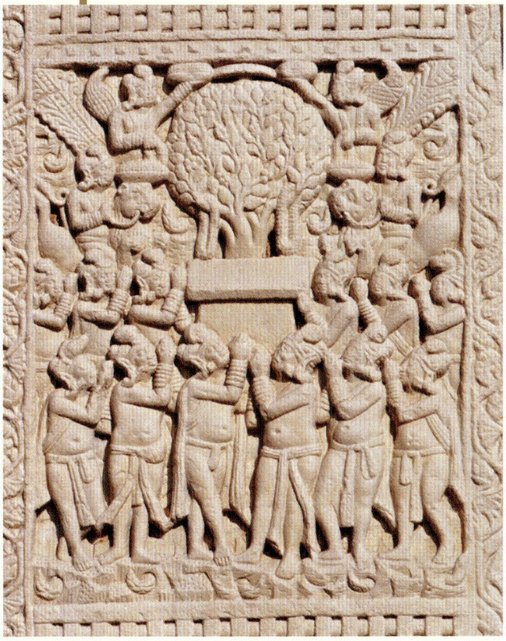

Objects of worship before Buddhist images

Buddhism was founded in the fifth century B.C., based on the teachings of Gautama Siddhartha (also known as *Shakamuni*), born in Kapilavastu, the capital of a small kingdom near the border between India and Nepal. By the third century B.C., Buddhism had spread throughout India. In the first few centuries after the death of *Shakamuni*, there were no Buddhist images made. This reflected the thinking dominant at that time that it was sacrilegious to make images of the enlightened *Shakamuni* Buddha.

Instead, adherents of Buddhism worshipped "the Wheel of the Law" (dharma-cakra in Sanskrit), a disk-shaped attribute that would open one's eyes to the Buddhist truth, the bodhi tree under which *Shakamuni* was believed to have attained enlightenment, or stones engraved with the Buddha's footprint (Buddhapada).

The Buddha's ashes were regarded as a symbolic representation of the Buddha, and after his death, the relics were distributed and housed in pagodas (stupas). The pagodas erected in temple compounds in China and Japan served the same purpose, with the five-story pagoda at *Hōryū-ji* temple in Nara being one example.

As Buddhist doctrine spread beyond the monastery to the larger population, representations of the Buddha in a more concrete and comprehensible form began to appear. The first image of the Buddha is believed to have been made in Gandhara (present-day province in northwest Pakistan) and in Mathura (now central northern India) in the first century A.D. This marked the beginning of Buddhist sculpture in Asia.

さまざまな仏像の誕生

悟りを得た釈迦の像（釈迦如来）だけではなく、次第にそれ以外の多くの種類の仏像も作られるようになりました。これは、仏教そのものの発展をもあらわしています。

修行によって自らの悟りや救いを得ることを目的とする、いわゆる「小乗仏教」に対して、自ら悟るとともに、あらゆる人々を悟らせ救済しようとする仏教の一派を、優れた乗り物にたとえて「大乗仏教」といいます。そうして、多くの人々を救うために、この世にあらわれた仏である釈迦の姿だけでなく、たくさんの仏たちが登場したのです。この教えを広めるために、釈迦の心のさまざまな側面を象徴する仏や、さまざまな役割を持った仏や菩薩などが数多く作られるようになりました。釈迦如来をはじめ、これら多くの仏像は、衆生を迷いの苦しみから救って悟りの世界に導く象徴であり、また、その案内役でもあったわけです。

また、仏教は、その広がりとともに、各地で古くから信仰されていた土着の神々を、仏の仲間として吸収していきました。たとえば仏教の成立以前からインド各地で信仰されていた神々は、仏教に取り入れられて、仏法の守護者として天（天部）という存在になりました。これが現在見られる四天王などです。

その後6～7世紀に、インドで仏教の一派として密教が盛んになると、そこでは五大明王像など密教特有の明王が作られました。この明王は、人々を畏怖させて従わせるという目的のために、多面多臂(複数の顔と腕を持つこと）の憤怒像などで表現されます。

本堂内部 奈良 新薬師寺
Main Hall (Hondō), interior, Shinyakushi-ji temple, Nara

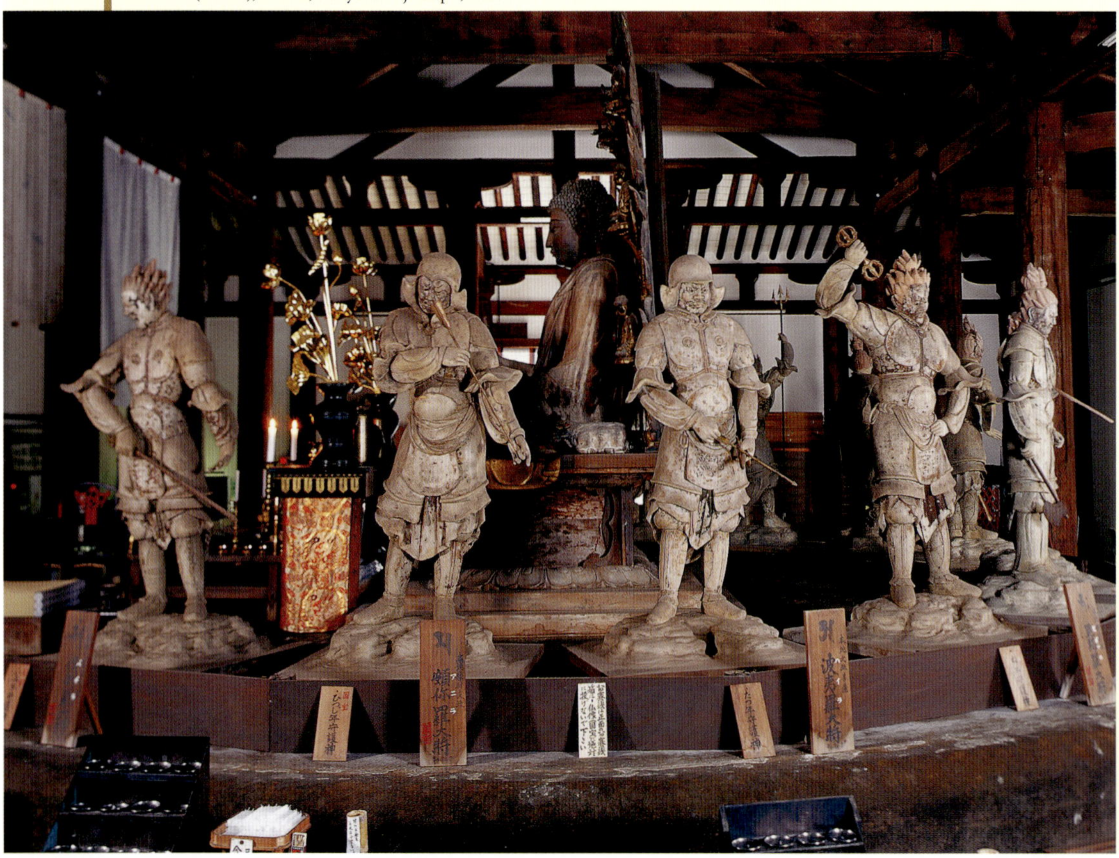

仏塔から仏像へ

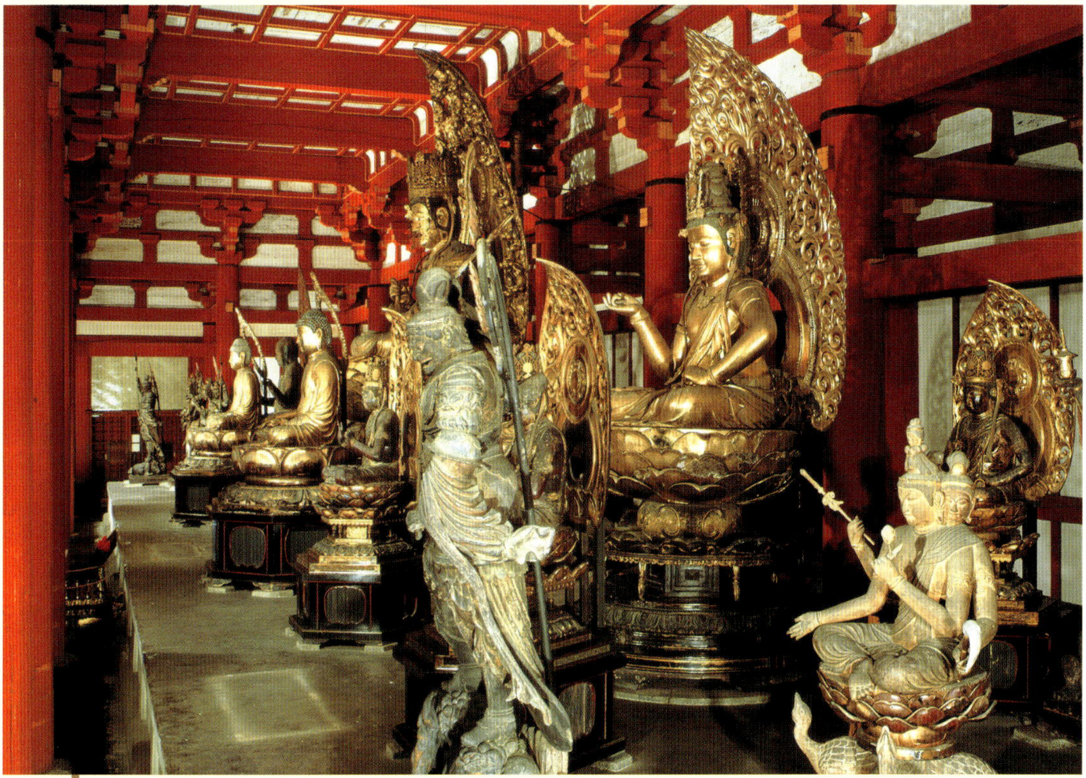

講堂内部 京都 東寺
Lecture Hall (Kōdō), interior, Tō-ji temple, Kyoto

Rise of multiplicity of Buddhist images

Soon there were sculptures not only of the historical *Shakamuni* after he attained enlightenment, called *Shaka Nyorai*, but a multiplicity of other Buddhist images was created. In part this reflects the developments in Buddhism itself.

The earlier form, known as Theravada ("Lesser Vehicle" [leading to enlightenment]), was focused on individual ascetic practice to attain salvation and enlightenment. The spread of Buddhism to the larger populace, who were unable to follow the monastic life, saw the rise of the Mahayana ("Greater Vehicle") doctrines, which emphasized the importance of working for the salvation of others as well as for one's own enlightenment. Besides the *Shaka Nyorai*, a multiplicity of Buddhist images symbolized the multiple paths open to the ordinary worshipper to attain salvation and enlightenment.

With its spread Buddhism absorbed local indigenous deities into the Buddhist pantheon. For example, in India the gods of Hinduism that pre-dated Buddhism were incorporated into Buddhism in the form of protective deities, manifested in Japanese forms such as the Four Heavenly Kings (*Shitennō*).

Furthermore, during the sixth and seventh centuries the Esoteric form of Buddhism became popular in India, bringing with it unique types of images, such as the Five Great Myō-ō (*Godai Myō-ō*), whose wrathful multi-headed, multi-armed manifestations must have struck worshippers with a sense of awe.

Background　Development of Japanese Buddhist sculpture

2 日本の仏像の発展

Background 2

日本の仏像の特徴

仏教は、インドからシルクロードを経て中国へ伝えられ、朝鮮半島を経由して、6世紀に日本へ伝えられました。アジア大陸諸地域の風俗習慣や文化の影響を受けながら、日本でも独自の発展を遂げました。日本の仏像制作者たちは、大陸で作られた仏像にさまざまな変化を加えて、日本人の感覚に合った、おだやかで上品な姿の仏像を生み出しました。また、繊細で優れた技術で作られた日本の仏像は、他の国の仏像には見られない緻密でていねいなできばえを示しています。

木彫像が多いのも、日本の仏像の特徴です。とくに平安時代以後（8世紀末以後）は、木彫像が中心になりました。

日本の仏像のもう一つの特色は、古代中世の古い時代の遺品が全国に数多く現存していることです。また、その多くが、今日でも寺院にまつられて実際に礼拝の対象とされていることも、他の国の彫刻と比べたときの大きな特徴です。

Characteristics of Buddha statues in Japan

Buddhism reached Japan in the sixth century through China and the Korean Peninsula via the Silk Road. Having changed styles and attributes under the influence of customs and cultures of various regions in the Asian continent, Buddhist sculpture (*Butsuzō*) followed an unique course of development after its arrival in Japan. With their sophisticated technique of construction, Japanese sculptors adapted the original continental styles and created imagery with a softer and more delicate appearance that met Japanese cultural taste.

In Japan, the most common material of Buddhist sculpture is wood, which became prevalent especially following the Heian period (the end of the eighth century). Many Buddhist statues from ancient and medieval times are still preserved at temples all over Japan and worshipped by Japanese people today.

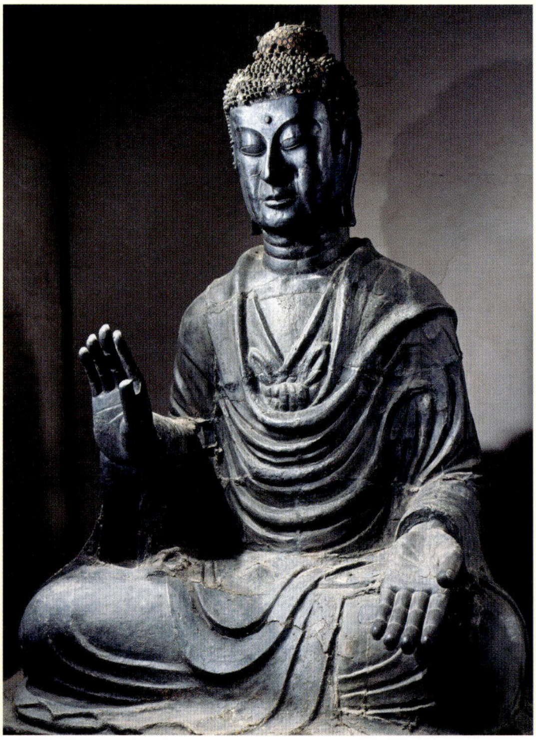

釈迦如来坐像（飛鳥大仏）奈良 飛鳥寺（安居院）
Seated Shaka Nyorai (Asuka Daibutsu), Asuka-dera temple (Ango-in temple), Nara

仏像の伝来
飛鳥時代の仏像（538年～709年）

飛鳥時代は、日本人が初めて大陸から伝わった仏像にふれ、その精巧さや造形力に驚いた時代です。この時代には、銅造で表面を鍍金（ときん）（金メッキ）した金銅仏と、クス材製の木彫が、仏像の素材の中心でした。623年に作られた奈良県法隆寺金堂銅造釈迦三尊像(→p.40)は、仏師鞍作止利（くらつくりのとり）によるもので、金銅仏の代表的作品です。木彫像の代表としては法隆寺夢殿救世観音像（→p.42）や奈良県中宮寺本堂菩薩半跏像などがあります。

飛鳥時代の仏像には、中国南北朝時代や朝鮮三国時代の仏像の影響が濃く、顔はまだ日本人離れして面長、鼻は高く、杏仁（きょうにん）形に見開いた眼をしています。アルカイックスマイル（古風な微笑み）という独特の表情が見られるのも飛鳥時代の仏像の特徴です。

The Arrival of Buddhist statues
Buddhist statues of the Asuka period (538~709 AD)

Japan was exposed to the sophisticated Buddhist culture of the Asian continent with the arrival of the first Buddhist statues in its history during the Asuka period. Gilt bronze statues (*Kondō Butsu*) and wood-carved statues (*Mokuchō-zō*) made of camphor wood were the primary forms of imagery during this period. The bronze Shaka Triad (→p.40) at the Golden Hall (*Kondō*) of *Hōryū-ji* temple in Nara, created by a famous sculptor *Kuratsukuri-no Tori* in 623, is one of the most prominent works of gilt bronze. *Guze Kannon* (→p.42) at *Yumedono* of *Hōryū-ji* temple and Seated Bodhisattva at Chūgū-ji temple in Nara are well-known examples of camphor wood carving.

Buddhist sculpture of the Asuka period developed under the strong cultural influence of Northern and Southern Dynasty China and the period of Three Kingdoms in Korea. They are characterised by un-Japanese facial features with a long faces, high noses and almond shaped large eyes as well as by the facial expression known as the 'archaic smile'.

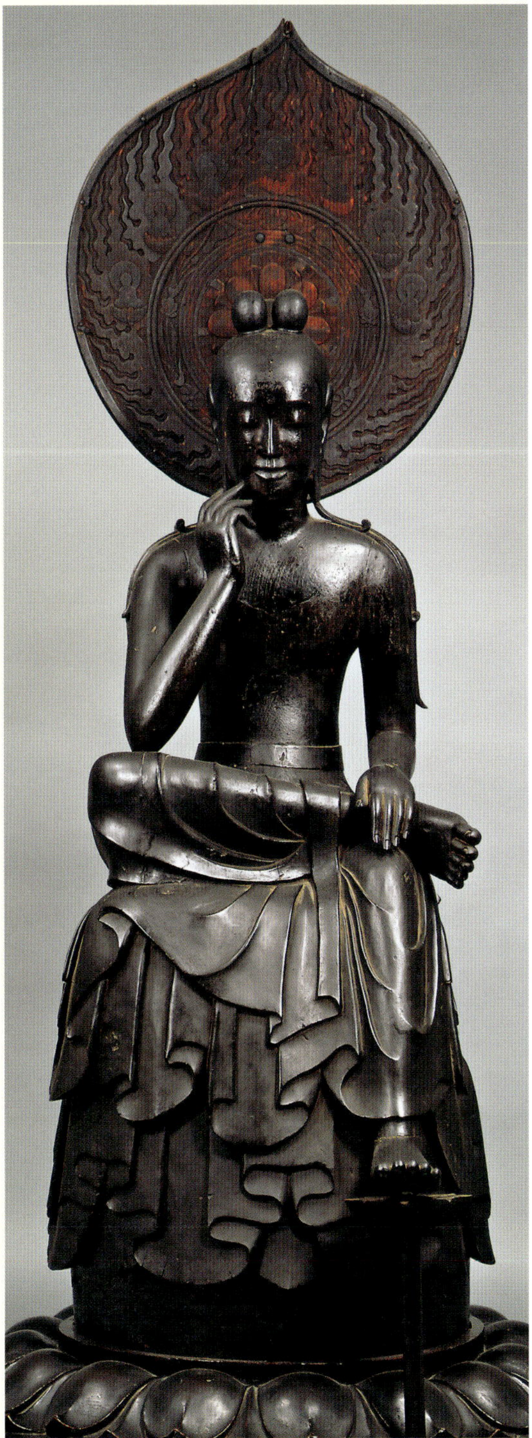

菩薩半跏像 奈良 中宮寺
Seated Bodhisattva, Chūgū-ji temple, Nara

古典的仏像の完成
奈良時代の仏像（710年〜783年）

710年に、都は奈良県の北部に位置する平城京に遷りました。奈良時代の始まりです。平城京には国営の寺院が数多く建てられ、優れた仏像が多く作られました。この時代は日本の仏像の古典時代ともいえます。

高い文化を誇った唐(中国)の彫刻の影響を受け、国際性を持ったスケールの大きな表現の仏像が作られました。奈良県薬師寺金堂銅造薬師三尊像（→p.46）はこの時代の初期の作品で、美しいプロポーションを持つ写実的な造形が特徴です。台座の装飾文様には、当時の大陸美術と共通する意匠が見られます。また、奈良県興福寺乾漆造八部衆像(→p.48)などには、人間らしさや親しみやすさがあらわされるようになりました。

奈良時代には、金銅仏に加えて、漆で布を固めて作る乾漆像や粘土を使った塑像などが作られ、制作技法の幅が広がりました。

Establishment of the classical style
Buddhist statues of the Nara period (710~783)

The Nara period began in 710 with the relocation of the capital to Heijō-kyō, located in northern part of present-day Nara prefecture. This period was marked by lavish court spending on temples, and many prominent Buddhist statues were created as a result. For this reason, the Nara period is often called the classical period of Japanese Buddhist sculpture.

During the Nara period, Japan was enamored of the sophisticated sculpture of the Tang Dynasty (China) and its continental outlook and large-scaled style predominated in Buddhist statues. The bronze Yakushi Triad(→p.46) of the Golden Hall (*Kondō*) at *Yakushi-ji* temple, created during the early phase of the period, is one of the most renowned statues, characterized by beautiful proportions and realistic delineation. The influence of the Tang Dynasty culture on this image is apparent in the decorative motifs on the pedestal.

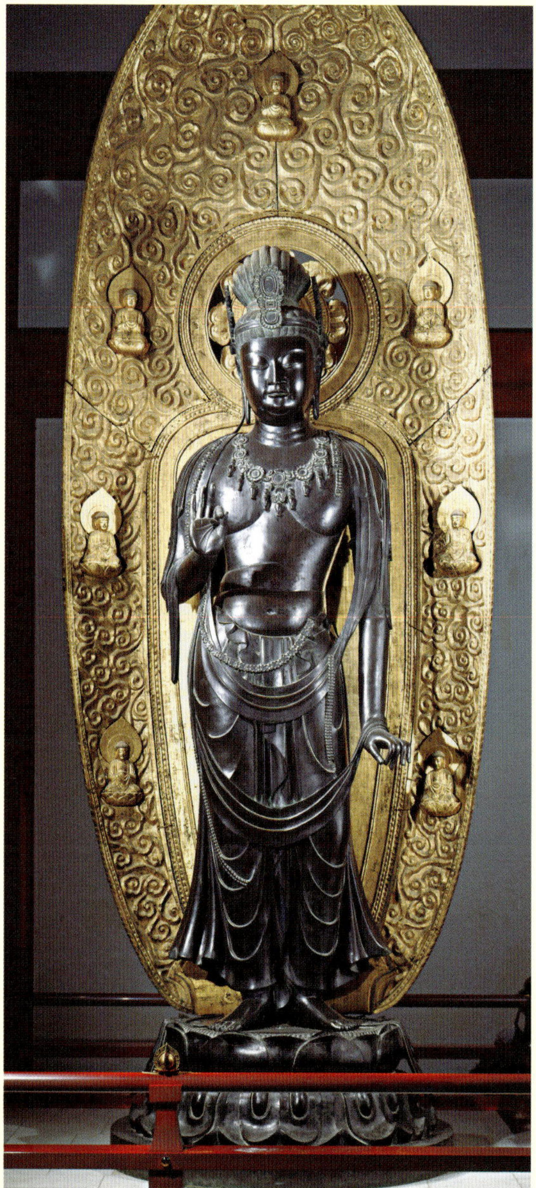

日光菩薩立像 奈良 薬師寺
Standing Nikkō Bodhisattva, Yakushi-ji temple, Nara

Humanness and the amiable facial expression, exemplified by the dry lacquer Eight Heavenly Beings (*Hachibushū* →p.48) of *Kōfuku-ji* temple in Nara, are also features prevalent in the images of this period.

In addition to gilt bronze, dry lacquer (hemp cloth soaked in lacquer applied to the surface), and clay were frequently used as materials, which widened the technical scope of sculptural production.

多彩な表現の仏像
平安時代前期の仏像(784年〜950年頃)

京都の平安京が政治の中心だった時代が平安時代です。この時代は約400年続きますが、仏像の歴史では、この時代を平安前期、後期の2つに分けて考えます。

平安前期は空海らが当時唐で流行していた仏教の新しい一派である密教を日本に伝えました。そして、密教に説かれる大日如来や多面多臂の五大明王像など、それまで知られていなかった新奇な仏像が作られはじめました。839年に作られた京都府東寺(教王護国寺)講堂の木彫諸尊はその代表作で、そこには、空海が考えた真言密教の原理が、まるで曼荼羅(まんだら)のようにあらわされています。東寺講堂の五大明王像や四天王像は憤怒を強調する、この時代独特の大胆な表現に特徴があります。また、大阪府観心寺如意輪観音像や奈良県法華寺十一面観音立像(→p.66)のように、大きな眼や長い髪が印象的な個性の強い仏像もたくさん作られました。これもこの時代の特徴です。

仏像の素材はそれまでの金銅仏や乾漆像に代わり木彫像が主流になります。木彫像には、表面をそのまま仕上げた素木(しらき)像、ていねいに彩られた彩色(さいしき)像や金色に輝く漆箔(しっぱく)像など、変化に富んだ仕上げ法が見られます。

Multiplicity of Buddhist images
Buddhist statues of the Early Heian period (784~950)

From the perspective of the history of Buddhist statues, the Heian period, during which *Heian-kyō* had been the political capital of Japan for four hundred years, can be divided into two phases.

The first phase of the Heian period is marked by the influence of Esoteric Buddhism (*Mikkyō*), which was prevalent in the Tang Dynasty and brought to Japan by the monks such as *Kūkai*. Various images of deities unique to esoteric Buddhism, including *Dainichi Nyorai* and the Five Great Myō-ō (*Godai Myō-ō*) who are multi-headed and multi-armed, were created during this period. Wooden sculptures (*Mokuchō Shoson*) at lecture hall (*Kōdō*) of *Tō-ji* temple in Kyoto, made in 839, is one of the best known example of such works. The wooden images of the deities represent the principles of the *Shingon* sect, founded by *Kūkai*, and depict the Buddhist world view as in the Mandalas. Among them, the bold expression and fierce outlook, that can be seen in the statues of the Five Great Myō-ō and the Four Heavenly Kings, are characteristics of the images created in this period. Also unique to the first phase of the Heian period are the statues with large eyes and long hair, which are apparent in *Nyoirin Kannon* at *Kanshin-ji* temple in Osaka, as well as the Eleven-headed Kannon (*Jūichimen Kannon* →p.66) at *Hokke-ji* temple in Nara.

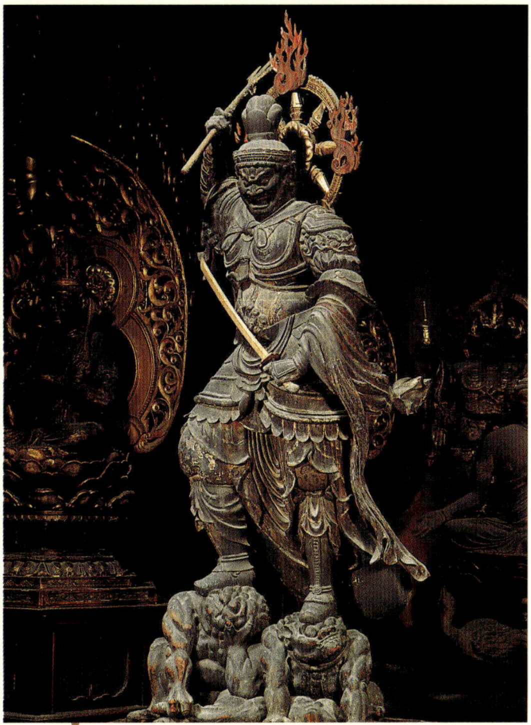

四天王立像(持国天)京都 東寺 講堂
Four Heavenly Kings (Jikoku-ten), Kōdō, Tō-ji temple, Kyoto

By this time, wood replaced gilt bronze and dry lacquer, and became the primary material of Buddhist statues. The variety of wooden images included natural wood (*shiraki*) statues, without any type of coating, painted (*saishiki*) statues, and statues that had applied gold foil on the surface (*shippaku*).

「和様彫刻」の完成
平安時代後期の仏像(950年頃〜1179年)

この時代には貴族文化が成熟し、社会のさまざまな面で、大陸文化からの影響を脱した日本的な文化が生まれました。仏像にも、日本人の容姿を写したような、丸顔で伏し目、鼻も低く、口は小さいおだやかな表現の仏像が作られるようになりました。1053年、仏師定朝作の京都府平等院鳳凰堂の阿弥陀如来坐像（→p.86）は平安時代後期の代表作です。そこに見られるいかにも日本的な姿の仏像は、作者の名をとって「定朝様」とも、また日本風という意味をあらわす「和様」とも呼ばれ、貴族たちに好まれて、全国で類似した仏像が流行しました。

この時代は仏法が力を失い世が乱れる「末法の時代」とされ、貴族たちは、極楽へ行くための善行として多くの仏像を作らせました。多くの仏像を短期間で作るためもあって、この時代には「寄木造」が発展しました。これは、細かい材木を規則的に組み合わせて大きい像を作る日本独自の合理的な木彫技法で、この後の仏像制作の基本技法となりました。

また、この時代には定朝をはじめ有力仏師たちの名が多く知られるようになりました。彼らは大勢の弟子を率いて、朝廷や貴族たちの建てる大寺院の造仏を数多く行いました。

Development of Japanese style Buddhist images
Buddhist statues of the late Heian period (950~1179)

The latter half of the Heian period saw the development of a new Japanese culture in many aspects of the society, reflecting the decline of influence from the Asian continent. Buddhist statues created during this period were affected by these changes, and came to have more Japanese-like facial features with round faces, downcast eyes, flat nose, small mouth and softness of expression. The *Amida Nyorai* image (→p.86) of Phoenix Hall (*Hō-ō-dō*) at the *Byōdō-in* in Kyoto is one of the most prominent examples, created by a sculptor *Jōchō* in 1053.

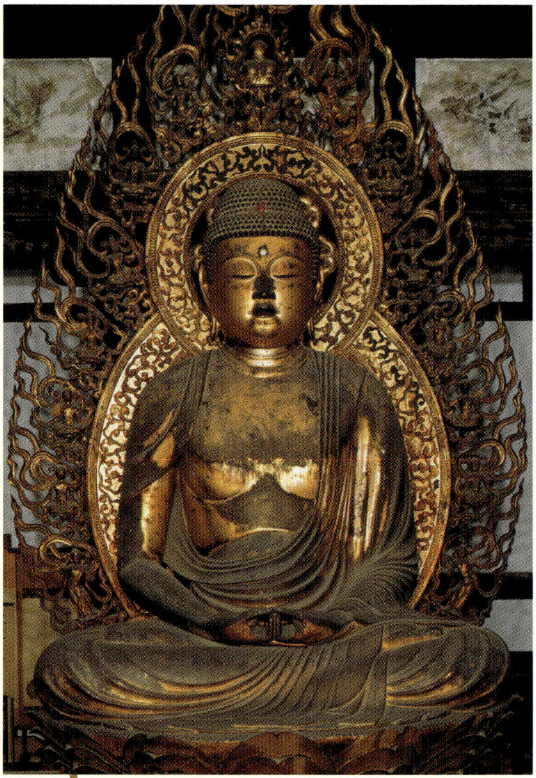

阿弥陀如来坐像 京都 法界寺
Seated Amida Nyorai, Hōkai-ji temple, Kyoto

Buddhist statues with similar features were called '*Jōchōyō* style', named after the sculptor, or '*Wayō* style' - meaning Japanese style - and became popular all over the country, especially among the aristocracy of the time.

This period was considered by people as the age of the "latter days of the law" (*Mappō*), when the power of the laws and truths of Buddha (*Buppō*) declined and led to a time of turmoil. Such a belief served as an important stimulus for the sponsorship of many Buddhist statues by aristocrats, who sought to accomplish good deeds in order to ensure their places in Pure Land Paradise (*gokuraku*) after death. The technique of joined wood construction (*yosegi-zukuri*) was developed in this period, partly due to the need for producing a large number of images within a short time. *Yosegi-zukuri* was a technique used to make the main part of a wooden statue out of two or more segments of wood, and became the prevailing method unique to Japan.

The late Heian period produced many prominent sculptors (*busshi*) including *Jōchō*, who undertook construction of Buddhist statues at large temples commissioned by the Imperial court and aristocrats.

生動感にみちた力強さ
鎌倉時代の仏像
（1180年～1333年）

鎌倉時代はそれまでの貴族に代わって武家が政権を担うようになりました。仏像も、それまでの貴族好みの仏像に代わり、躍動的で力強い表現の仏像が好まれました。

この時代を代表する仏師が運慶（うんけい）です。運慶が指揮をとって、一門の仏師たちを率いて1203年に制作した奈良県東大寺南大門の金剛力士立像（仁王像→p.60）は、高さ８メートルを越す巨像で、鎌倉時代を代表する傑作です。

この時代の仏像の容姿は変化に富み、また、水晶製の眼球をはめ込む「玉眼（ぎょくがん）」と呼ばれる新技法などを盛んに採用して、リアリズムや人間くささが見られることにも特色があります。

室町時代以後も仏像はたくさん作られました。しかし、次第に過去の時代の仏像を踏襲することが目立つようになり、それまでの仏像のように創造性に富んだ傑出した作品は少なくなりました。

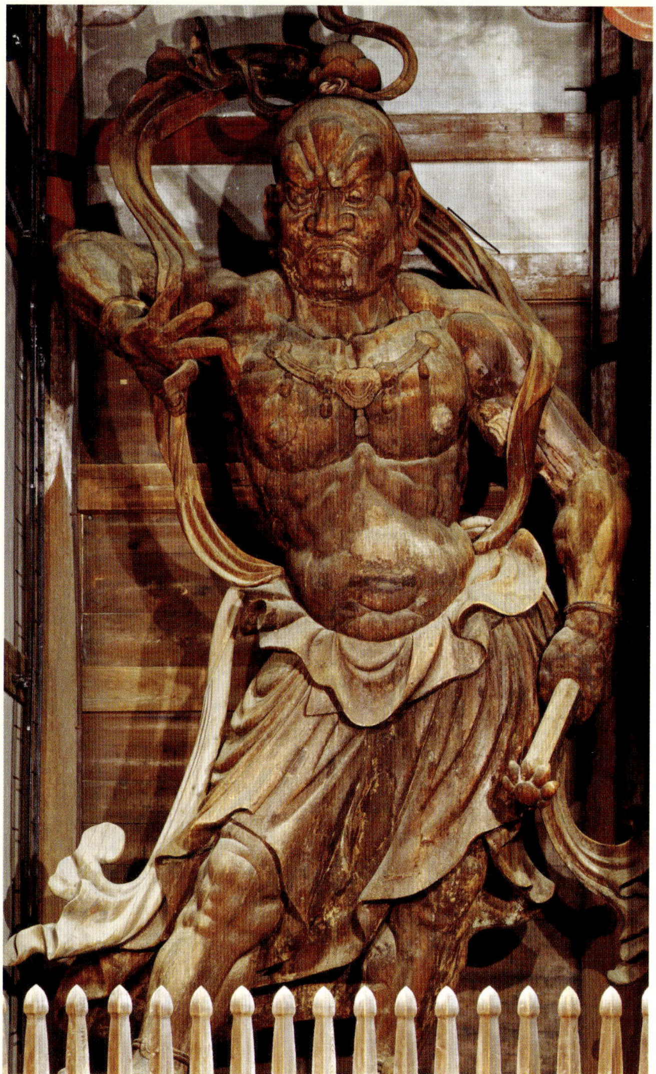

金剛力士立像 奈良 東大寺 南大門
Standing Guardian King, Great South Gate, Tōdai-ji temple, Nara

Realism and dynamism Buddhist statues of the Kamakura period (1180~1333)

Reflecting the nature of the military government, which seized political power from the aristocracy, Buddhist statues of this period are characterised by their dynamic and energetic expression.

Unkei is one of the most prominent Buddhist sculptors of the time who produced the statue of Two Guardian Kings (*Kongō Rikishi* →p.60) standing in *Tōdai-ji's* Great South Gate (*Nandai-mon*). Created in 1203, this 8 meters tall image is considered to be a masterwork of the period.

Sculptures from this period vary widely, and a number of new techniques were also applied to produce a realistic and human-like appearance, including *gyokugan*, eyes made of crystal that were inserted into the head of statues.

While an equally large number of sculptures were produced during the subsequent Muromachi period, Buddhist statuary of this period was marked by the decline of creativity and artistry, with a focus on replicating the style of masterpieces from the past.

Background

Nyorai, Bosatsu, Myō-ō, Ten

3 如来、菩薩、明王、天

さまざまな仏

仏像には、仏陀となった釈迦をあらわしたものだけではなく、それ以外の様々な仏たちの姿をあらわしたものがあります。これら数多くの尊像は、如来、菩薩、明王、天の4種類に分かれます。それらは仏教の世界でそれぞれ違う役割を持ち、髪型や衣服、持ち物、印相(いんそう)(手のしぐさ)などの表現にも特徴があります。

Identifying a variety of Buddhist statues

Buddhist statues represent a large variety of deities besides the image of the enlightened *Shakamuni*. Most of these images can be classified into four categories, *Nyorai*, *Bosatsu*, *Myō-ō* and *Ten*. Each has its own characteristic hairstyle, garment, accessory and hand gesture (*insō*), with a particular role to play in the Buddhist teachings.

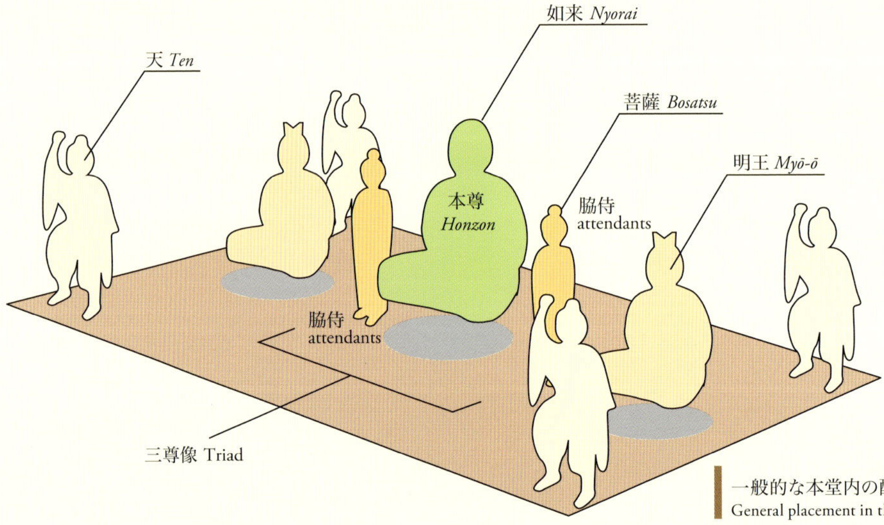

一般的な本堂内の配置
General placement in the Main Hall

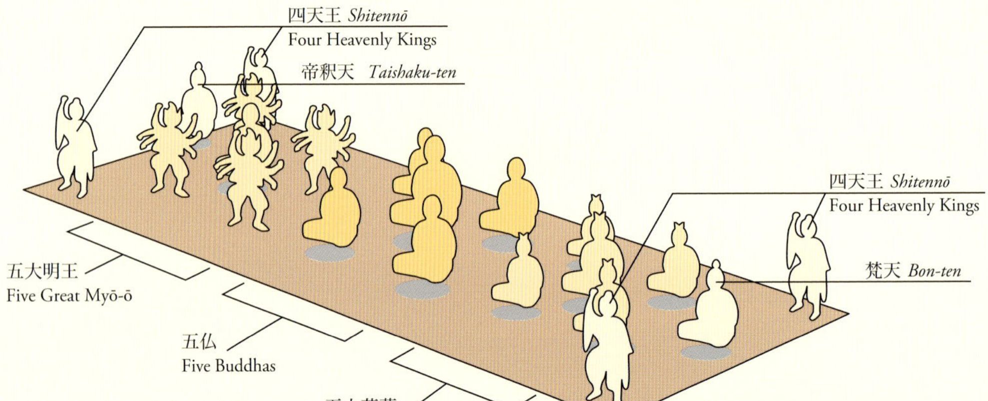

東寺立体曼荼羅の配置
The placement of the three-dimentional Mandala at Tō-ji temple

悟りをひらいた仏、如来

如来には釈迦如来、阿弥陀如来、薬師如来、盧舎那仏（るしゃなぶつ）、大日如来などがあります。

釈迦如来は、最初に悟りを開いた仏陀（釈迦）の姿をあらわした仏です。世俗の迷いを超越した釈迦は、宝冠や首飾りなどは捨て、1枚の粗末な衲衣（のうえ）を身に着けた姿にあらわされます。これが如来の姿の基本形です。

阿弥陀如来は、西方にある極楽浄土に住むとされる仏です。「南無阿弥陀仏」と唱えることで人々は極楽に往生できるとされています。

薬師如来は、現世での病の苦しみから救ってくれる仏です。左手にはその働きを象徴する薬壷（やっこ）を持つことがあります。

これらの如来を統率し、頂点にいると考えられた仏が盧舎那仏です。その光背（こうはい）には多数の化仏（けぶつ）（仏の化身）があらわされます。奈良県東大寺の大仏は盧舎那仏をあらわしたものです。

大日如来は、空海が平安時代前期に中国から伝えた真言宗の中心的な尊像です。宇宙全体の中心にいる最高の存在とされる、いわば観念的な存在の仏像です。この如来は他の如来とは違い、宝冠や首飾りを着け、菩薩のような姿をしています。

Nyorai – enlightened Buddha

The most commonly depicted *Nyorai* are *Shaka Nyorai, Amida Nyorai, Rushana Butsu, Dainichi Nyorai.*

Shaka Nyorai is the image of Buddha (*Shakamuni*) who was the first to attain true enlightenment. *Shaka Nyorai* is the basic form of *Nyorai* image, and is typically portrayed wearing simple robes without accessories or jewelry, symbolizing the historical Buddha's transcendence from worldly desires and suffering.

Amida Nyorai (Amitabha) presides over the Great Western Paradise (*Gokuraku Jōdo*) and rebirth in the Pure Land Paradise (*Gokuraku*) can be attained by faithfully reciting his name - '*namu amida butsu*' in Japanese.

Yakushi Nyorai (Bhaisajyaguru) is the Buddha of healing and medicine, and often holds a small jar of medicine in his left hand.

Rushana Butsu (Vairocana) is thought to be the central Buddha of universe, personficaton of the Buddhist doctrine (dharma). The halo (*kōhai*) is usually adorned with one hundred images of transformed Buddhas (*kebutsu*). The Great Buddha (*daibutsu*) enshrined in *Tōdai-ji* temple in Nara is one of the most prominent examples.

Dainichi Nyorai (Mahāvairocana) is the most important of all Buddhas in Japan's Esoteric Buddhist teachings, such as the *Shingon* sect, which was brought to Japan by *Kūkai*. *Dainichi Nyorai* is considered the supreme Buddha at the center of the universe of whom all other Buddhas are an aspect. He is typically depicted in the guise of *Bosatsu* (Bodhisattva) wearing a crown and jewels.

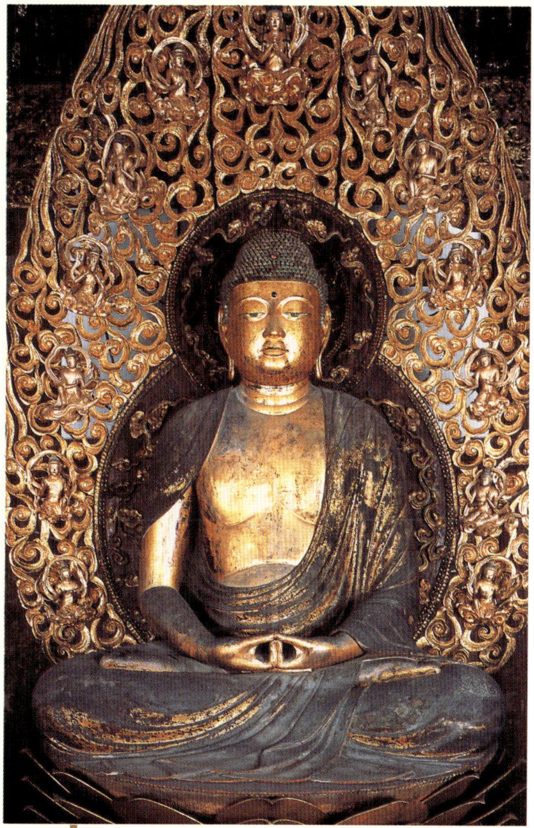

阿弥陀如来坐像 京都 平等院 鳳凰堂
Seated Amida Nyorai, Hō-ō-dō, Byōdō-in, Kyoto

悟りのために修行を続ける菩薩

菩薩とは菩提薩埵の略で、悟りを開いて如来になるために修行している仏です。菩薩は如来に続く地位にあり、如来を補佐する役目にあります。悟りを開く前の釈迦がモデルなので、古代インドの王族の姿をしています。冠や豪華な首飾り、腕輪などの装身具を身に付けています。左肩から斜めに条帛をかけ、腰には裙という巻きスカート、両肩に天衣という細長い衣をかけて足もとまで垂らしています。見る者に華麗で優美な印象を与えます。

菩薩の中でも特になじみがあるのが観音菩薩です。観音は人々の救いを求める声を聞き、慈悲をもって自在に救いの手を伸べる存在です。左手に水瓶や蓮華を持ち、冠の前に如来の化仏をあらわす姿が基本形で、これが聖観音と呼ばれます。この聖観音は、さらに多くの人々を救うために、十一面観音、千手観音というようにその姿を変化させます。それがいわゆる変化観音です。不空羂索観音、如意輪観音、馬頭観音なども変化観音の一種です。

菩薩にはこのほかにも、56億7千万年後に如来となってこの世に出現するという弥勒菩薩をはじめ、文殊菩薩、普賢菩薩、地蔵菩薩、虚空蔵菩薩など多くの種類があります。

菩薩像は単独像としてまつられるほか、如来像の両脇にあらわされて三尊像としてまつられることもあります。薬師如来の脇侍像である日光・月光菩薩などはその例です。

Bosatsu – deity seeking enlightenment

Bosatsu (Bodhisattva) is an abbreviation of *bodai satta*, or one who trains to attain enlightenment and become *Nyorai*, to which he is assigned to serve as an attendant. Modeled on *Shaka* prior to his enlightenment, *Bosatsu* are usually represented in the form of royalty in ancient India wearing ornaments including crowns, necklaces, armlets and earrings. They are also characterized by *jōhaku* (a decorative scarf draped diagonally across the upper body and over the left shoulder), *kun* (a skirt-like garment covering the lower part of the body), as well as *tenne* (long narrow strips of ornamental cloth hanging down onto the ground) – which give *Bosatsu* a florid and elegant appearance.

Kannon Bosatsu, who listens to the prayers of worshippers and offers them helping hands with compassion, is one of the most widely worshipped divinities in Japan. Typically, *Kannon* holds a small bottle or lotus in the left hand, and the crown displays a small image of *Amida* (*kebutsu*). The basic form of *Kannon* is known as *Shō Kannon*, and often changes form, and appears with eleven heads or a thousand arms (called *Jūichimen Kannon* or *Senju Kannon* respectively), in order to save people according to their circumstances. These transformed manifestations are generally called *henge* (transformation) *Kannon*, and include *Fukūkensaku Kannon*, *Nyoirin Kannon*, and *Batō Kannon*.

Other types of bodhisattvas include *Miroku Bosatsu*, believed to appear 5.67 billion years after the death of *Shaka Nyorai*, *Monju Bosatsu*, *Fugen Bosatsu*, *Jizō Bosatsu*, and *Kokūzō Bosatsu*.

Bosatsu statues are often displayed singly or at both sides of a *Nyorai* as part of a triad (*sanzon*). *Nikkō Bosatsu* and *Gakkō Bosatsu* (Solar and Lunar radiance), represented as part of the Yakushi Triad, are one such example.

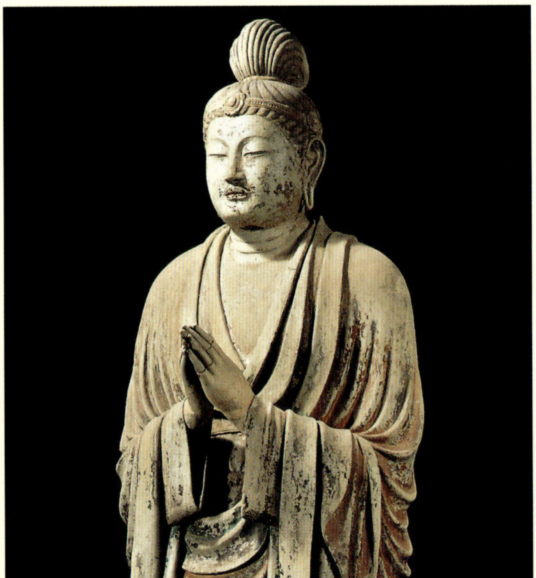

伝日光菩薩立像 奈良 東大寺
Standing Nikkō Bodhisattva, Tōdai-ji, Nara

密教の憤怒像、明王

明王は密教で信仰され、仏に逆らう仏敵をこらしめ、信心を持たない衆生を、畏怖によって帰依させようとする仏です。顔と腕を複数持つ多面多臂の姿で、武器を持ち、髪は炎のように逆立ち、憤怒の形相をとることが特色です。

明王像の代表が、不動明王を中心として、降三世明王、軍荼利明王、大威徳明王、金剛夜叉明王からなる五大明王です。燃え上がる炎の光背をあらわし、右手に剣、左手に羂索を持ち、歯をむき出した顔で睨みつけている不動明王像は、平安時代以後、数多くの密教寺院にまつられるようになりました。

Myō-ō – fierce looking deities of Esoteric Buddhism

Myō-ō (Wisdom Kings) are deities revered by practitioners of Esoteric Buddhism, believed to chastise those who defy Buddhist teachings, and to convert obdurate nonbelievers. Typically, they are represented with many faces, many arms, and flame-like hairstyle, and hold weapons in their hands.

The Five Great Myō-ō (*Godai Myō-ō*) is one of the most prevalent groups, consisting of *Fudō Myō-ō*, *Gōzanze Myō-ō*, *Gundari Myō-ō*, *Daiitoku Myō-ō*, *Kongōyasha Myō-ō*. *Fudō Myō-ō* is the central figure among the Five Great Myō-ō, usually depicted with a halo of fire behind him, a sword in his right hand, *kensaku* (a rope with five different colored strands) in his left hand as well as glaring facial expression. He became one of the most worshipped deities in many Esoteric Buddhist temples following the Heian period.

仏法の守護者、天

インド古来のバラモン教やヒンドゥー教の神々が、仏教に取り入れられたのが「天」です。大きく分けると、四天王、金剛力士、十二神将などの仏の守護の役目を持つグループ、そして梵天、大黒天、帝釈天、聖天などインド古来の神々のグループ、吉祥天、弁才天、鬼子母神などの天女(女神)のグループがあります。神将像は甲冑を着け、また、吉祥天などは華やかな衣装を着た姿にあらわされ、仏像の世界に変化に富んだ彩りを添えています。

このほか、仏像の仲間には、釈迦の弟子である十大弟子像や羅漢像、また聖徳太子や鑑真など実在した人物の像などがあります。

Ten – the Heavenly Guardians of the Buddhist law and doctrine

Ten (the Heavenly Guardians) were originally derived from Hindu and Brahmanic myths and incorporated into the Japanese Buddhist beliefs. They include those who serve as guardians of Buddha, such as the Four Heavenly Kings (*Shitennō*), Two Guardian Kings (*Kongō Rikishi*), and Twelve Heavenly Generals (*Jūni Shinshō*), those who originated from Hindu myths such as *Bon-ten*, *Daikoku-ten*, *Taishaku-ten*, *Shō-ten*, as well as goddesses such as *Kisshō-ten*, *Benzai-ten* and *Kishibojin*. Some deities wear armor or richly embellished gowns, such as *Shinshō* and *Kisshō-ten* images, and add a delicacy and elegance to the world of Buddhist images.

There are also some statues depicting actual historical Buddhist characters that include *Jūdai Deshi* (the Ten Chief Disciples of the historical Buddha), *Rakan* (the Highest Disciple of *Shaka*), *Shōtoku Taishi* (a well-known prince regent of Japan), and the Tang dynasty priest *Ganjin*.

Background The Characteristics of Buddhist images

4 仏像の特徴

仏像を見るポイント

仏像は、その姿について経典のなかに各種の決まりごとが記されています。それは、各時代の仏師にとっては守るべき大切な規則でした。仏像の姿のだいたいの決まり事を知ることは、制限の中で発揮される作者個人の創意工夫を見るために大切なことです。ここではその規則のいくつかを見ることにしましょう。

Essentials of Buddhist statues

For the production of Buddhist statues, there were a number of specifications set by the scriptures that the sculptors (*busshi*) had to follow strictly. By understanding some of those essential rules of iconography, we can appreciate the sculptors' creative efforts to make the most of their artistic genius within restrictions. The following are examples of those specifications.

独特の手つき、印相

仏像は印相と呼ばれる独特の手つきをしていて、これらにはそれぞれ意味があります。釈迦如来なら施無畏印(せむいいん)と与願印(よがんいん)、阿弥陀如来なら弥陀定印(みだじょういん)と、仏の種類によって決まっていることが多く、その意味によって役割を示しています。

Hand gestures (mudra)

Buddhist sculptures have various hand gestures, called *insō* (mudra, in Sanskrit), each of which have specific meanings. *Shaka Nyorai* often employs the combination of *Semui-in* and *Yogan-in*. *Amida Nyorai* uses *Mida-Jō-in*. Each hand gesture suggests the role of the deities.

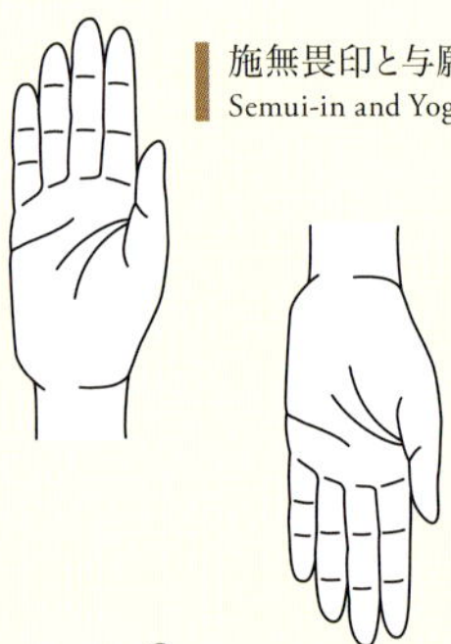

施無畏印と与願印
Semui-in and Yogan-in

釈迦如来に多い。人々の不安を払い、願いをかなえる印相
Most often associated with *Shaka Nyorai*. *Semui-in* grants the absence of fear, and *yogan-in* grants wishes.

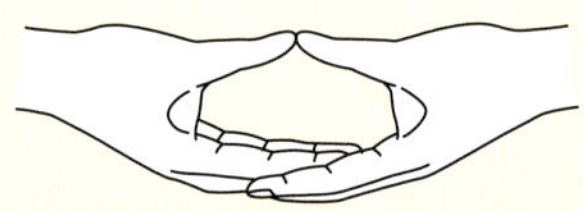

禅定印
Zenjō-in

悟りを開いたときの釈迦が座禅をするときの印相
Hand gesture symbolized *Shakamuni's* enlightenment through Zen meditation.

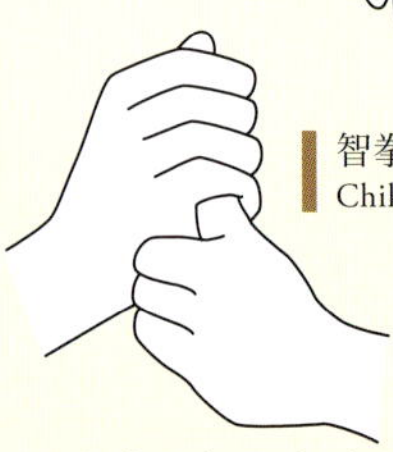

智拳印
Chiken-in

大日如来の迷いを粉砕する印相
Dainichi Nyorai uses this to symbolize knowledge which clears away ignorance.

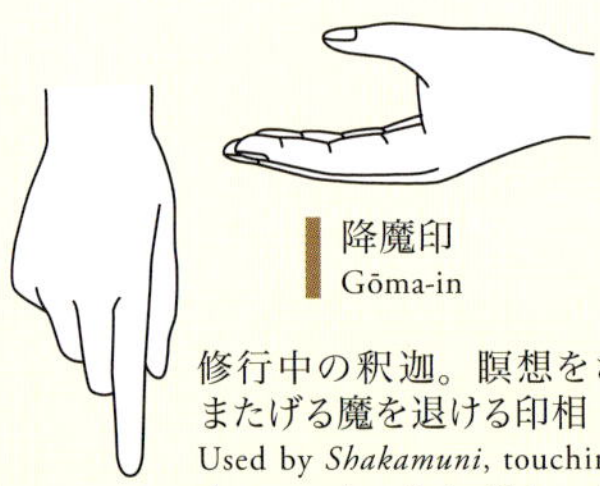

降魔印
Gōma-in

修行中の釈迦。瞑想をさまたげる魔を退ける印相
Used by *Shakamuni*, touching the ground and signifying the subjugation of the demons.

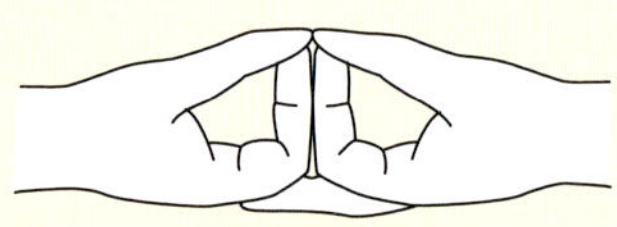

弥陀定印
Midajō-in

阿弥陀如来の極楽へ導く印相
Amida Nyorai's hand gesture for guiding believers to the Pure Land Paradise.

仏の体の特徴

悟りを開いた釈迦は、普通の人間とは異なるさまざまな肉体上の特徴を持っていたといいます。この特徴を三十二相といいます。

如来の粒々の髪型は螺髪(らほつ)といいます。これは修行中に伸びた髪が縮れて丸まったことをあらわしています。頭頂部がコブのように盛り上がっているのは仏の智恵をあらわした肉髻相(にっけい)です。眉間に生えたという長い白毛が巻き毛状になったものが白毫相(びゃくごう)です。仏像では水晶珠などで表現されます。

このほかに、耳たぶは長く、首には三道(さんどう)というシワがあります。手足の指の間にある水かき状のものは、衆生をもらさず救いあげる如来の働きを象徴しています。足の裏には煩悩を砕くという法輪と吉祥(きっしょう)相の模様があります。これらの特徴は多くの仏像に実際に再現されています。

Iconographic characteristics of Buddha

The enlightened *Shakamuni* is belived to have thirty-two iconographic traits, embodied as thirty-two physical characteristics (*sanjū-ni-sō*) that symbolize his super-human qualities.

Buddha's head is covered with *rahotsu*, spiral shaped curls of hair that grew during the period he sought enlightenment through ascetic training. The protuberance on the top of the head, known as *nikkei-sō*, represents the nobility and wisdom of Buddha. The clockwise whorl of white hair is called *byakugō-sō*, which is usually represented in sculptures by precious stones such as crystal.

Buddha also has long ear lobes and three horizontal grooves on the neck, known as *sandō*. *Nyorai's* webbed fingers and feet symbolizes his ability to 'scoop up' and save as many people as possible, while the bottoms of his feet have the Wheel of Law (*hōrin*) motif that is an emblem of his renunciation of desire, and symbols of fortune (*kisshō-sō*). These features can be seen in many statures of Buddhas.

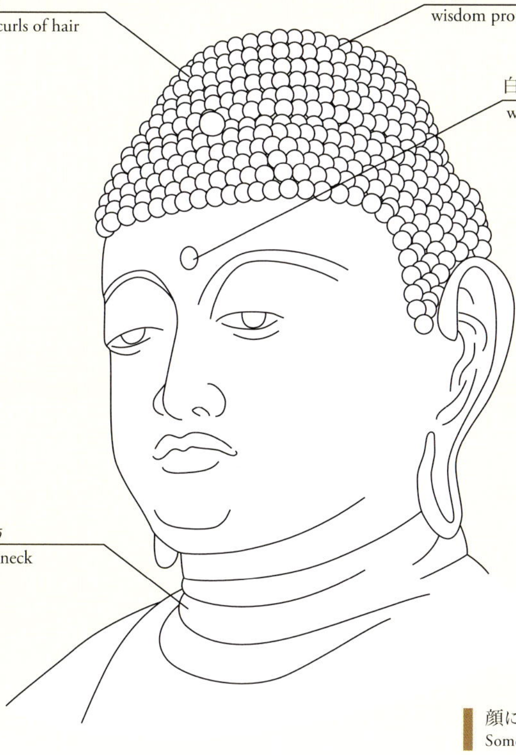

顔にある主な三十二相
Some of thirty-two physical characteristics on the face

仏像の服装

如来は衲衣という大きな布を体にまといます。悟りを開いたあとなので質素な姿をしています。

菩薩は、肩から胸に条帛という幅の狭い布を懸け、両肩に天衣を懸けて体の両側にその端を垂らし、下半身には裙という巻きスカート風の衣を着けます。悟りを開く前の王子だった釈迦の姿がモデルなので、宝冠や耳飾りなど華麗な装身具を身に付けています。

明王は、裸に近い上半身に条帛を、下半身には短い裙を着けています。天は鎧や兜で身を固めるなど、明王も天も敵と戦うための格好をしています。

Garments

As beings who have attained enlightenment, *Nyorai* Buddha images typically wear plain monk's robes draped around the body.

Bodhisattva images are modeled on the historical Buddha, *Shakamuni*, before his enlightenment, when he was a prince, wearing crowns and earrings. The garments are likewise elaborate, characterized by a flowing sash (*jōhaku*) draped diagonally across the upper body over the left shoulder, a long narrow scarf (*tenne*) hanging down from both shoulders, and a skirt-like garment (*kun*) covering the lower part of the body.

While the *Myō-ō* also wear the sash and skirt-like *kun*, the guardian figures (*ten*) are depicted in armor and casque, reflecting their role as combatants against the enemies of Buddhism.

如来 *Nyorai*
Buddha

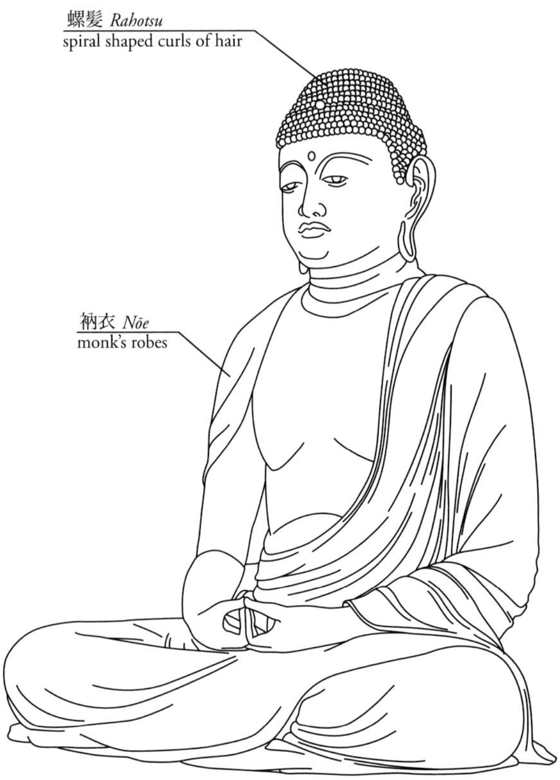

阿弥陀如来坐像
Seated Amida Nyorai

菩薩 *Bosatsu*

Bodhisattva

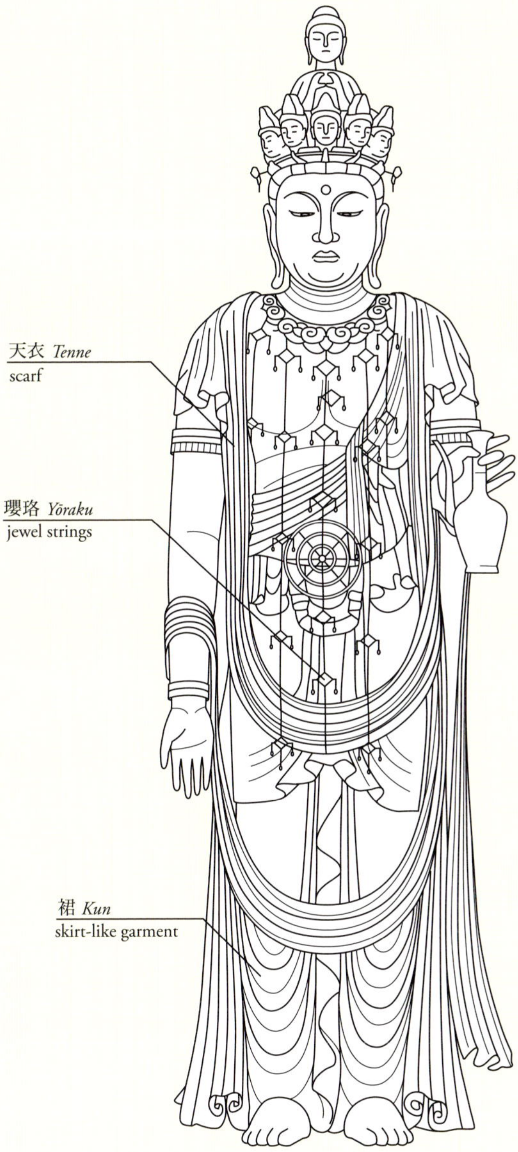

十一面観音立像
Standing Eleven-headed Kannon

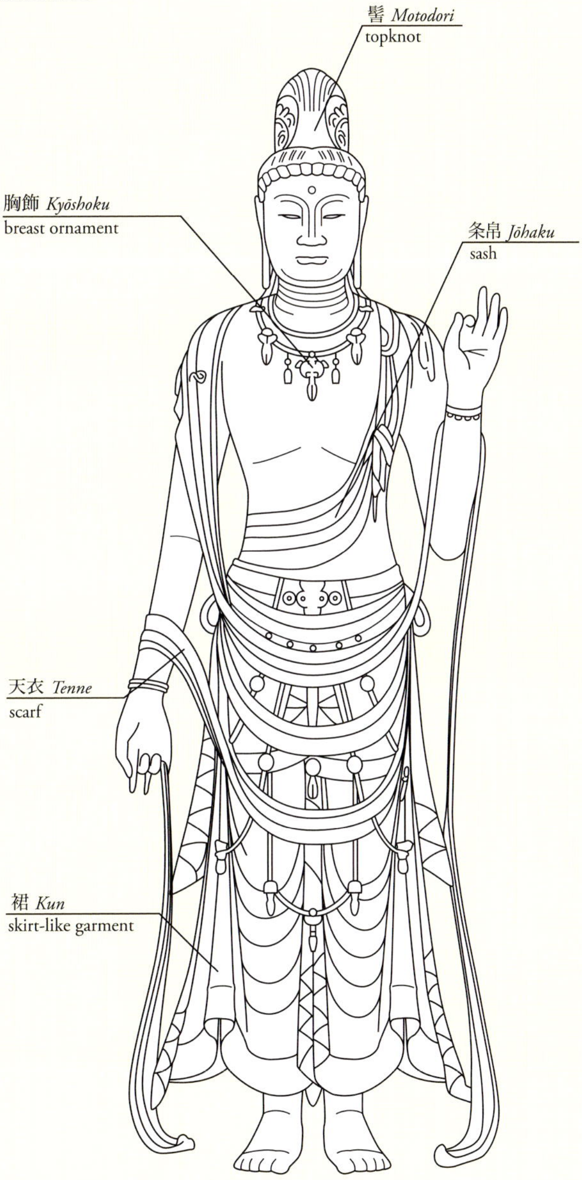

観音菩薩立像（聖観音）
Standing Kannon (Shō Kannon)

明王　*Myō-ō*

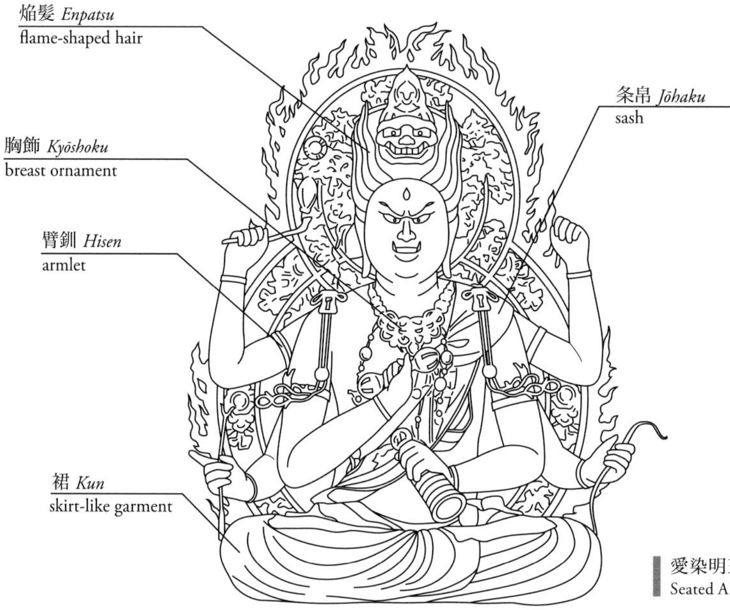

愛染明王坐像
Seated Aizen Myō-ō

天　*Ten*

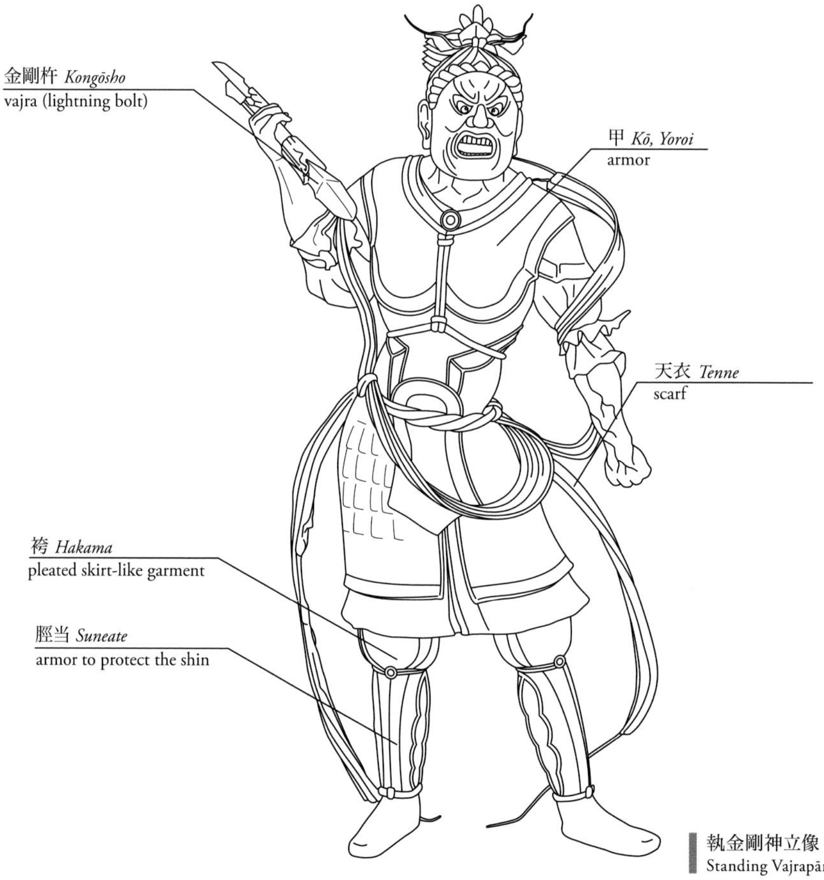

執金剛神立像
Standing Vajrapāni

仏像の持ち物

仏像は、その役割を示す持物を持つことがあります。

たとえば薬師如来は薬壺を持っています。中には万病を治す薬が詰まっていて、いくら使っても尽きることはないとされています。

菩薩は、悟りの象徴である蓮華やすべての願い事を叶えてくれる水が入った水瓶、衆生を救い集めたり煩悩をとらえたりする投げ縄である羂索、如意宝珠、錫杖、法輪など役目に応じたさまざまな持物を持っています。とくに千手観音はその手一つひとつにそれぞれ違う数多くの持物を持っています。

明王や天部は、その働きをあらわす剣や戟などの武器を持つものが目立ちます。

Attributes

Buddhist statues often have attributes which they hold, which indicates the roles of particular images.

Yakushi Nyorai, for instance, has a medicine jar that contains unlimited reserve of veritable panacea(*yakko*).

Bosatsu images are characterized by attributes including the lotus (*renge*) symbol of enlightenment, ritual water vessel (*suibyō*) that fulfill everyone's all wishes, the rope (*kensaku*) to save people by capturing their worldly desires, sacred jewels (*nyoihōju*), a priest's staff (*syakujō*) topped with a metal finial, and the wheel (*hōrin*). The thousand-armed Kannon (*Senju Kannon*), images usually hold variety of attributes in each hand.

Weapons like swords and *geki* are often found as attributes of guardian Buddhist figures such as *Myō-ō* and *Ten*.

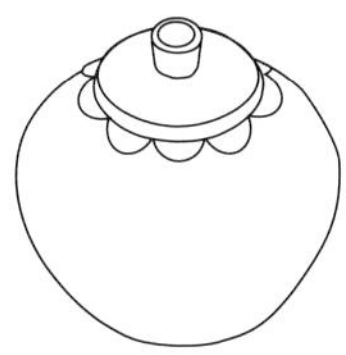

薬壺 薬を入れた壺
Yakko: medicine jar

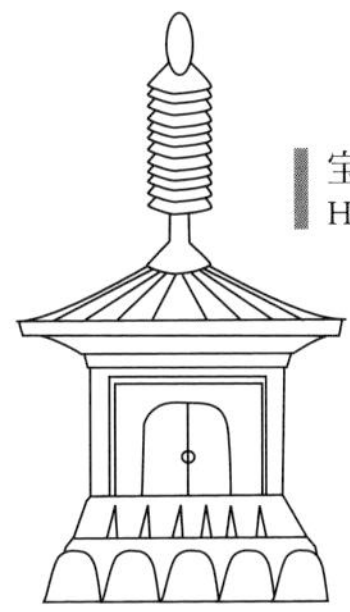

宝塔
Hōtō: stupa

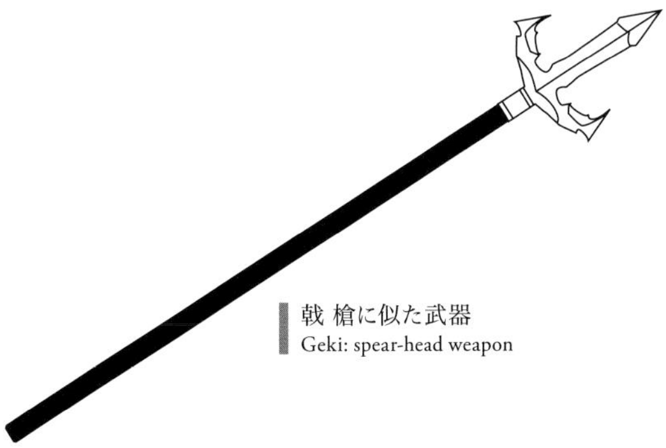

戟 槍に似た武器
Geki: spear-head weapon

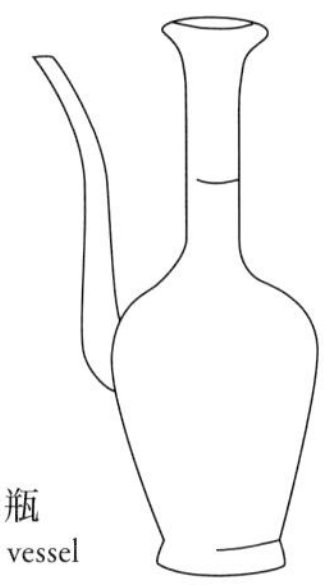

水瓶 水を入れた瓶
Suibyō: ritual water vessel

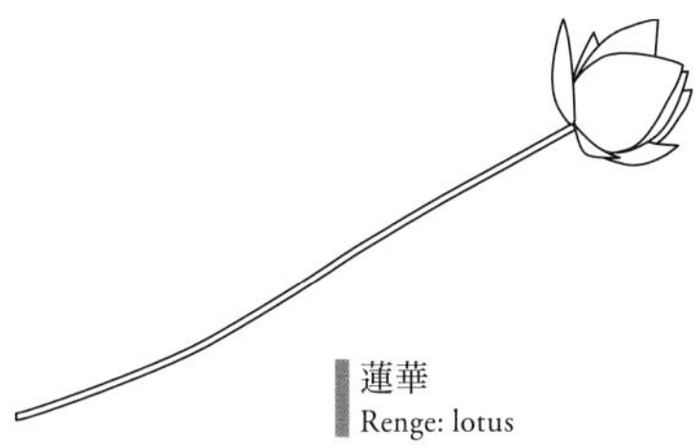

蓮華
Renge: lotus

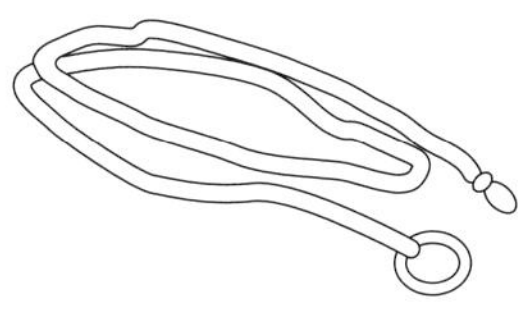

羂索 魔を捕えるロープ
Kensaku: rope

Background 4

光り輝く体をあらわす光背

彫刻として作られた仏像の背後には、板状の光背があります。釈迦は悟りを開いたときに全身が金色に輝いたといわれ、光背はその光を表現したものです。

光背には円形や蓮弁形、火焔形など様々な形があります。そこには、雲や蓮華、化仏などさまざまな意匠があらわされます。たとえば盧舎那仏の光背には多数の化仏が付けられます。光背は、作られた時代によっても変化があり、仏像本体と同じように、見どころの多いものです。阿弥陀如来が発する光線を矢のようにあらわした放射光は、鎌倉時代に作られるようになり、その後長く流行しました。

Halo

Many of Buddhist images are depicted with halo (*kōhai*) which represents the light said to be emitted by the Buddha when he attained enlightenment.

Decorative motifs of the halo include free-standing ring, lotus-petals and flame-shaped designs, representing images such as clouds, lotus-petals, and small transformed Buddha (*kebutsu*). For instance, numerous *kebutsu* figures are found on the halo of Rushana Buddha. Patterns of the halos vary according to the period the statues were produced, and often add unique features to Buddhist images. The radial nimbus, featuring radiating lines, is one such example that became widely used after the Kamakura period for images of *Amida Nyorai*.

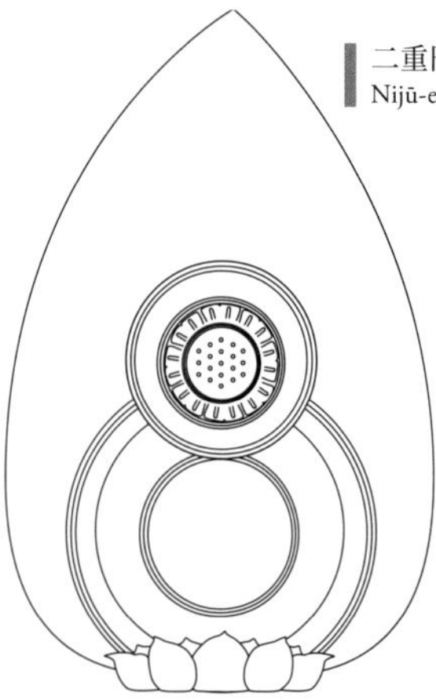

二重円相光
Nijū-ensō-kō: double ring halo

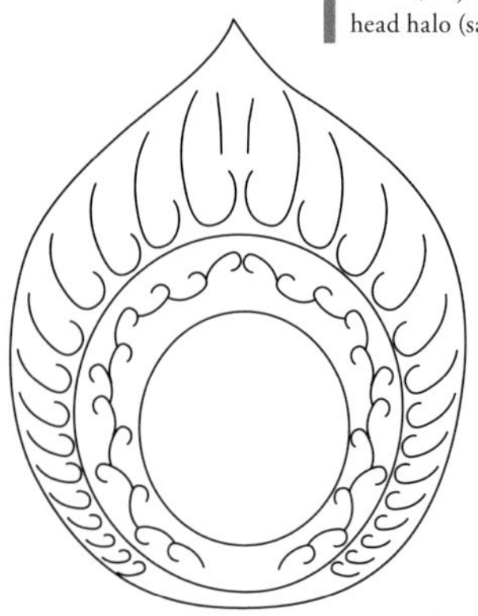

頭光（宝珠形）
Zukō (Hōju-kei): head halo (sacred gem shaped)

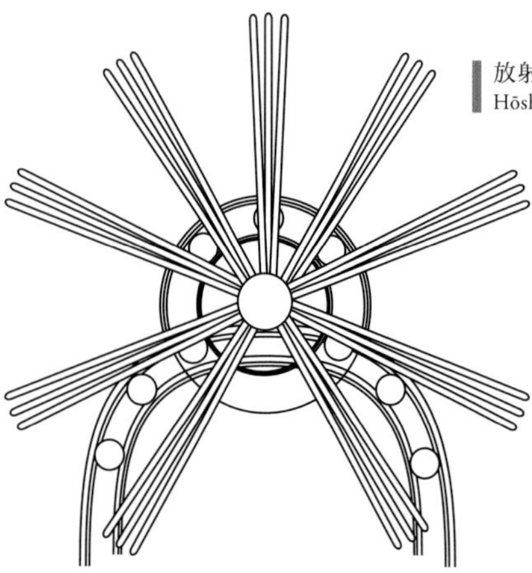

放射光
Hōsha-kō: radiating halo

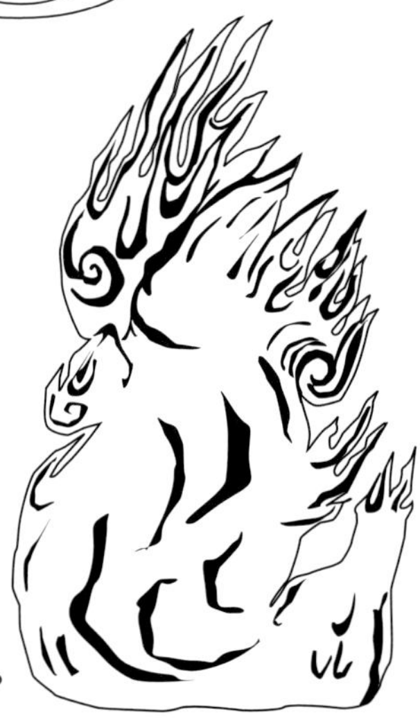

火焔光
Kaen-kō: flame-shaped halo

仏像の台座

仏像が座ったり、立ったりする台が台座です。方座をはじめとくに多くみられるのが、蓮の花をかたどった蓮華座です。

その他、台座と似たものに、四天王像が踏みつける邪鬼や、菩薩や明王などが乗る獅子、象、鳥、水牛などの動物があります。これらの仏像本体以外の造形にも、各時代の優れた意匠や技術が見られます。

Pedestal

Pedestals (*daiza*) are the commonly used base on which to place Buddhist images, among which lotus pedestals are the most widely used form.

Other forms include *Jaki* (demon spirits) that appear in sculptures as a small figures being crushed under the feet of *Shitennō* as well as animals such as lions, elephants, birds and buffalos, upon which some Bodhisattva and *Myō-ō* images stand. The designs and techniques applied to various types of pedestals are equally artistic and sophisticated as those of the sculptures themselves.

蓮華座
Renge-za: lotus pedestal

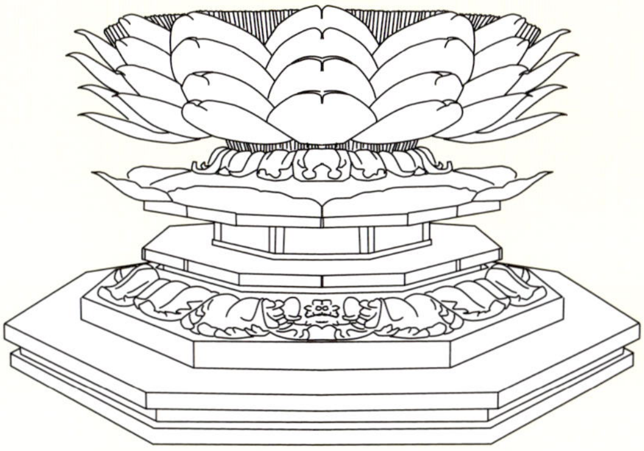

宣字座
Senji-za: two-tiered pedestal

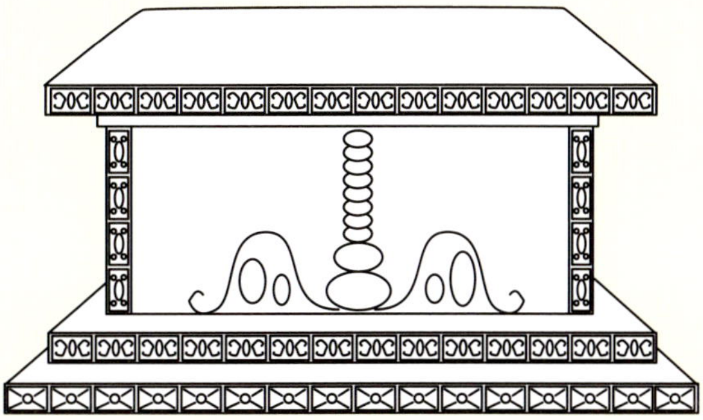

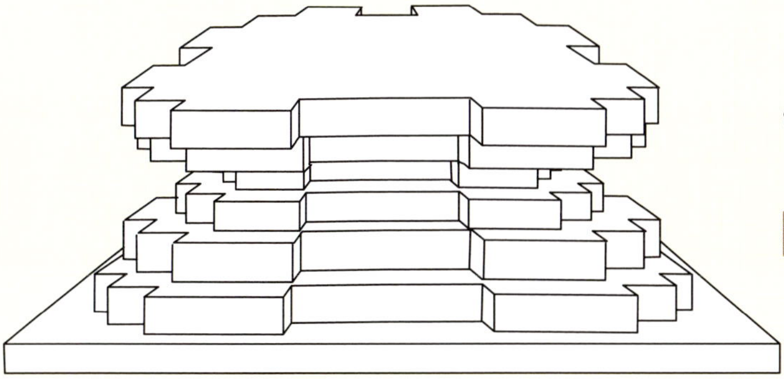

しっしつ
瑟瑟座
Shitsushitsu-za: Piled rock pedestal

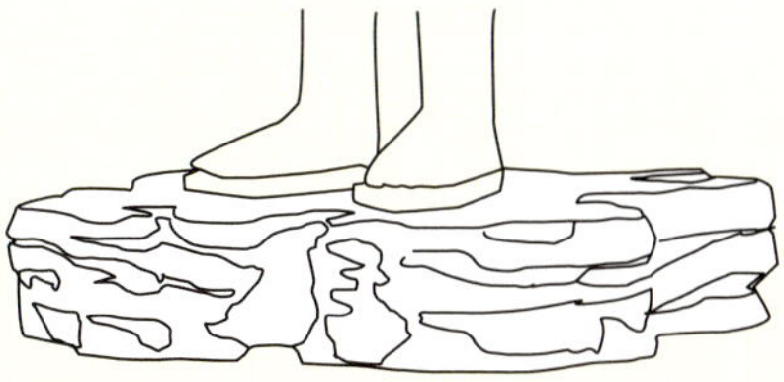

洲浜座
Suhama-za: pedestal representing shoreline rock

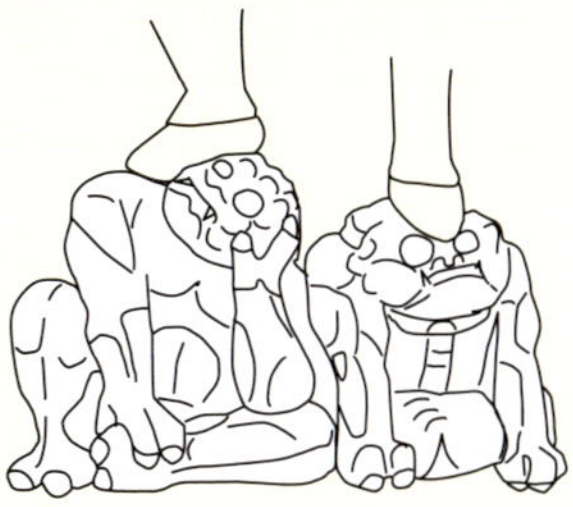

邪鬼
demon spirits

Background Making Buddhist statues

5 仏像の作り方

日本の仏像の多様な技法

日本の仏像には、銅像（金銅仏）、乾漆像、塑像、木彫像などがあります。ほかに石仏や鉄仏、銀仏や金仏などもありますが、数は多くありません。

このうち、もっとも多いのは木彫像で、日本に現存する仏像のおよそ9割以上は木彫像です。

Materials and techniques of Japanese Buddhist sculpture

In Japan, the primary forms of Buddhist statues by material were bronze (*dō-zō*), gilt bronze (*kondō-zō*), dry lacquer (*kanshitsu-zō*), clay (*so-zō*) and wood (*mokuchō-zō*). Although stone (*seki-butsu*), cast iron (*tetsu-butsu*), silver (*gin-butsu*) and gold (*kin-butsu*) were also common, these techniques are rarely seen in Japan. The most frequently used material of Buddhist statues in Japan is wood, encompassing more than 90 percent of the extant images.

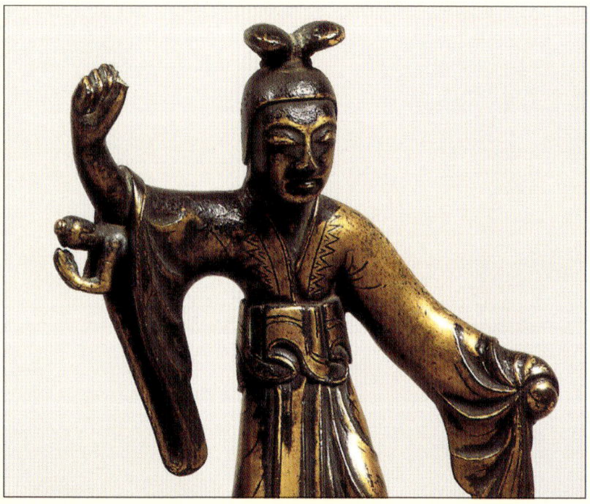

金銅仏 Kondō-butsu
Bronze

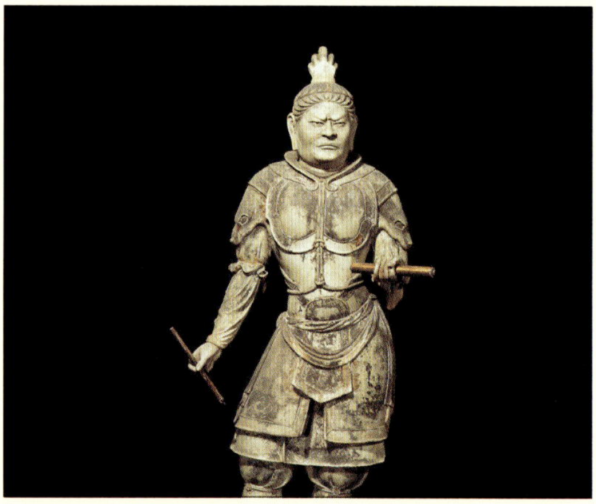

塑像 Sō-zō
Clay

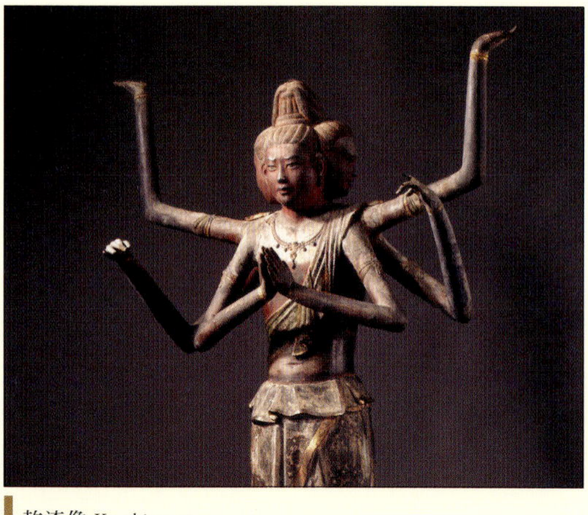

乾漆像 Kanshitsu-zō
Dry lacquer

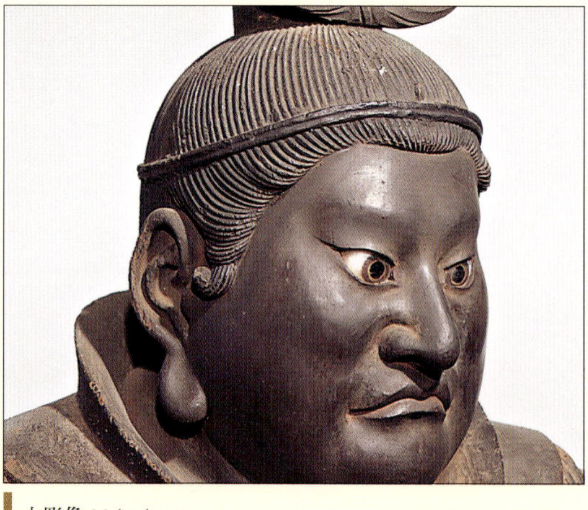

木彫像 Mokuchō-zō
Wood

飛鳥、奈良時代中心の金銅仏

銅（実際には合金である青銅）で鋳造して、表面に金メッキ（鍍金）をほどこした仏像を金銅仏といいます。大陸より技法が伝えられ、飛鳥・奈良時代に盛んに作られました。それ以後の時代にもときどき作られ、たとえば鎌倉時代の作である神奈川県高徳院阿弥陀如来像（鎌倉大仏）は銅造の仏像です。

飛鳥、奈良時代の金銅仏は、蝋型鋳造技法によって作られました。これは､粘土でおよその形を作り、その上を覆った蜜ロウに仏像を彫刻します。その際に湯道という銅をそそぐ部分を作ります。この原型全体を粘土で覆い、窯の中で高温で焼くとロウが溶けて流れ出して、その部分に空洞ができます。そこへ溶かした銅を流し込み、冷えて固まったら周りの粘土を壊して像を取り出します。表面をきれいに整え、金メッキをすると完成です。

現在残る古い金銅仏の多くは銅の地金があらわれていますが、作られた当時は金色に光り輝いていたのです。

Gilt Bronze (Kondō-zō)

Gilt bronze images made of bronze (or copper, in some cases) and gilded with a thin layer of gold (*tokin*) are called *kondō-zō*. This technique was brought to Japan and widely used in the Asuka and Nara periods. Some gilt bronze sculpture was made in later periods as well. The cast bronze seated figure of *Amida Nyorai* in the *Kōtoku-in* temple in Kamakura (also known the *Kamakura Daibutsu*) was created in the Kamakura period and became one of the most famous examples.

The primary technique used to make bronze statues in the Asuka and Nara period was the lost-wax (*rōgata*) method. This technique involves creating a basic clay model of the desired statue as the first step. It was then covered with a layer of beeswax, which was molded to the required shape and engraved with surface details. An outer layer of soft clay was then applied over the wax. The entire construction was then fired, causing the mold to harden and the wax to melt and run out. Molten metal was then poured into the gap left by the wax, between the outer mould and the inner core. After the metal had cooled and hardened, the inner and outer molds were removed, and the sculpture was finished by smoothing the surface.

Although most of the gilding which covered the surfaces is lost from many of the surviving *kondō-zō* images now, they used to reflect the gold and add regal splendor to the statues.

金銅像の制作工程
Production process of gilt bronze

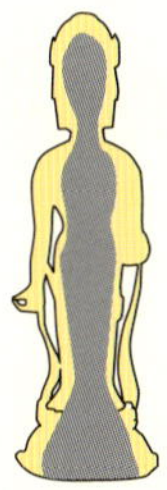

粘土の芯に蜜ロウを盛って原型を作る
The core body is made of clay. It is then covered with beeswax to be shaped into the basic model.

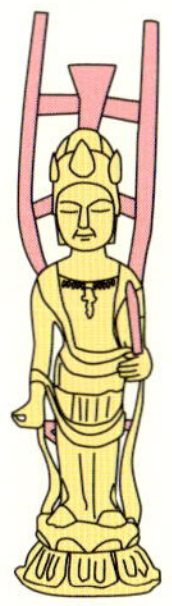

銅を注ぐ道をつける
The tubes are attached for casting molten bronze.

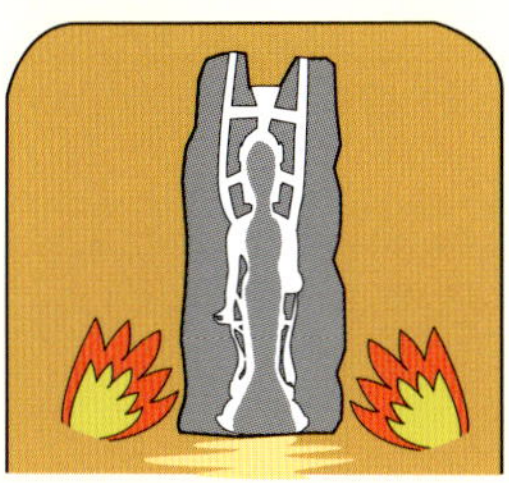

全体を粘土で包み、窯で焼く。蜜ロウは溶けて流れ出す
The basic model is covered with the outer clay. The beeswax flows out of the mold while being fired in the kiln.

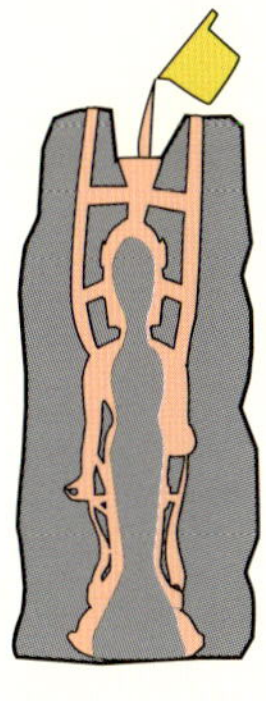

空洞に溶かした銅を流し込む
The molten bronze is cast into the gap.

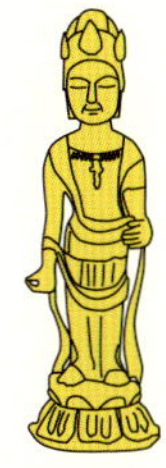

仕上げて完成
The surface is finished.

漆の特性を生かした乾漆像

日本を代表する工芸品に漆器がありますが、この漆器に使われる漆を利用して作る仏像が、乾漆像です。

粘土でだいたいの形を作り、その表面に麻布を漆を用いて貼り重ねます。それが乾いて硬化したら、像の背面などを切り開いて、麻布の層の下にある粘土をかき出して像の内部を中空にします。これで麻布を漆で固めた張り子ができあがります。この表面に、漆に木の挽き粉（おがくずなど）を混ぜてペースト状にした漆（木屎漆＝乾漆）を盛って、細部を塑形します。これが脱活乾漆技法です。

乾漆像は手間と時間がかかり、高価な漆が大量に必要なため、奈良時代以降はあまり作られなくなりました。

Dry Lacquer (Kanshitsu-zō)

Dry lacquer sculptures (*kanshitsu-zō*) were created by applying the dry lacquer coating technique - still used for lacquer wares (*shikki*) - one of the most widely known Japanese crafts.

A rough core was first modeled in clay and then layers of hemp cloth soaked in lacquer were applied over the surface, each layer being left to dry before the next layer was added. The clay core was then removed, forming a lightweight hollow statue. Surface details were modeled with a thick paste known as *kokuso-urushi*, a paste made by adding wood powder to lacquer. This technique is called *dakkatsu kanshitsu* (hollow dry lacquer) method.

The dry lacquer technique was widely used throughout the Nara period. However it gradually became obsolete during the following periods, as it required a lot of work, time, and large amount of expensive lacquer.

乾漆像の制作工程
Production process of dry lacquer

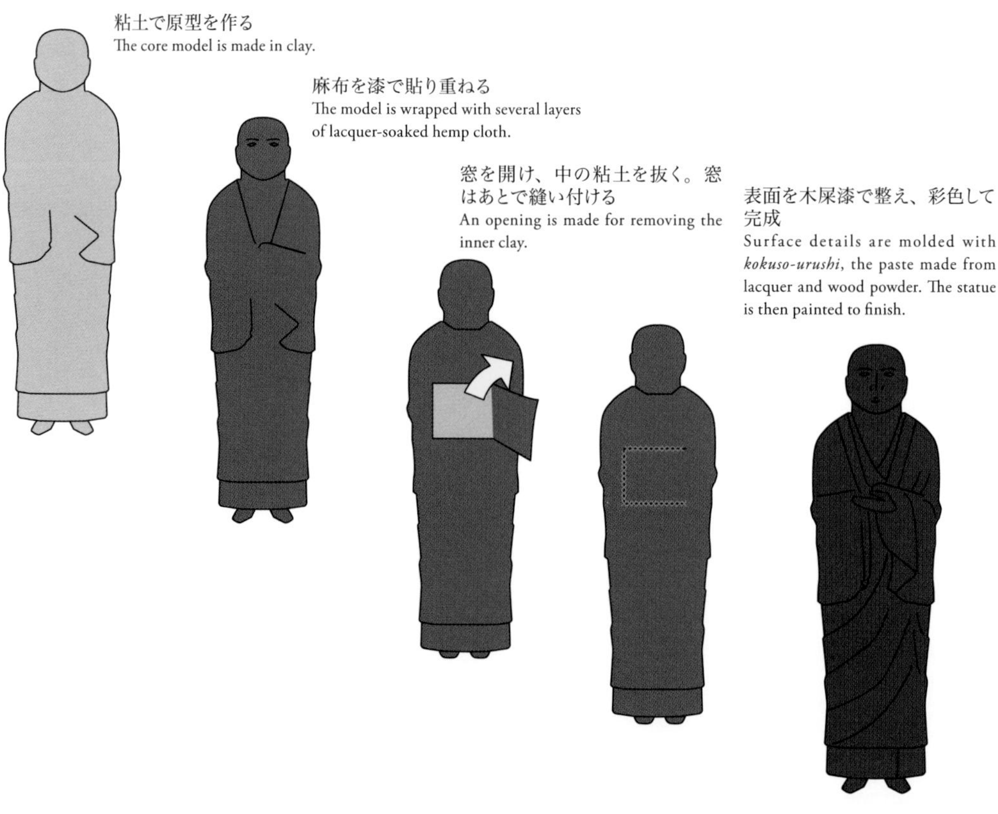

飛鳥、奈良時代中心の塑像

粘土で作られる塑像は、金銅仏や乾漆像にくらべて手間は少なく、飛鳥時代後期から奈良時代には盛んに制作されました。複雑な形の像や、大きな像では、木製の心木を立て、腕などは針金を芯にして、そこに粘土を盛りつけて作ります。8世紀中頃に作られた奈良県東大寺戒壇堂四天王像などが、日本の塑像の代表作です。

塑像は材料費は安価ですが、重くて壊れやすいという欠点があり、木彫が主流となった日本では、平安時代以後はあまり作られていません。

Clay (So-zō)

Clay statues (*so-zō*) became common during the late Asuka period and the Nara period, partly due to the relative ease of production compared with the gilt bronze and dry lacquer techniques. Its basic form involves preparing a simple wooden core wrapped in straw or cloth, which was then thickly coated with clay. Materials such as wire were often used to form the core of statues' arms for very detailed or large images. The Four Heavenly Kings (*Shitennō-zō*) in the *Kaidan-dō* hall of the *Tōdai-ji* temple are among of the most well-known statues made with this technique.

While clay allowed low-cost production and very detailed modeling, the clay images (*so-zō*) were virtually discontinued after the Nara period partly owing to the fragility and weight of the material.

塑像の制作工程
Production process of clay

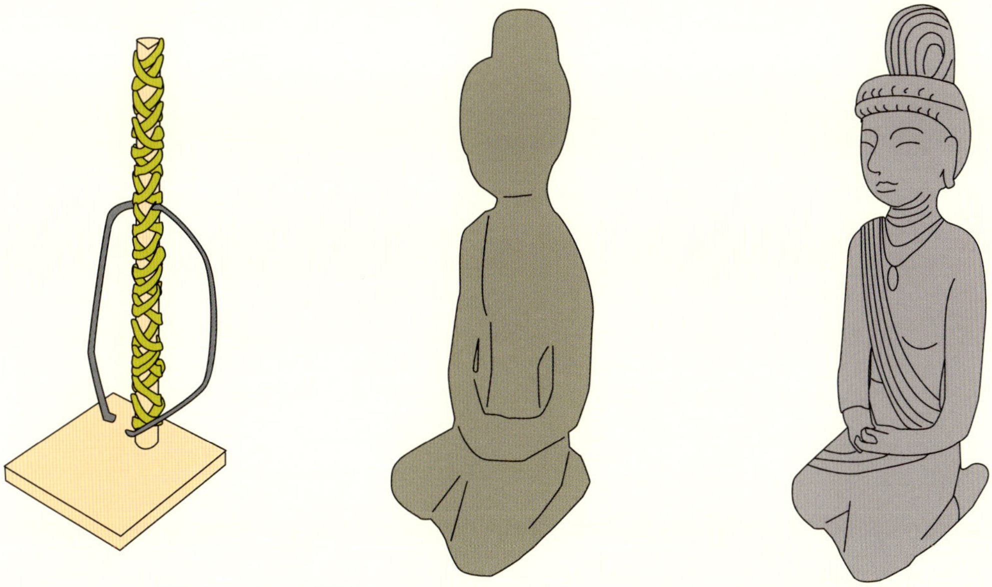

木に縄や針金を巻きつける
A wooden core is coiled with rope and metal wire.

粘土で整形する
The basic model is wrapped with clay and molded.

細部を仕上げ、彩色して完成
Surface details are carved and painted to finish.

平安前期までの木彫、一木造（いちぼくづくり）

飛鳥時代から平安時代前期頃までの日本の木彫像は、像をだいたい一本の木材から彫り出す、いわゆる「一木造」によって作られました。

坐像では、前に上げた腕や手、組んだ両足などの突出部には、別の材木を使うこともありますが、像の主要部である頭部と胴体がだいたい１本の材木で作られていれば一木造といいます。飛鳥時代の木彫像はほとんどクスノキで作られ、平安時代前期にはカヤが多く使われました。

木彫像の表面には、漆箔仕上げによって金色に仕上げられたり、多種の顔料によって極彩色に彩られたりしました。

一木造の制作工程
Production process of single-block carving

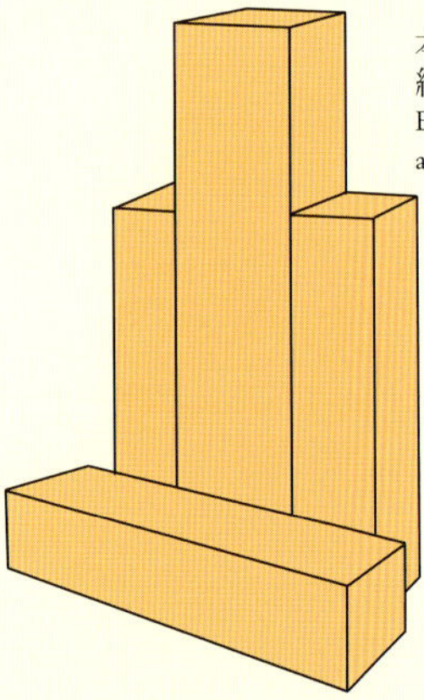

本体の材木を中心に大まかに組みあげる
Every pieces of wood is roughly assembled around the central block.

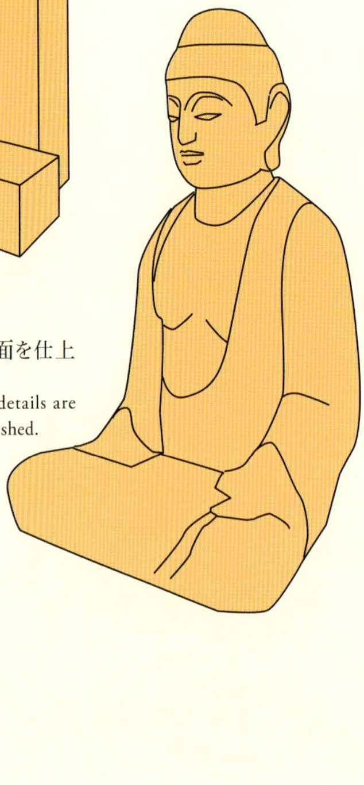

彫り上げる。細部、表面を仕上げて完成
The statue is carved. The details are carved and the surface is finished.

一木造と寄木造
Single-block carving and joined-block carving

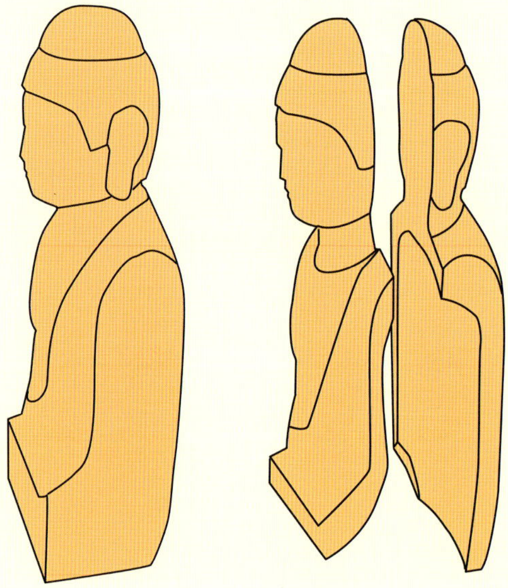

一木造は、像の本体が１本の材木から彫り出される
In ichoboku-zukuri, the statue is carved from a single-block.

寄木造はいくつかの材木をあわせて彫り出し、内部をくり抜く
In yosegi zukuri, joined block is carved and hollowed out.

Carved wood and single-block carving (Mokuchō and ichiboku-zukuri)

Most of the wooden images during the Asuka period and the early Heian period were produced employing a technique called single-block contruction (*ichiboku-zukuri*), in which the main part of a statue was made from a single block of wood.

The term is used even if projecting parts, such as the hands, arms, or knees of a seated figure, are made separately and joined to the single-block main body. Most wooden works in the Asuka period were made of *kusunoki* (the broadleaf camphor trees), while *kaya* (Japanese nutmeg trees) were used as the primary materials during the early Heian period.

The surface of wooden images were often coated with gold foil (known as *shippaku* technique) or richly colored with a variety of pigments.

日本独自の合理的技法、寄木造

一木造の技法では、仏像の大きさは材木の太さによって限定されます。また、木彫像には、完成後の木材の乾燥によって生じる干割れを防止するためや、像を軽量化するために、像の内部に内刳りが施されますが、一木造の像では、内刳りが十分にはできません。

これらの欠点を改善した技法が、平安時代後期に生まれた寄木造です。この技法は、複数の木材を規則的に束ねて、像を彫ります。つまり、この技法によって、細い材木でも大きな仏像を作ることができるようになり、また、一度彫った仏像を途中で部材ごとに解体して内部を大きく内刳りすることもできるようになりました。1053年に仏師定朝によって作られた京都府平等院鳳凰堂阿弥陀如来像にはこの技法の典型が見られます。

平安時代後期には、等身大程度の仏像でも、前面部と背面部の2本の材木を組んで作られることが多くなりました。合理的で経済的な寄木造は、日本独自のすぐれた木彫技法であり、その後の木彫像制作の基本として長く利用されました。

Joined-block construction (Yosegi-zukuri)

Joined-block construction (*Yosegi-zukuri*) is a sophisticated technique unique to Japan that is used to make the main section of a wooden statue out of two or more pieces of wood. It was developed in part to overcome the technical limitations of the *ichiboku-zukuri* method. For one, the size of statues was severely curtailed by the size of the tree trunk from which they were carved – therefore unsuitable for creating larger images. Moreover, it posed technical difficulties to sufficiently hollow out the interior of a wooden statue for the purpose of reducing weight and preventing the wood core from developing large cracks (called *uchiguri*).

The joined-block method was developed in the late Heian period and provided solutions for these problems. By carving a statue in a piecemeal fashion from several blocks of wood, this technique enabled Japanese artisans to create large-scale statues of Buddhist divinities, as well as to hollow the inside of the image further by dis-assembling individual parts. The *Amida Nyorai* image of the *Hō-ō-dō* (Phoenix Hall), at *Byōdō-in* in Kyoto, is one of the finest examples of the Buddhist sculptures which is executed in this technique.

By the late Heian period, this method became widely-used even allowing for the production of life-size statues by combining hollowed front pieces and back pieces. As a technique enabling an efficient use of sometimes scarce materials, *yosegi-zukuri* was adopted as the most prevalent method for wooden statues.

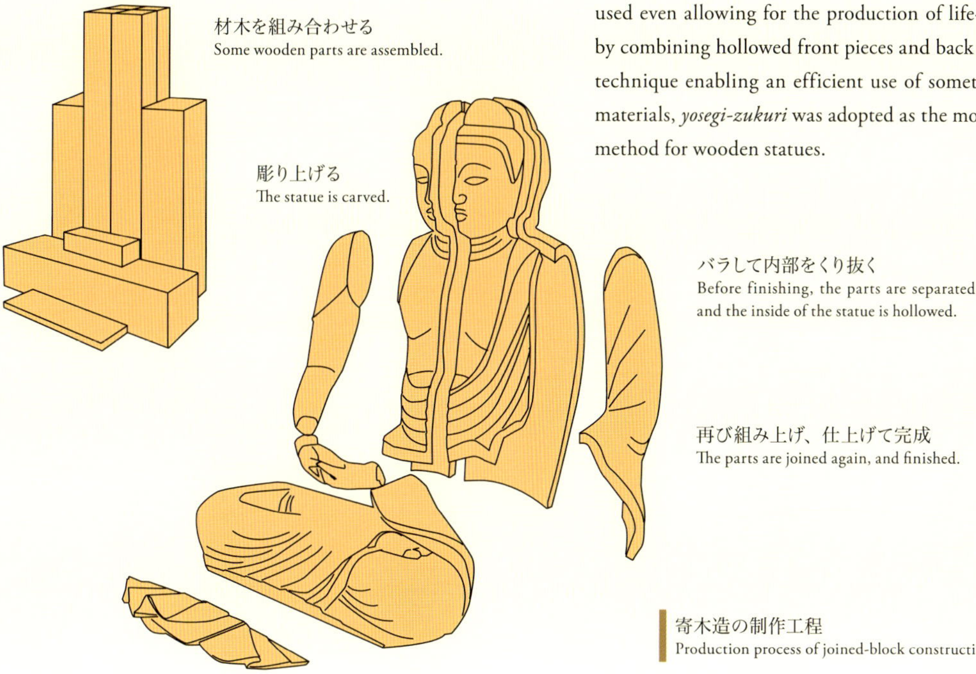

寄木造の制作工程
Production process of joined-block construction

Background Extra 仏像拝観の作法

Etiquette when visiting Buddhist sculptures

寺院を参拝するときは

寺院に安置されている仏像はただの彫刻ではなく、信仰の対象として長い歴史を通じて多くの人々に敬われてきた存在です。美術品として鑑賞するだけでなく、仏像を介して仏様を敬う気持ちを持つことができれば、仏像の魅力がさらに深まるでしょう。

Proper manners when visiting temples

Buddhist statues are not only sculptures but objects of worship for the Japanese people who have respected them through their long history. Appreciating the statues as works of art is only one aspect of visiting a temple. It can be an even more fascinating experience if you visit with an awareness of Buddist practices.

礼拝の仕方

1.堂内に入るときは、一礼をする
2.両手をあわせ(合掌)、一礼する
※寺院では拍手(パンパンと鳴らすこと)はしない(これは神社の作法です)
3.堂を出るときは、一度後ろを向き、一礼してから出る

How to worship the images (in the hall)

1. Bow once when you enter the hall.
2. Join your hands quietly in front of the statue and bow once.
   *Don't clap your hands twice as you do in shrines.
3. Before you exit the hall, turn around and bow once more.

手水(ちょうず)の仕方

神社や寺院の入り口には、参拝の前に手を清める「手水舎(ちょうずや)」が建っている場合があります。

1.右手で柄杓を持ち、水をすくって左手にかける
2.左手に持ち替えて右手に水をかける
3.右手に水をため、口をすすぐ(柄杓に口をつけない)
4.柄杓をもどす
※すべての手順をひとすくいの水で行います。

How to use the Chōzu, the purifying water (at the entrance of temples)

Most shrines and temples have *Chōzu-ya* (the purifying font) near the gate. This is where you purify yourself with water before viewing the Buddhist statues.

1. Take the dipper (*hishaku*) with your right hand. Scoop water and rinse your left hand.
2. Take the *hishaku* with your left hand and rinse your right hand.
3. Pour some water into your cupped right hand and rinse your mouth. You should not put your mouth directly on the *hishaku*.
4. Place the *hishaku* back to its original position.
   * Complete the whole process with one scoop of water.

第 2 章

各地の仏像を訪ねる

Chapter 2

Visit to Japanese Buddhist Sculptures

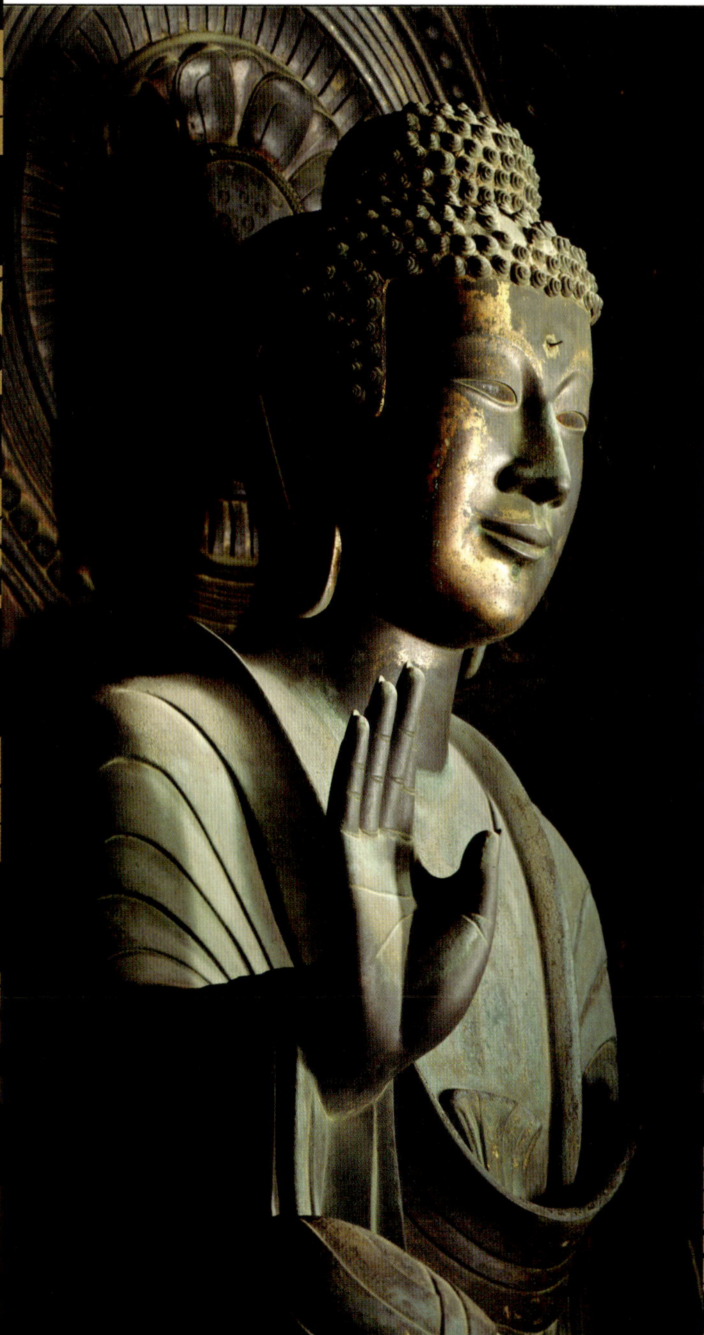

釈迦三尊像 奈良 法隆寺
Shaka Triad, Hōryū-ji, Nara

Area1

奈良の仏像

Buddhist sculpture in Nara

日本の仏像の原点

日本に本格的に仏教が伝えられ、仏像もさかんに作られるようになった7世紀から8世紀の都が平城京、すなわち奈良の都です。

東大寺、興福寺、薬師寺など、雄大な伽藍が数多く建てられ、そこではにぎやかな仏教文化が花開きました。寺院には数多くの仏像が作られ、その手法も、金銅仏や木彫像だけでなく、塑像や乾漆像など、多岐にわたるさまざまな素材が用いられ、新しい仏像彫刻への挑戦が行われていました。また、平城京の南の飛鳥は、7世紀に都が置かれ、日本最初の寺院である法興寺(今の飛鳥寺)が建てられた地です。

今でも国宝に指定されている仏像の約半数は奈良県にあります。日本の仏像にとって、奈良はまさに原点ともいえる地域です。

近鉄奈良駅周辺には、興福寺、東大寺、新薬師寺、奈良国立博物館などがあり、西ノ京には薬師寺、唐招提寺があります。法隆寺は奈良市の南西にある斑鳩(いかるが)にあります。これらはバス、鉄道などの公共交通機関で訪ねることができます。円成寺や京都南部の浄瑠璃寺など、市域から少し離れた古寺を訪れるには、レンタカーなどを利用してもよいかもしれません。

法隆寺
Hōryū-ji temple

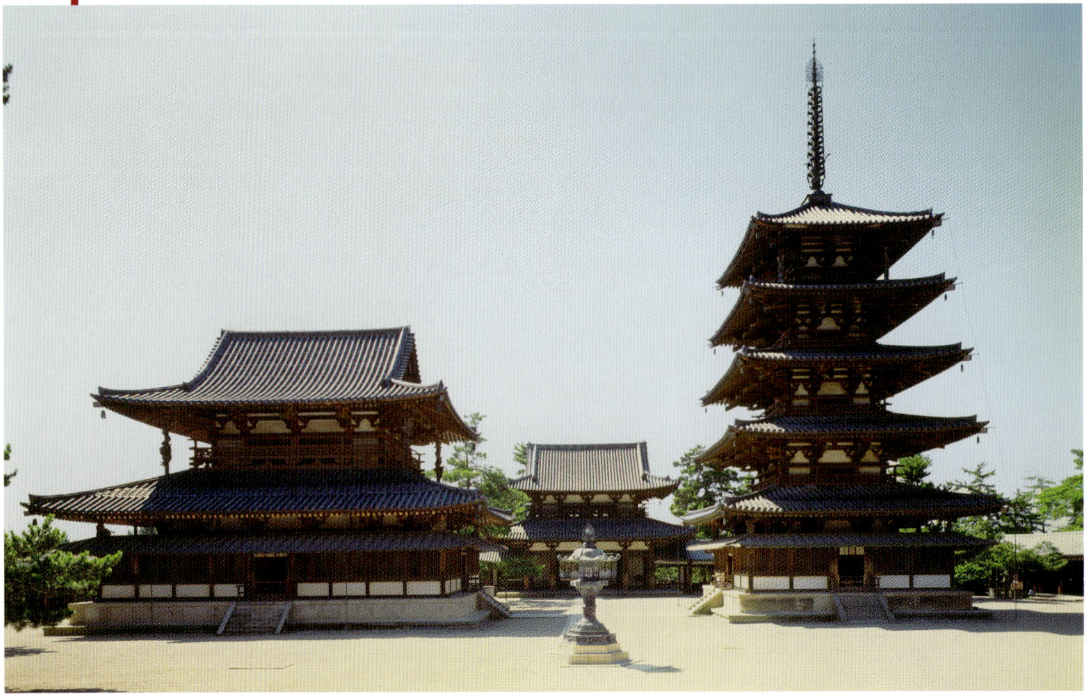

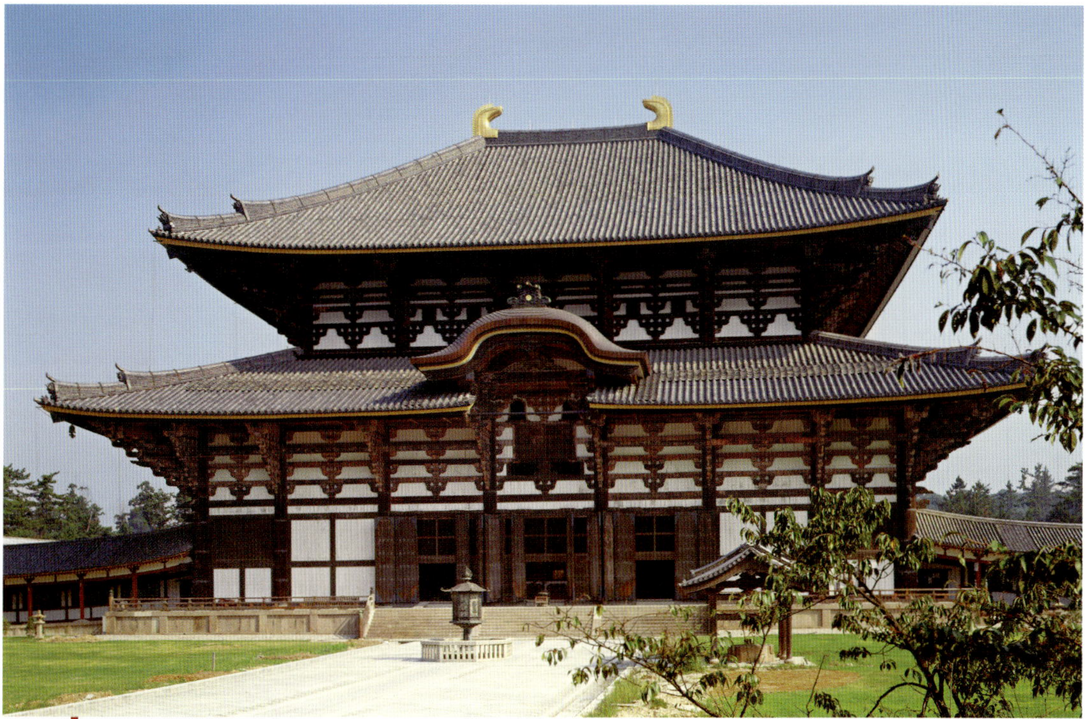

東大寺大仏殿
Daibutsu-den, Tōdai-ji temple

The origin of the Japanese Buddhist statues

From the seventh to eighth century, the capital city of Japan was called *Heijō-kyo*, or *Nara-no-miyako*, and Buddhism was widely introduced, with many Buddhist statues being made.

A multitude of grand temples were built, such as *Tōdai-ji*, *Kōfuku-ji* and *Yakushi-ji*, and the Buddhist culture was in full bloom in Nara. Numerous Buddhist sculptures were created during the Asuka period to the Nara period, using various techniques. The sculptors met the challenge to forge new styles using not only metal and wood, but also clay or lacquer. The area south of *Heijō-kyō* was called Asuka, which was the capital city in the seventh century, and *Hōkō-ji*, now called *Asuka-dera*, was the oldest temple in Japan.

Even now, Nara prefecture still houses approximately half of the Buddhist statues which are designated as National Treasures. Nara is considered the starting point for Japanese Buddhist sculpture.

The prominent temples like *Kōfuku-ji*, *Tōdai-ji*, *Shinyakushi-ji*, and Nara National Museum are located near the Kintetsu Nara station. *Yakushi-ji* and *Tōshōdai-ji* are in the Nishi-no-kyō area. The famous *Hōryū-ji* temple is in Ikaruga, southwest of Nara city. You can visit these temples by bus or train. Some temples like *Enjō-ji*, and *Jōruri-ji* which is in south Kyoto, are far from the city center. You may rent a car to visit those old temples in the outskirts.

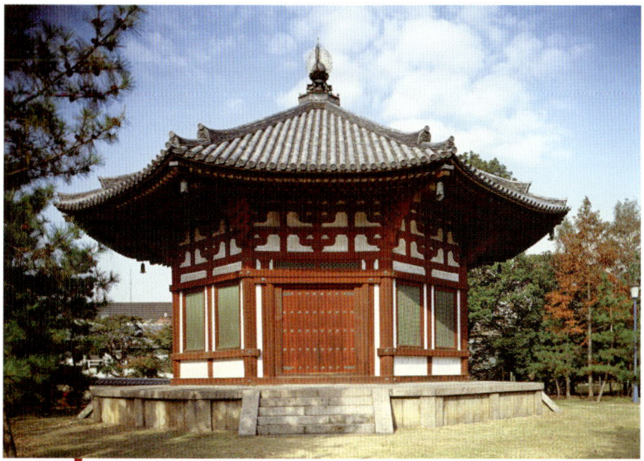

興福寺北円堂
Hokuen-dō, Kōfuku-ji temple

止利作釈迦三尊像
Shaka Triad *Made by Tori [Busshi], Completed in 623*

静かに微笑む高貴な姿に悠久の時を感じて
The eternal time in a serene smile

日本最古の仏像 | 法隆寺は聖徳太子が建立したと伝えられる寺で、世界遺産にも登録されています。世界最古の木造建築として知られる伽藍の一つ、金堂へ入ると、中央に両脇侍を従えた釈迦如来像が安置されています。釈迦三尊像は聖徳太子の病気平癒のために発願されました。願むなしく太子は亡くなりましたが、その翌年にあたる推古31年（623）に仏像は完成しました。作者は当時の代表的仏師、鞍作止利（くらつくりのとり）です。現存する日本最古の仏像ともいえる作品で、1つの大光背に三尊を並べる形式（一光三尊（いっこうさんぞん））など朝鮮半島や中国南北朝時代の仏像様式を取り入れながら、日本独自の表現を加えた作品となっています。

神秘的なアルカイックスマイル | 中尊はアルカイックスマイルと呼ばれる古風な笑みを浮かべ、宣字座（せんじざ）という高い台座の上で結跏趺坐（けっかふざ）（足を組む座り方）をしています。衣文は鋭い曲線を描いて台座上段を覆い、左右でほぼ同形の両脇侍が台座下段から延びた蓮華に乗って並んでいます。この三尊像は蝋型鋳造（ろうがたちゅうぞう）によるブロンズ（青銅）製で、作られた当時は全身に鍍金（ときん）（金メッキ）がほどこされていました。

Japan's oldest Buddhist sculptures | Prince Shōtoku (also called *Shōtoku Taishi*, 574-622) is credited with building *Hōryū-ji* temple, which is a registered UNESCO World Heritage site. The Main Hall (*Kondō*), one of the world's oldest extant wooden structures, houses a statue of *Shaka Nyorai* flanked by two attendant bodhisattvas. This Shaka Triad was commissioned in 622 as an offering to assure Prince Shōtoku's recovery from an illness. The sculptures were completed the following year, however, after his death. The sculptor of the triad was *Kuratsukuri-no Tori*, one of the best and most representative of his time. The triad comprises the earliest extant Japanese Buddhist sculptures. The three statues share a single large halo (*ikkō sanzon*), a style that originated from the Korean peninsula and China, yet elements of a specifically Japanese style are present here as well.

The enigmatic "archaic smile" | The central figure of the triad, Shaka Buddha, has a serene expression, the so-called "archaic smile." He is seated in a cross-legged pose (*kekka fuza*) on a tall two-tiered pedestal (*senji-za*). The folds of the sharply delineated robes cover the upper part of the pedestal. The attendant bodhisattvas stand on lotus petals that extend from the lower tier of the pedestal. The three sculptures are made of bronze, cast in the lost wax technique (*rōgata chuzō*) and covered with gilding.

飛鳥時代
止利作釈迦三尊像

Asuka period
Tori saku Shaka Sanzonzō

Data

釈迦如来及び両脇侍像
奈良 法隆寺 金堂
推古31年（623）
像高 中尊 87.5cm
左脇侍 92.3cm
右脇侍 93.9cm
止利作
国宝
銅造 鍍金

Shaka Nyorai and flanking attendants
Main Hall, Hōryū-ji temple, Nara
AD 623 (Suiko 31)
Central image: 87.5 cm
Left: 92.3 cm
Right: 93.9 cm
Made by Tori [Busshi]
National Treasure
Gilt bronze

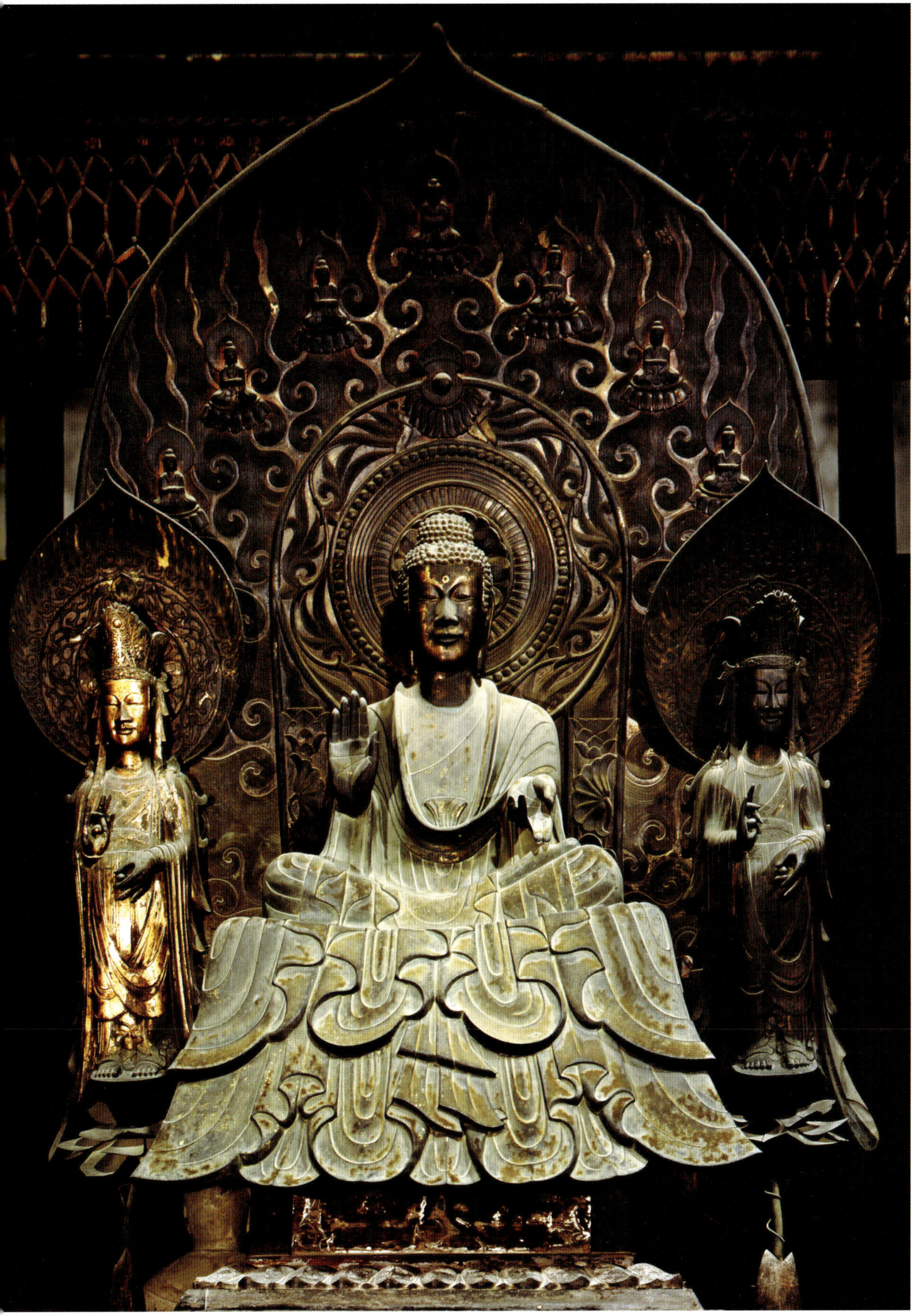

止利作釈迦三尊像 ｜ Shaka Triad

観音菩薩立像（救世観音）
Standing Guze Kannon *"Salvation" Avalokitesvara*

見る者を魅了し続けるいにしえの秘仏
Ancient secret Buddhist image that continues to captivate viewers

フェノロサが再発見した秘仏 | 行信僧都（ぎょうしんそうず）が斑鳩宮跡に聖徳太子を偲んで奈良時代に建立したのが現在の法隆寺東院です。その中心となる夢殿（国宝）は珍しい八角形の木造建築です。明治17年（1884）、米国の美術史家フェノロサは、日本政府の依頼で奈良の古美術調査を行いました。そのとき、それまで数百年間秘公開だった夢殿の厨子を、寺僧を説得して開け、この救世（ぐぜ）観音（夢殿観音）を再発見しました。彼はこの像について「驚嘆すべき世界に唯一なる影像」と記録を残しています。

飛鳥時代を代表する木彫像 | 像はすべてクス材一木から彫りだされ、金箔押しで仕上げられていて、横からの視線も意識した立体的な造形で美しい曲線をかたちづくっています。さらに、左右に垂れた髪や、大きく張りだした天衣が像全体にゆるやかな上昇感を与えています。金銅透彫りの宝冠と宝珠の火焔はみごとなデザインで、火焔文と唐草文を配した光背とともに、飛鳥時代の優れた意匠が随所に見られます。

The "hidden image" rediscovered by Fenollosa | The present-day Eastern Precinct (*Tō-in*) of *Hōryū-ji* temple is believed to have been built on the former site of Prince Shōtoku's Ikaruga Palace by the priest *Gyōshin Sōzu* (d. 750). Here he erected as the central hall an unusual octagonal building called the *Yumedono* (literally, "Dream Hall"), which is a registered National Treasure. In 1884 the American art historian Ernest Fenollosa (1853-1908) conducted an investigation into Nara's antiquities at the request of the Japanese government. He persuaded the temple priests to open the shrine containing sculptures and sutras that had been kept hidden away for hundreds of years. Inside was this *Guze Kannon* (also called *Yumedono Kannon*). In his notes Fenollosa describes it as "this marvelous statue, unique in the world."

A wood sculpture that typifies the Asuka style | This statue was carved from a single piece of camphor wood and finished with gold leaf. The image has a three-dimensionality that makes it equally satisfying seen in profile, with gently curving lines. Furthermore, the lines of the hair falling over the shoulders and the wide outward-curving scarves (*tenne*) lend an upward sweep to the whole. The gilt bronze openwork crown and flaming jewel are superbly designed. These and the halo, with its finely incised flames and scrolling arabesque motifs attest to the skilled craftsmanship of the Asuka period sculptors.

飛鳥時代
観音菩薩立像（救世観音）

Asuka period
Kannon Bosatsu Ryūzō (Guze Kannon)

Data

観音菩薩立像
奈良 法隆寺 夢殿
7 世紀前半
像高　179.9cm
国宝
木造 クス 金箔押し

Standing Avalokitesvara
Yumedono, Hōryū-ji temple, Nara
First half of the seventh century
179.9 cm
National Treasure
Wood (Camphor; kusu) with gold leaf

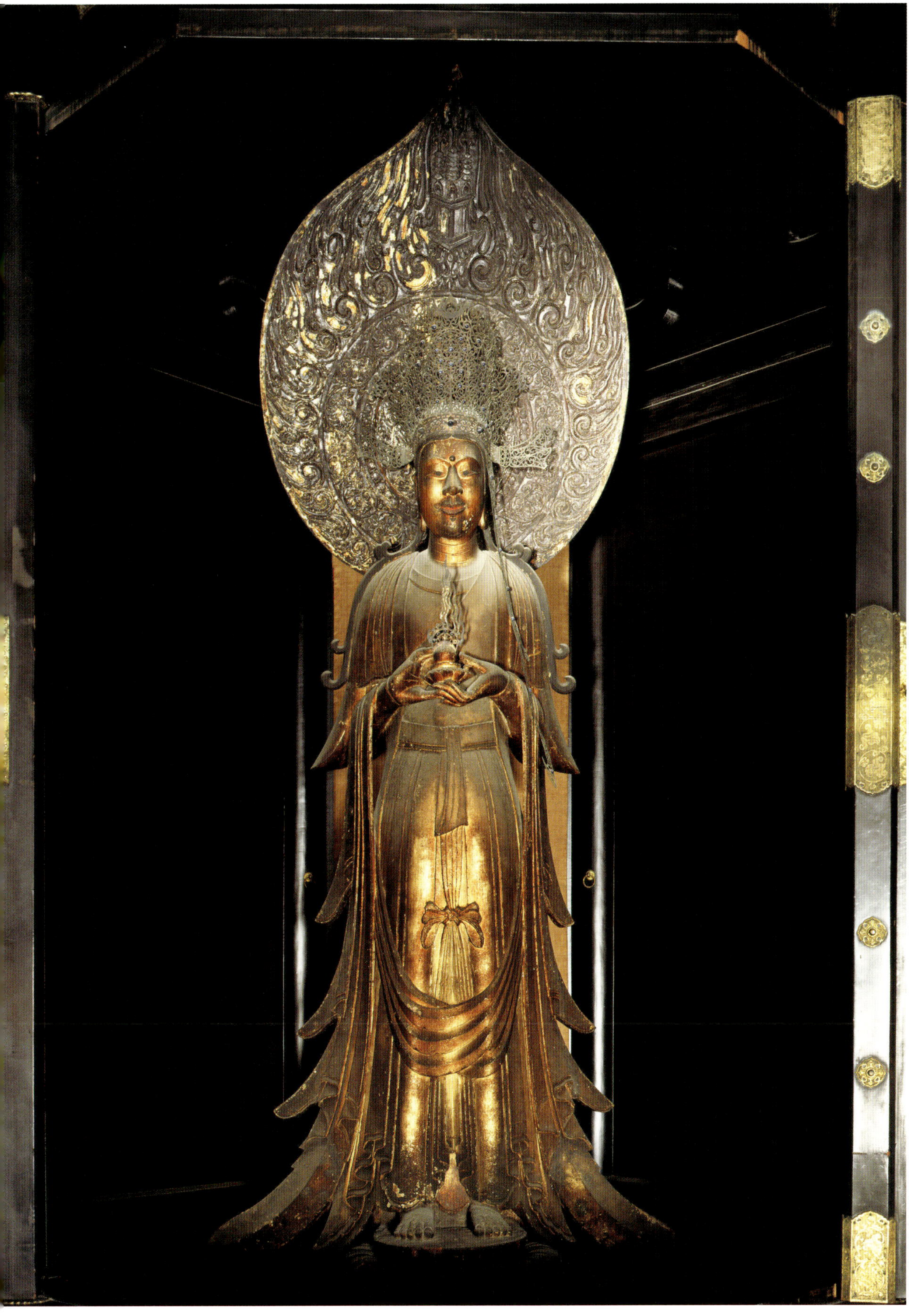

観音菩薩立像（救世観音）　|　Standing Guze Kannon

塔本四面具
Four Walls of a Pagoda

仏教経典を再現した壮大な塑像群
Spectacular panorama of scenes from the Buddhist scriptures

日本最古の五重塔 | 日本各地には古い木造の五重塔がいくつもありますが、法隆寺五重塔はそのなかで最古のものです。その初層内部の四方には、100体近い塑像によってジオラマのように、仏教の経典にあるシーンがあらわされています。
四面にあらわされたさまざまな場面 | 東面には、仏教経典の一つである維摩経に書かれた維摩居士と文殊菩薩の討論の場面が再現されています。北面にはクシナガラ城外における釈迦入滅の場面、西面には釈迦の荼毘と分骨を描いた分舎利仏土、そして南面には釈迦入滅の56億7千万年後にこの世にあらわれる弥勒浄土のようすがそれぞれ再現されています。特に釈迦の最期をあらわした北面は、菩薩や弟子たちの嘆く姿がたいへん印象的で、日本の彫像には珍しい表現です。
「塑壁」と呼ばれる貴重な塑像群 | これらの塑像は、心木の上に藁縄を巻き、粘土で塑形し、彩色をほどこして仕上げられています。こうした群像は唐時代の中国で「塑壁」と呼ばれ、盛んに作られました。しかし、今では中国のものはほとんどがすでに失われ、この法隆寺の塑像群は世界的にもたいへん貴重なものです。

The oldest five-story pagoda in Japan | Numerous wooden five-story wood pagodas are extant in Japan, and among them the one at *Hōryū-ji* temple is the oldest. Inside, on the four walls of the ground floor of the pagoda, nearly one hundred clay sculptures are arrayed in diorama-like scenes which illustrate sutra texts. The east wall has a scene from the Yuima sutra of the discussion of Buddhist teachings between the venerable Yuima and the bodhisattva Monju. The nirvana, or passing of the historical Buddha Shakamuni is depicted on the north wall. The west side grouping illustrates the distribution of Shaka's sacred ashes after his cremation, and on the south wall is the paradise of *Miroku*, the future Buddha who will appear 5.67 billion years after Shaka's death. The north wall scene of Shaka Buddha's last moments, is particularly impressive for its rare depictions of the vivid expressions of grief among the mourners.
"Dry clay" group of rare sculptures | These sculptures are made by first wrapping straw ropes around a wood core, and then covering the whole with clay, which is allowed to dry, and then adding pigments. The practice of placing clay statuary groups in pagodas was common in seventh-century Tang dynasty China. The Chinese examples are, however, no longer extant, so these *Hōryū-ji* panoramas are extremely important.

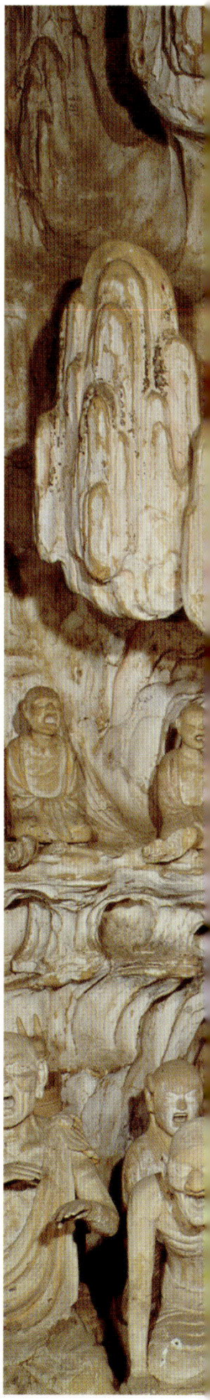

奈良時代 **塔本四面具**
Nara period **Tōhonshimengu**

Data

塔本四面具（北面）
奈良 法隆寺 五重塔
和銅４年（711）
像長　98.0cm（涅槃釈迦像）
国宝
塑像 彩色 漆箔

Panorama of sculptural scenes (north wall)
Five-story pagoda, Hōryū-ji temple, Nara
AD 711 (Wadō 4)
98.0 cm (Shaka Nirvana sculpture)
National Treasure
Dry clay, Pigments, Gold foil applied with lacquer

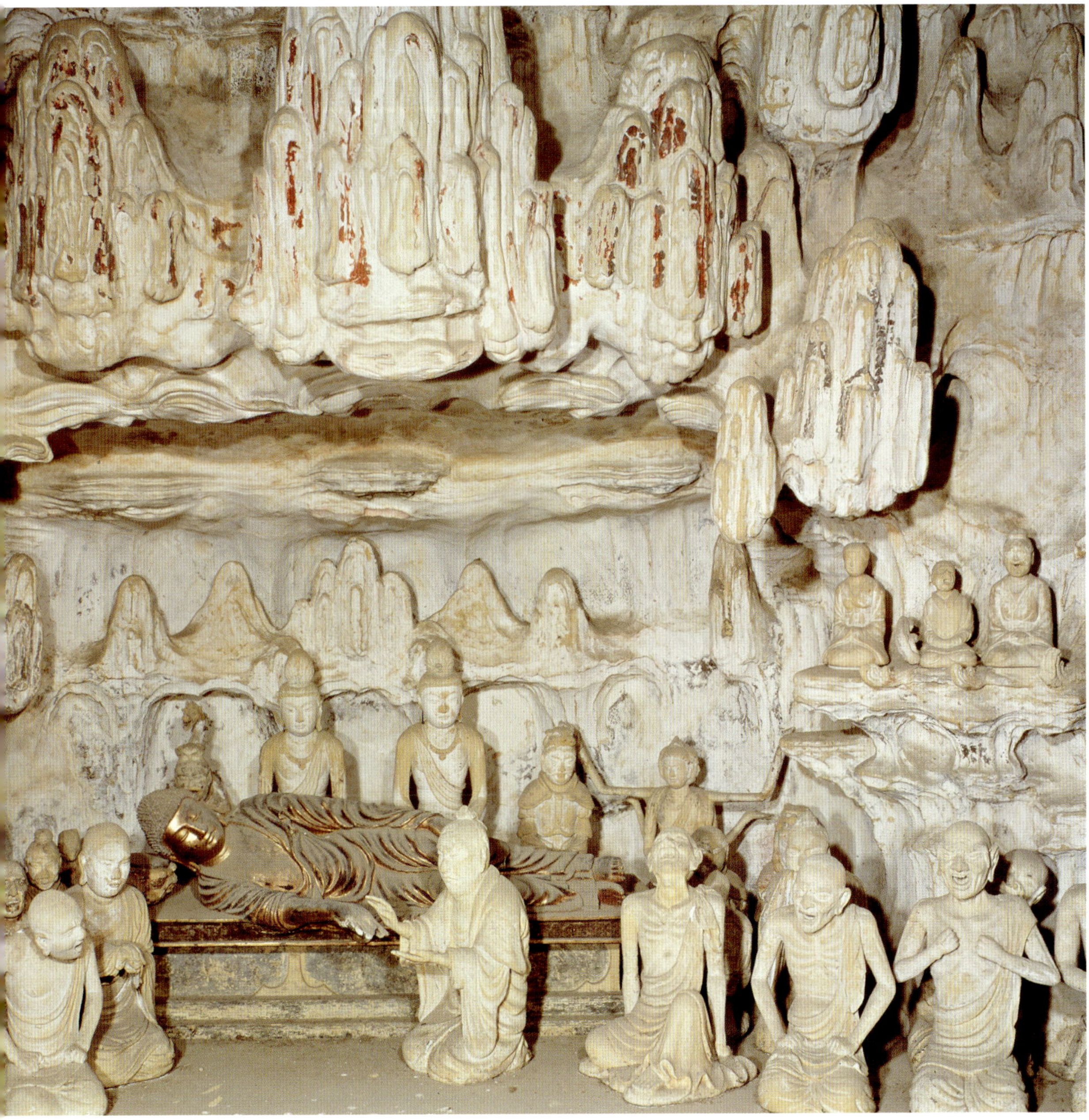

薬師三尊像
Yakushi Triad

技術の粋を尽くした金銅仏の最高峰
Pinnacle of gilt bronze Buddhist sculptural technique

古代東アジアの仏像の集大成 | 薬師寺は天武9年（680）、天武天皇が皇后の病気平癒を祈り飛鳥の地に造営させました。平城京遷都にともなって養老2年（718）、現在の地に移転されました。金堂本尊である薬師三尊像は、平城京遷都前後、7〜8世紀に作られた奈良時代初期の代表的金銅仏です。その柔軟で写実的な表現や、台座の意匠には、中国唐時代の仏像の作風との共通性が多く見られます。まさに当時の東アジアの仏像の集大成ともいえる作品です。

とろけるような美しさ | 中尊の薬師如来像は、丈六（じょうろく）（仏像の身長の基準である4.84メートル）の金銅仏で、もとは輝く金色でしたが、今では黒く光る銅の地肌があらわれています。その「やわらかい硬さ」が、えもいわれぬ滑らかさ、美しさを生みだしています。切れ長の目、ふっくらしたほほ、やわらかな鼻すじや唇の作る表情は、人間を超えた叡智を感じさせ、哲学者で文化史家でもある和辻哲郎はその著書『古寺巡礼』で「とろける美しさ」と記しています。その体は自然な立体感にあふれ、張りがあり、衣のひだも現実のもののように巧みに仕上げられています。

Amalgam of Buddhist sculpture in ancient East Asia | *Yakushi-ji* temple was established by Emperor Temmu in the Asuka area in 680 to pray for the recovery of the empress. The temple was moved to its present site in 718 when the capital was relocated to *Heijō-kyō* (present-day Nara). The Yakushi Triad is the central icon of the *Kondō*. Made in the seventh or eighth century before or after the move of the capital, the triad is representative of early Nara period gilt bronze sculpture. The soft, naturalistic expression, and the design of the pedestal show parallels with the style of the Tang dynasty China. Indeed, these sculptures show the amalgamation of Buddhist imagery across ancient East Asia.

Sculpture of "awesome beauty" | The central image of *Yakushi Nyorai* (Healing Buddha) is gilt bronze, and measures one *jōroku* (4.84 m, the standard height for gilt bronze Buddhist sculptures). Once covered with gold, the surface is now a reflective black bronze. This "soft firmness" generates an indescribable smoothness and grace. The expression created by the narrow slits of the eyes, the plump cheeks, soft ridge of the nose and mouth communicates a transcendent wisdom. The philosopher and cultural historian *Tetsurō Watsuji* wrote in his book "*Koji Junrei*" that the sculptures have an "awesome beauty." The torsos are imbued with a natural three-dimensionality and a tension, and the surface of the robes gives the lend a certain realism to the sculptures.

奈良時代
薬師三尊像

Nara period
Yakushi Sanzonzō

Data

薬師如来及び両脇侍像（中尊）
奈良 薬師寺 金堂
7〜8世紀
像高 254.7cm
国宝
銅造 鍍金

Yakushi Nyorai and flanking attendants (Central image)
Main Hall, Yakushi-ji temple, Nara
Seventh or Eighth century
254.7 cm
National Treasure
Gilt bronze

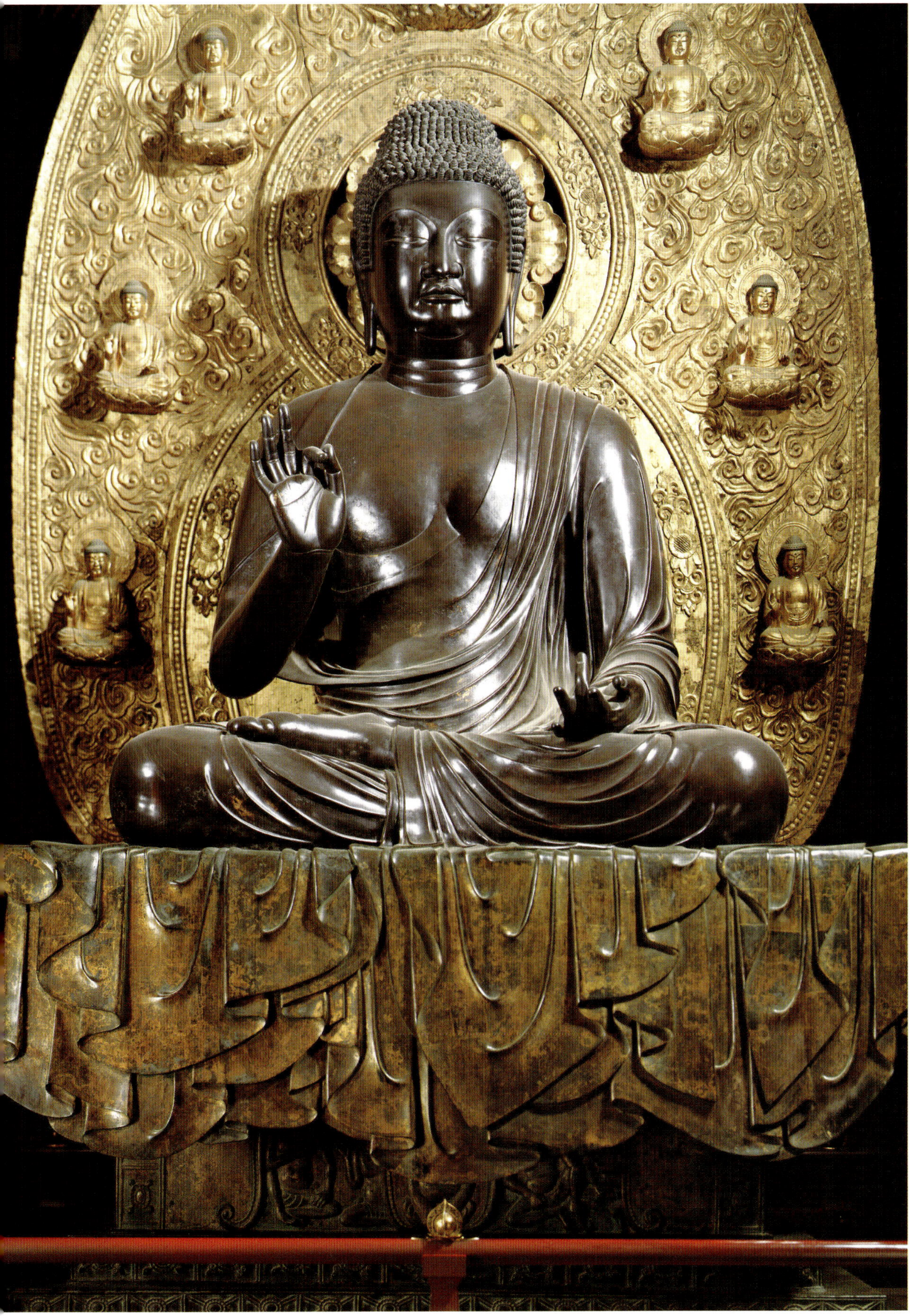

阿修羅像（八部衆像）
Ashura *one of the Eight Heavenly Beings*

時代を超えて伝えられる天平の息づかい
The timeless aura of the Tempyō era

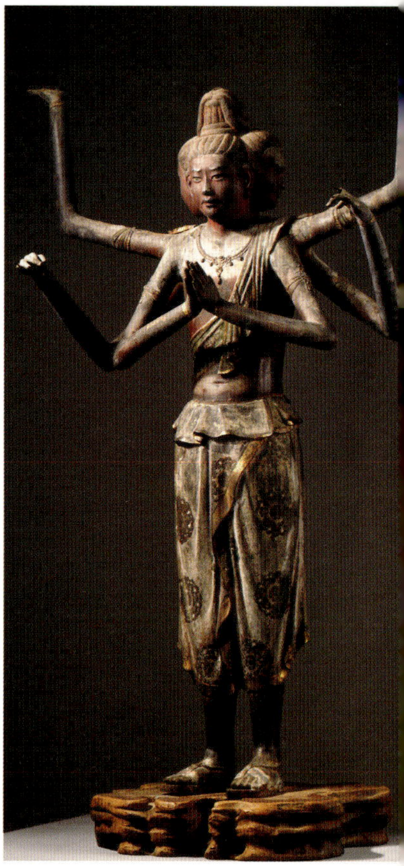

戦火をくぐりぬけた天平の名品 | 天平6年（734）、光明皇后は母のために興福寺に西金堂を建立し、ここに釈迦三尊像をはじめ釈迦十大弟子像、八部衆像など28体の諸像を安置しました。永い年月のあいだに、戦火などで建物は焼亡し、多くの仏像も失われました。しかし、十大弟子像と八部衆像の一部は奇跡的に現存しています。これらの像は内部が空洞になっている乾漆像です。乾漆像は重量が軽く、持ち出しが容易です。そのこともあって焼失を免れたのでしょう。十大弟子像と八部衆像はいずれも細身で直立した姿勢で、明るく、さわやかな作風を示しています。獣や鳥の頭をもつ異形の八部衆像のなかでも、少年の表情を見事にあらわした阿修羅像は一際目を引きます。

少年のような表情の阿修羅像 | 3つの顔に6本の腕を持つ阿修羅像の姿には本来の闘争的な性格があらわされています。顔の両側に作られた2つの面には厳しさと苦渋の表情が浮かびます。しかし、正面の顔ははるか遠くを見つめ、その表情には一点の濁りもありません。天平時代の息づかいがそのまま伝わってくるような、名品中の名品です。

Masterpieces of the Tempyō era that survived the ravages of warfare | In the 6th year of the Tempyō era, that is, in 734, the Empress Kōmyō established the *Saikondō* (West Golden Hall) on the grounds of *Kōfuku-ji* temple, for the repose of the soul of her mother. There she enshrined twenty-eight sculptures, including a Shaka Triad, Ten Great Disciples of Buddha (*Jūdai Deshi*), and the Eight Heavenly Beings (*Hachibushū*). Through the centuries, many of the buildings and sculptures at *Kōfuku-ji* have been destroyed through the ravages of war and nature, but miraculously, most of the group of Ten Great Disciples and Eight Heavenly Beings survived to the present day. They were all made using hollow dry lacquer construction, making them lightweight and easy to transport, and which may in part account for their survival. Both groups are slender standing figures, exhibiting a clear and fluent style. Some of the images have bird or animal heads. The image of Ashura, skillfully depicted as a youth is especially noteworthy.

The youthful Ashura | The three-faced, six-armed Ashura was originally an icon of combativeness, evolved from Indian mythology, and the two faces at the side of his head exhibit violent or vehement expressions. The central face, however, seems to be gazing into the distance, showing not one a trace of rancor. It is a masterpiece among masterpieces that transmit the timeless aura of the Tempyō era.

奈良時代
阿修羅像（八部衆像）

Nara period
Ashura (Hachibushū Zō)

Data

八部衆立像（阿修羅）
奈良 興福寺 国宝館
天平６年（734）
像高　153.0cm
国宝
脱活乾漆造 彩色

Eight Heavenly Beings (Ashura)
Hall of National Treasures,
Kōfuku-ji temple, Nara
AD 734 (Tempyō 6)
153.0 cm
National Treasure
Hollow dry lacquer, Pigments

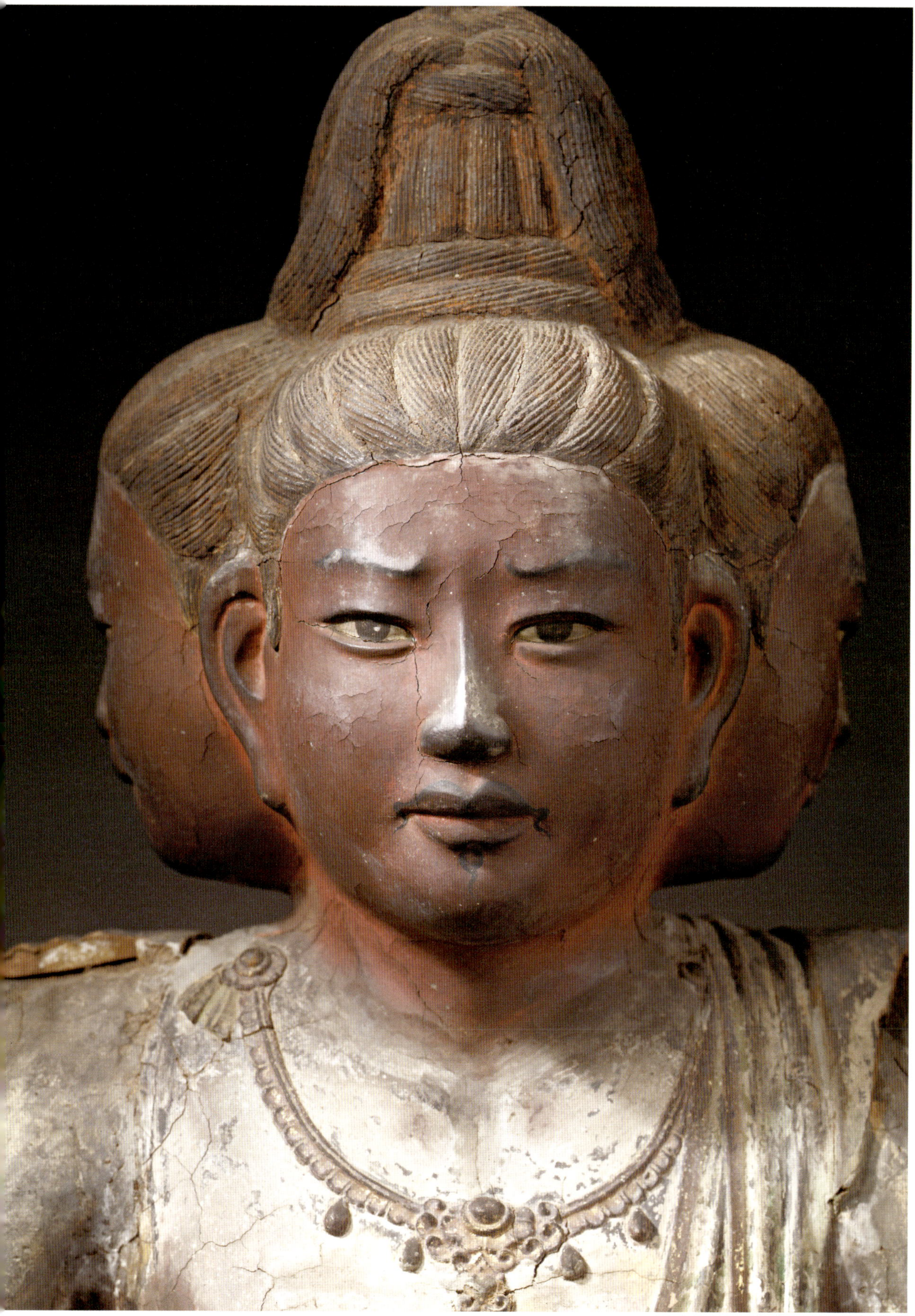

阿修羅像（八部衆像）｜Ashura

康慶作不空羂索観音坐像
Seated Fukūkensaku Kannon *Made by Kōkei (act. 1175-1200)*

康慶の情熱が込められた力強い造形
Powerful creation imbued with Kōkei's passion

興福寺の復興事業 | 治承4年（1180）に、当時政権を握っていた平家は、対抗勢力である奈良の東大寺、興福寺などを焼き討ちし、このとき奈良時代以来の古仏の多くが焼失しました。奈良仏師たちは、京都仏師たちほど活躍していませんでしたが、まもなく始まった東大寺と興福寺の復興事業で多くの造仏を任され、大きく躍進しました。奈良仏師のリーダー康慶は、一派を率いて文治5年（1189）に興福寺南円堂に、中尊不空羂索観音像と四天王像および法相六祖像を作りました。

古典を取り入れた新たな作風 | 巨大な丈六の不空羂索観音像は、復興前の像の印象を残しながら、鎌倉時代の仏像の新しい魅力に満ちています。大きな目とうねるような唇の顔は、明確な意志を感じさせ、がっしりとした体にダイナミックな衣文が刻まれます。それまでの定朝様（じょうちょうよう）のおとなしい仏像とは異なった力強さがあります。独特の形の光背は、旧像の形をそのまま写したものです。古きよきものを残しつつ新たなスタイルを生み出す、これは、奈良の地で古典に触れる機会の多かった奈良仏師だからこそできた、いわば仏像のルネッサンスなのです。

The reconstruction of *Kōfuku-ji* temple | In the 4th year of the Jishō era (1180), in its drive to seize power, the Taira clan (*Heike*) burned down *Tōdai-ji*, *Kōfuku-ji* and other temples they perceived to be centers of opposition. A great number of Buddhist images from the Nara period were destroyed. Although Kyoto had become the center of Buddhist art, the sculptors in Nara now saw a revival of their activities, as they worked on the reconstruction of *Tōdai-ji* and *Kōfuku-ji* soon after their destruction. To refurbish *Kōfuku-ji* temple, the leading sculptor of the time, *Kōkei* and artisans from his atelier created works such as the *Fukūkensaku Kannon* (central image), the Four Heavenly Kings (*Shitennō*), and the six patriarchs of the *Hōsō* sect at *Nanen-dō* in 1189.

A new style based on the classical | The colossal seated *Fukūkensaku Kannon* (one *jōroku* tall, or 4.84 m, a standard size for Buddhist statuary) retains classical Nara period features, combined with innovations of the twelfth-century Kamakura period. There is a clear strength in the face, with its large eyes and swelling lips, and there is a dynamism to the carving of the folds of the robes over the compact torso. These features differ from the softer style of *Jōchō* in the past. Yet the unique shape of the halo is in the traditional style. The sculptors in Nara had no doubt seen and studied the traditional Buddhist works and were thus able to re-create the style, resulting in a renaissance of Buddhist sculpture.

鎌倉時代
康慶作不空羂索観音坐像

Kamakura period
Fukūkensaku Kannon Zazō
Kōkei saku

Data

不空羂索観音坐像
奈良 興福寺 南円堂
文治５年（1189）
像高　344.7cm
康慶作
国宝
木造 ヒノキ 漆箔

Seated Fukūkensaku Kannon (Amoghapasa)
Nanen-dō, Kōfuku-ji temple, Nara
AD 1189 (Bunji 5)
344.7 cm
Made by Kōkei
National Treasure
Wood (Japanese cypress; hinoki), Gold foil applied with lacquer

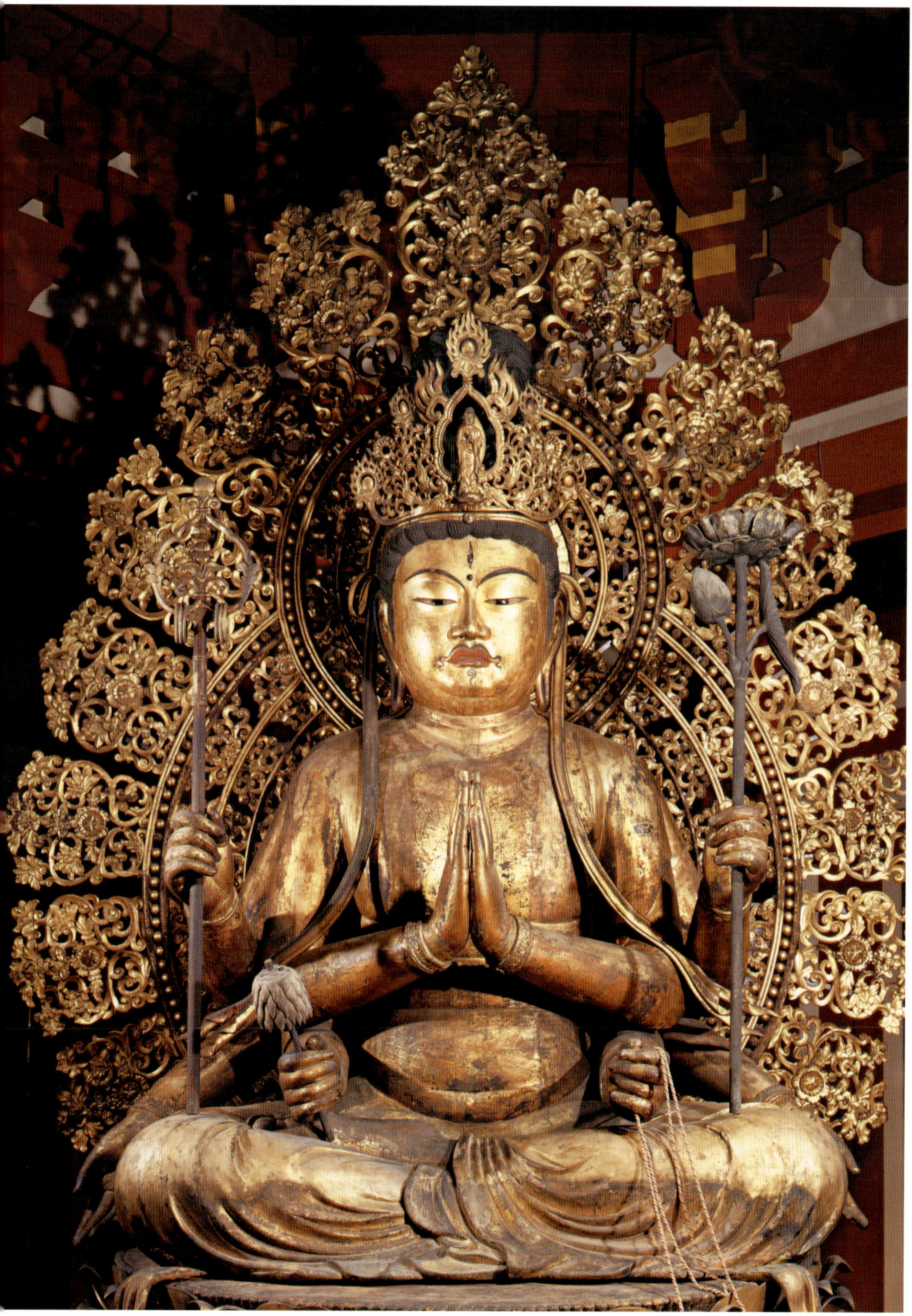

康慶作不空羂索観音坐像　|　Seated Fukūkensaku Kannon

運慶等作無著菩薩立像、世親菩薩立像
Mujaku and Seshin *Made by Unkei and his atelier*

仏師運慶がついに到達した静かなる存在感
The serenity achieved by the masterful sculptor Unkei

運慶と北円堂の造仏｜興福寺の北円堂は藤原摂関家の始祖ともいえる藤原不比等(ふひと)の供養のために奈良時代に建てられた仏堂です。北円堂は、二度の焼失を経て、仏師康慶の子、運慶の手により復興造仏が行われました。北円堂の諸像は運慶の造仏の集大成ともいえる作品で、建暦2年（1212）に作られた中尊の弥勒仏坐像と無著菩薩立像、世親菩薩立像が今に伝わります。諸像は、それぞれ運慶の息子や弟子たちの作と記録されていますが、総監督の運慶の構想下で造仏が行われたものと考えられます。

卓越したリアリティ｜これら北円堂の諸作品には、鎌倉時代の代表的仏師である運慶の円熟した境地がうかがわれます。兄の無著と弟の世親は、仏教発展に重要な役を果たしたインドの高僧で、リアルで存在感のある表情や、まるで本物のような衣文のディテールに驚かされます。東大寺南大門の金剛力士阿形像など、かつての運慶の作品にあったような、観る者を驚かせる激しい表現は影をひそめ、静寂さを感じさせる落ち着きのある表現が完成されています。運慶は約30年の創作活動を経て、ついにこのような作風を完成させたのです。

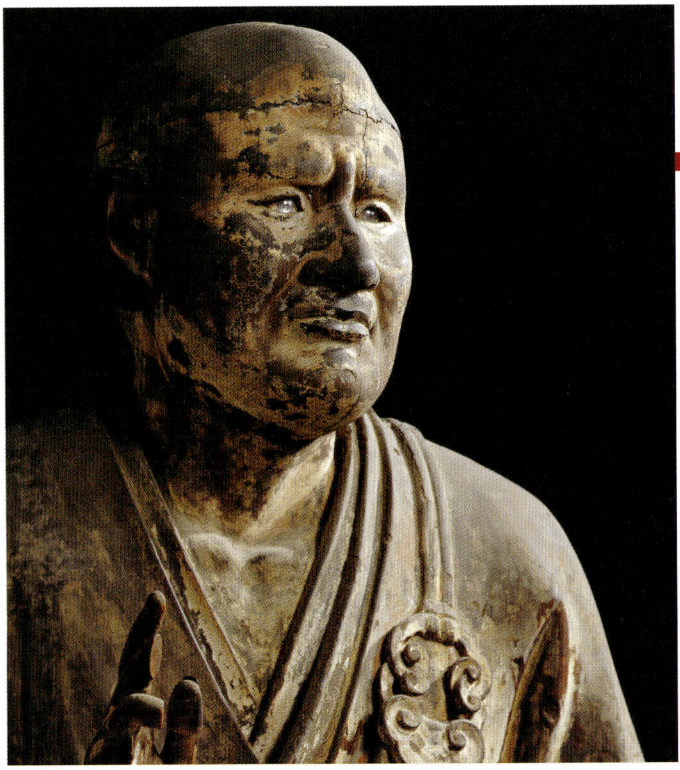

鎌倉時代
運慶等作無著菩薩立像、世親菩薩立像

Kamakura period
Mujaku Bosatsu Ryūzō, Seshin Bosatsu Ryūzō
Unkei nado saku

Data
無著菩薩立像、世親菩薩立像
奈良 興福寺 北円堂
建暦２年（1212）
像高　193.0cm（無著像）
国宝
木造 カツラ 彩色 玉眼

Mujaku and Seshin bodhisattva
Hokuen-dō, Kōfuku-ji temple, Nara
AD 1212 (Kenreki 2)
193.0 cm (Mujaku)
Made by Unkei and his atelier
National Treasure
Wood (katsura), Pigments, Crystal inset eyes

Unkei and the creation of Buddhist sculpture for Hokuen-dō | The *Hokuen-dō* at *Kōfuku-ji* temple is a Buddhist hall that was built by the powerful *Fujiwara* family during the Nara period as a tutelary shrine commemorating their earliest ancestor *Fujiwara-no Fuhito*. *Hokuen-dō* was twice destroyed by fire, and *Unkei* (d. 1223), the son of the sculptor *Kōkei*, worked on the refurbishing of the temple. Among the statuary still extant at *Hokuen-dō* are the central seated Miroku Buddha, and the two bodhisattva, *Mujaku* and *Seshin*. Records state that they were made in 1212 by Unkei's son and others in his workshop, but most likely these sculptures were made under Unkei's supervision and reflect his high standards.

Superb realism | The sculptures at *Hokuen-dō* represent the mature Kamakura style of the master *Unkei*. *Mujaku* and *Seshin* were originally brothers who became high-ranking priests important to the spread of Buddhism in India. The realistic depiction of their facial expressions and details of their robes are astounding. Unlike the fierce guardian figures such as those at the Great South Gate of *Tōdai-ji* temple by *Unkei*, these Indian patriarchs exude serenity and beneficence. They are the epitome of the style developed by *Unkei* over his thirty-year career.

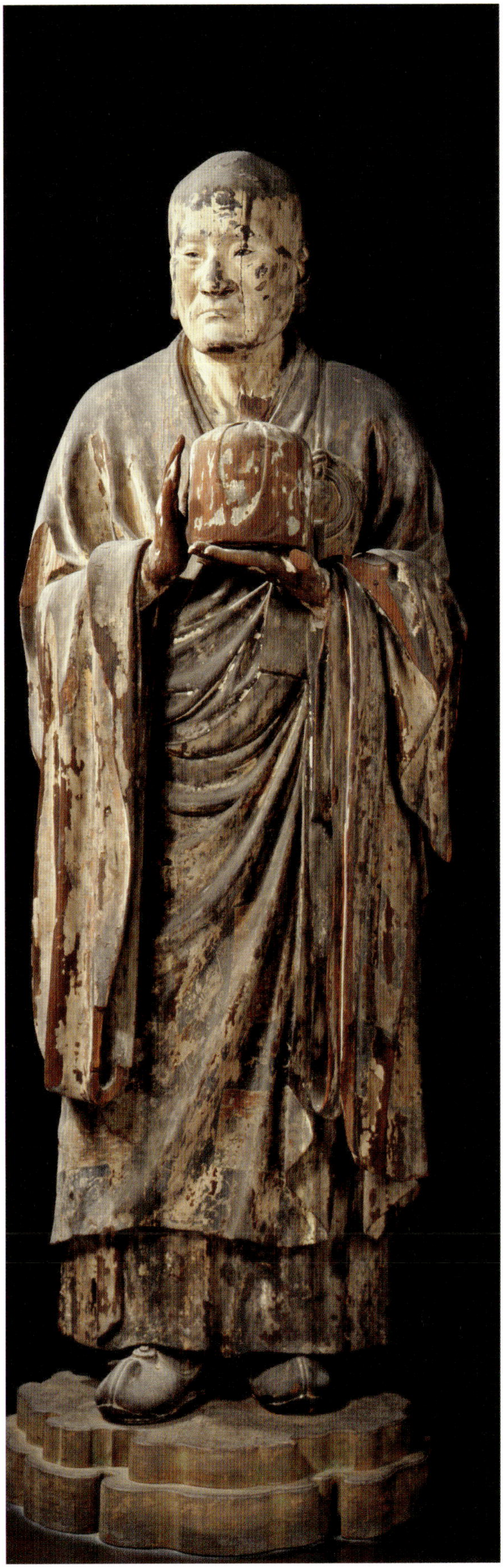

運慶等作無著菩薩立像、世親菩薩立像 | Mujaku and Seshin

不空羂索観音立像
Standing Fukūkensaku Kannon

豪華な宝冠を戴く三目八臂の大観音像
Three-eyed, eight-armed statue of Kannon with a luxurious crown

堂宇を守る王者の風格 | 東大寺伽藍の東端に位置する法華堂（別名三月堂）は仏像が安置される正堂と礼拝のための礼堂が一つになった珍しい作りの仏堂です。その法華堂創建当初からの本尊とされるのが、4メートル近い堂々たる威容の不空羂索観音像です。3つの目に8本の腕、あとから着せかけたように装着された鹿皮をまとい、四天王像など一群の天平古像を従えて立つ姿はまるで王者のように見えます。脱活乾漆造の大像は、ほほを豊かに張り、正面を直視します。肩の豊かな肉付け、厚みのある体躯にはしなやかで美しいモデリングが見られます。どっしりとした落ち着きが威厳ともなり、天平時代盛期8世紀中頃の仏像を代表する傑作です。
他に類を見ない華やかさ | また、豪華な首飾りや瓔珞（ようらく）が全身を飾り、両肩にかけた天衣は腰の前をわたって反対の手首にふわりとかかります。よく見ると合掌した両手には大きな水晶が挟まれています。とりわけすばらしいのが宝冠で、翡翠、琥珀、水晶、真珠など多くの宝玉をちりばめ、正面には銀製の化仏立像を配し、周囲を銀製鍍金の透彫り宝相華（ほうそうげ）で飾っています。

Majestic presence | The *Hokke-dō* (Lotus Hall, also known as *Sangatsu-dō*, the Third Month Hall) at the eastern end of the *Tōdai-ji* compound is unusual in that it combines in one building an inner hall (*hondō*) where the statues are enshrined, and an outer hall (*raidō*) where worship takes place. The principal icon (*honzon*) of the inner hall is the magnificent eighth-century *Fukūkensaku Kannon*, nearly 4 meters tall. With his three eyes and eight arms, wearing a deer skin garment, the image presides majestically over the hall, which includes a group of the Four Guardian Kings. The *Fukūkensaku Kannon* is constructed in the hollow dry lacquer technique (*dakkatsu kanshitsu*), with full cheeks and the gaze of the eyes directed straight downward. The ample shoulders and thick torso are beautifully modeled. The effect is one of monumentality and dignity. This sculpture is a masterpiece of Buddhist statuary of the mid-eighth century, at the height of Tempyō era.
Unprecedented magnificence | Furthermore, this Kannon sculpture is swathed in elaborate necklaces and adornments, with flowing scarves extending from both shoulders, overlapping at the front and wrapped around the wrists. A closer look reveals a large crystal ball in the pair of hands clasped in prayer. The magnificent crown is embedded with jade, agate, crystal, pearls and other precious stones. At the front center of the crown is a silver Amida Buddha, surrounded by gold-plated silver openwork floral motifs.

奈良時代
不空羂索観音立像

Nara period
Fukūkensaku Kannon Ryūzō

Data

不空羂索観音立像
奈良 東大寺 法華堂
8 世紀中頃
像高　362.0cm
国宝
脱活乾漆造 漆箔

Standing Fukūkensaku Kannon
Hokke-dō, Tōdai-ji temple, Nara
Mid-eighth century
362.0 cm
National Treasure
Hollow dry lacquer, with gold leaf applied with lacquer

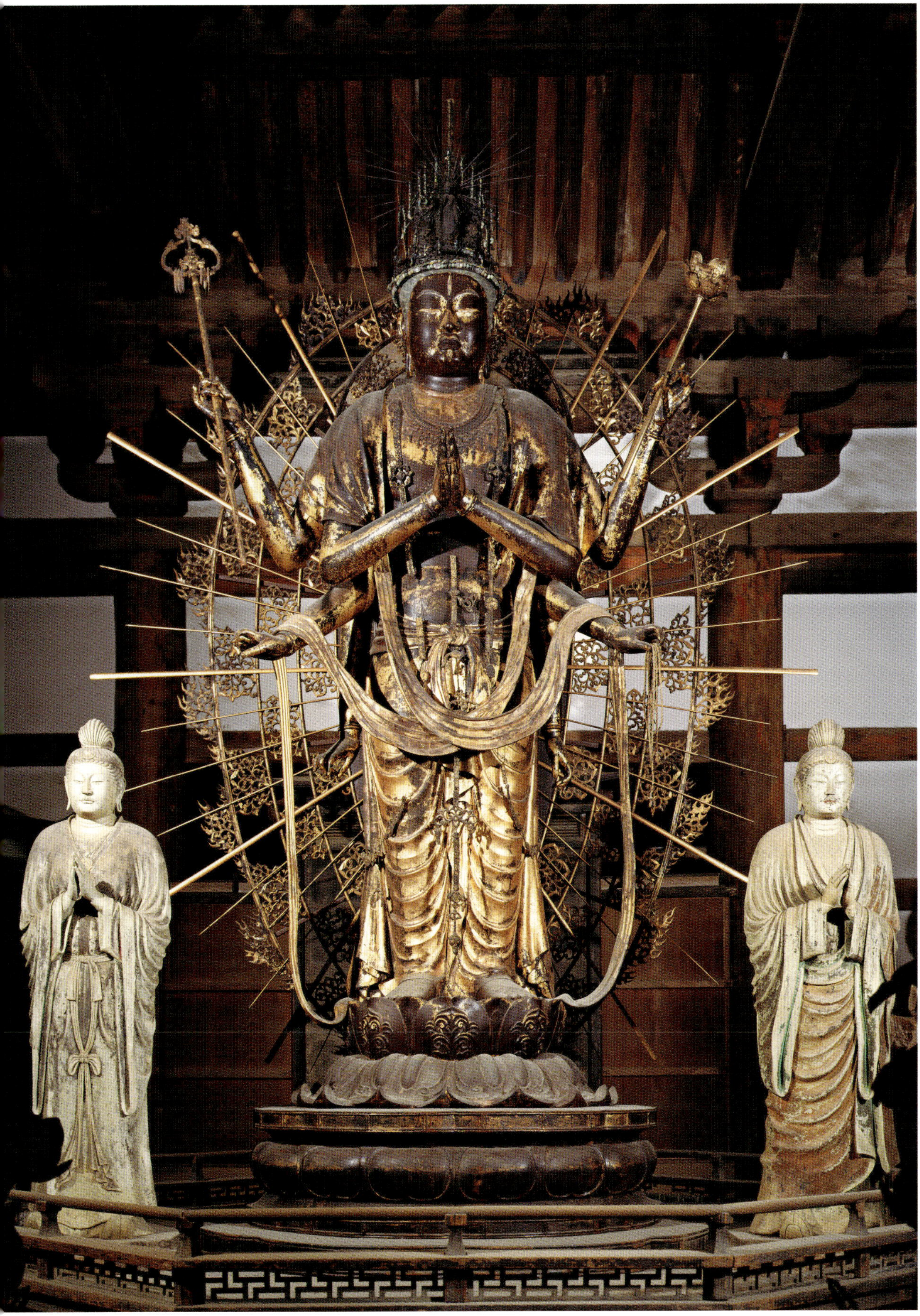

不 空 羂 索 観 音 立 像　｜　Standing Fukūkensaku Kannon

四天王立像（広目天）
Four Heavenly Kings *Kōmoku-ten in the Kaidan-dō, Tōdai-ji temple, Nara*

深い怒りを内に秘めた四天王像の名作
Masterpiece of controlled power

天平塑像の名品｜大仏殿を挟んで法華堂とは反対、境内の西側に戒壇堂があります。ここには日本の四天王像の代名詞ともいえる4体の塑像が安置されています。現在の建物は江戸時代に再建されたもので、そのときおそらく法華堂から移されてきたのがこの四天王像です。法華堂の日光､月光菩薩像と技法や表現が共通し､もともとは一具の像だったとも考えられています。今は彩色がほとんど剥げ落ち、全体にあらわれた塑土の白さが独特な印象を生んでいますが、よく見ると鎧や袴の細部に造立時の美しい彩色や切金文様が残っています。

仏敵を排除する強い威圧感｜アジア西域にルーツのある革製のような甲冑を身に着けた自然な姿勢は、法華堂の巨大な四天王像に比べると、表現の細やかさがめだちます。ヘラさばきはみごとの一言につき、深い内面性をあらわした表情は、時をへだてた現代人にも多くのことを訴えてきます。大きく口を開けた増長天像に対して、広目天、多聞天、持国天像は口を閉じ、静かに沈黙しています｡とりわけ広目天の半眼の目は､はるか遠くすべてを見つめているようで、ここを訪れる者の心をとらえて放しません。

A polished jewel of Tempyō era sculpture | The *Kaidan-dō* (Ordination Hall) is situated on the west side of the temple precincts, that is, on the opposite side of the *Daibutsu-den* from the *Hokke-dō*. The *Kaidan-dō* houses an exemplary group of clay sculptures of the Four Heavenly Kings (*Shitennō*). The present building dates to the Edo period, when these four images were moved here probably from *Hokke-dō*. These statues are similar in style and technique to the pair of sculptures known as *Nikkō* and *Gakkō Bosatsu* (Bodhisattvas of Solar and Lunar radiance) in the *Hokke-dō*, and they may all have originally been part of the same group. Their original color has deteriorated, exposing the white clay underneath, giving them a unique aura. Close examination reveals remnants of the original colors and cut gold leaf patterns on the robes and armor.

Strength to ward off threats against Buddhism | The Four Heavenly Kings are posed naturalistically, wearing armor and helmets, which resemble the leather gear from western Asia. Compared with the larger set of guardians in the *Hokke-dō*, this group is more sensitively rendered. One, *Zōchō-ten*, is open-mouthed, while the other three have closed mouths. The *Kōmoku-ten* in particular has a far away look, gazing at the world through half-open eyes that captures the visitor's attention.

奈良時代
四天王立像（広目天）

Nara period
Shitennō Ryūzō (Kōmoku-ten)

Data

四天王立像
奈良 東大寺 戒壇堂
8世紀中頃
像高　162.7cm（広目天）
国宝
塑像 彩色 切金

Four Heavenly Kings
Standing Kōmoku-ten
Kaidan-dō, Tōdai-ji temple, Nara
Mid-eighth century
162.7 cm
National Treasure
Clay, with traces of pigment and cut gold

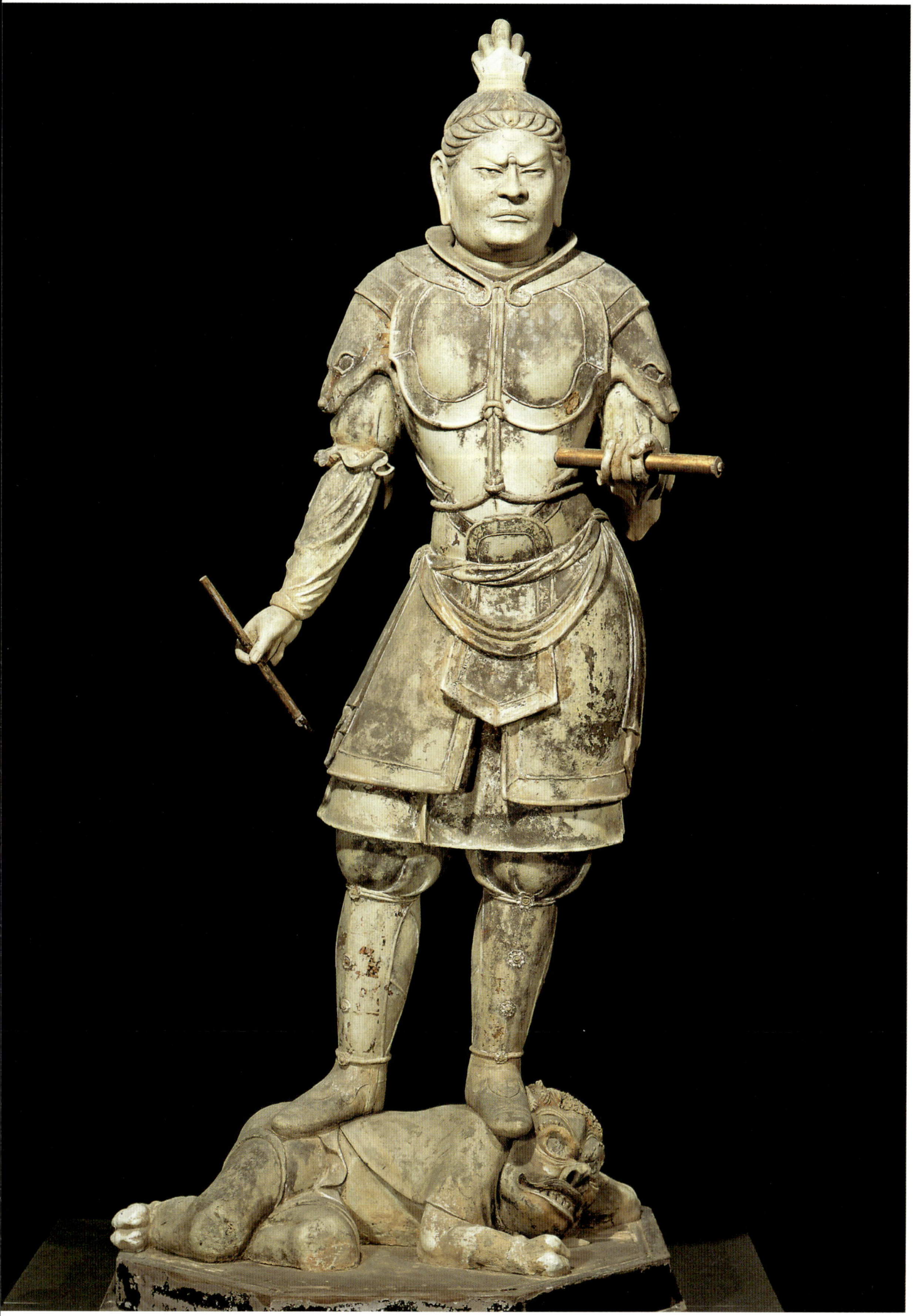

四天王立像（広目天）　|　Four Heavenly Kings

盧舎那仏坐像（奈良の大仏）
Seated Vairocana (the Great Buddha of Nara)

世界最大の銅像、奈良の大仏
The largest bronze statue in the world, the Great Buddha of Nara

3度の大修復 | 世界最大の木造建築と言われる大仏殿は世界遺産でもあり、見る者を圧倒する威容を誇ります。その本尊盧舎那仏坐像、いわゆる奈良の大仏も世界最大の銅像です。大仏は当時の国威発揚の手段の一つとして作られ、天平勝宝4年（752）に開眼供養が行われました。しかし、大仏と大仏殿はその後の多くの戦乱や天災により破壊、焼失しました。なかでも治承4年（1180）の平家による焼き討ちでは甚大な被害を被りました。永禄10年（1567）にも戦火で焼け、このときは、修復が行われるまでに実に100年以上もの歳月を必要としました。現在、天平の造立当時の姿は脚部と台座蓮弁の一部に残されています。

かつては全身が金色だった | この巨大な大仏は削り中型（なかご）と呼ぶ方法で作られたと考えられています。これは塑像を原型とし、その外側に外型を作り、原型を銅を流す厚さの分を削って中型として、そのすき間に溶けた銅を流し込む技法です。一度に全体を鋳造するのではなく、3年をかけて8回に分けて下から鋳造したとされます。さらに表面を仕上げ、金メッキをほどこして完成。完成した当初は全身が金色に輝いていました。

Three major restorations | The *Daibutsu-den* (Great Buddha Hall) is said to be the largest extant wooden structure in the world, and is registered as a Worlde Heritage site. It has a great dignity about it that dazzles visitors. Its main image, Vairocana (*Rushana Butsu*), or the so-called *Nara no Daibutsu* (Great Buddha of Nara) is the largest bronze statue in the world. The sculpture was a symbol of national prestige, and it was dedicated with an "eye-opening" ceremony in 752. After that time, however, both the *Daibutsu* and the *Daibutsu-den* were subject to destruction during civil wars and natural disasters. The most severe damage was caused in 1180 when the temple was burned down during the civil wars by Taira clan (*Heike*). Another civil war in 1567 caused more destruction by fire, requiring over one hundred years until the restoration was completed again. Of the present *Daibutsu* image, only the legs and part of the pedestal remain from the Nara period.

Originally completely covered with gold leaf | The enormous image of Buddha is believed to have been made using a technique called *kezuri nakago*. That is, a clay prototype was used to make an outer mold. Then the clay prototype was ground down to leave room between it and the outer mold for molten bronze to be poured. The casting began from the bottom of the sculpture and was accomplished in eight separate castings over a three year period. The entire image was then covered with gold leaf, reflecting its radiance.

奈良時代
盧舎那仏坐像（奈良の大仏）
Nara period
Rushana Butsu Zazō (Nara no Daibutsu)

Data

盧舎那仏坐像
奈良 東大寺 大仏殿
天平勝宝４年（752）
像高　1473cm
国宝
銅造 鍍金

Vairocana, or the Great Buddha of Nara
Seated Vairocana
Daibutsu-den, Tōdai-ji temple, Nara
AD 752 (Tempyō Shōhō 4)
1473 cm
National Treasure
Bronze with gilding

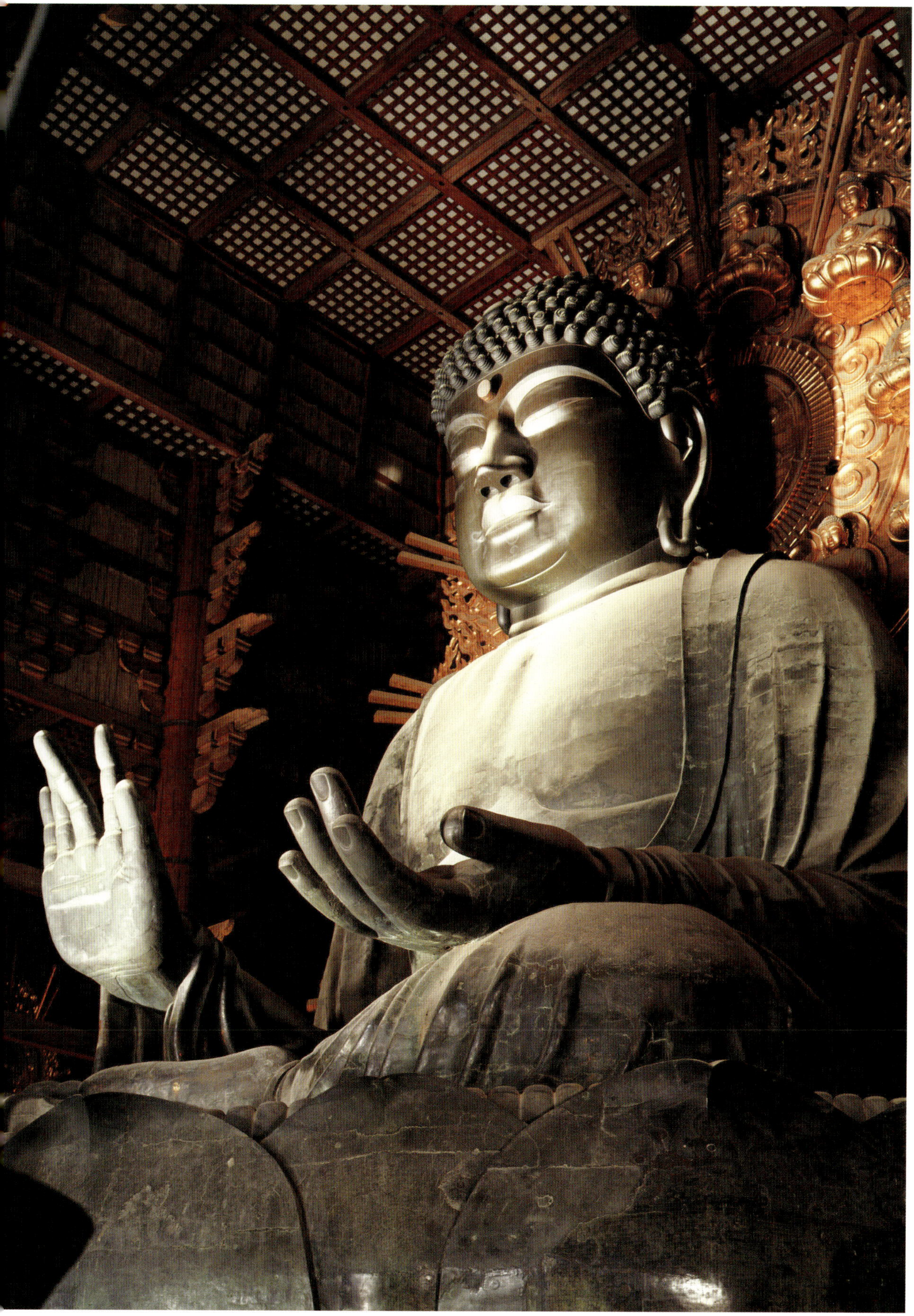

盧舎那仏坐像（奈良の大仏）　｜　Seated Vairocana (the Great Buddha of Nara)

運慶・快慶等作金剛力士立像
Two Guardian Kings (Vajrapani) *Unkei, Kaikei and their studio*

慶派の総力を結集した大作、南大門仁王像
Guardian Kings (Ni-ō) of the Great South Gate, masterpieces of the collective talent of the Kei school

東大寺復興の締めくくりの2体 | 鎌倉時代初頭に行われた東大寺復興の際に建てられたのが現在の東大寺南大門で、大仏様建築の代表的なものとして知られています。門に向かって左側には口を開いた阿形(あぎょう)像、右には口を閉じた吽形(うんぎょう)像の2体の金剛力士立像が立っています。この巨像は、像内や納入品に書かれた銘などから、建仁3年(1203)に、仏師運慶が総指揮をとり、仏師定覚(じょうかく)、運慶の子湛慶(たんけい)、快慶をはじめ二十余人の慶派仏師らによって作られたことが知られます。

快慶らしい阿形像と運慶らしい吽形像 | 吽形像は全体のイメージを司る運慶の作風が全面にあらわれた力強い作品として完成しました。阿形像の整ったシルエットには絵画的ともいわれる快慶ならではの雰囲気もうかがえます。両像はヒノキ材の寄木造で、8メートルを超える像はそれぞれ8、9本の太い角材を束ねた上に厚い板を張り、それに彫刻されています。完成時は全身に彩色がほどこされ、今でも衣の裏側などに文様が残っています。いかにも慶派仏師の作らしい筋骨たくましい肉体と迫力ある表情を持つ2体の像は、日本の仁王像のなかでも最高の傑作です。

Two sculptures that crown the reconstruction of *Tōdai-ji* temple | The Great South Gate (*Nandai-mon*) was erected during the reconstruction of *Tōdai-ji* temple in the early Kamakura period, in the so-called *Daibutsu* (or "Indian") style of architecture. On the left side of the gate is a sculpture of open-mouthed *Agyō*, and on the right, *Ungyō*, with his mouth closed. These two sculptures of standing Guardian Kings (*Kongō Rikishi*) were executed around 1203 under the supervision of *Unkei* by over twenty sculptors of the *Kei* school, including *Jōkaku*, *Tankei* (Unkei's son), and *Kaikei*, judging from the names recorded inside the sculpture and in the dedicatory scrolls and objects.

Kaikei-style *Agyō* and Unkei-style *Ungyō* | The dynamism and power of Unkei's style is dominant in the image of *Ungyō*, while Agyō's painterly silhouette reflects the refined naturalistic atmosphere of Kaikei's style. Both statues are made from Japanese cypress (*hinoki*) in the joined-block technique, and stand over 8 meters tall. The sculptures are made up from eight or nine large blocks of wood joined together, over which another layer of thick planks of wood were attached. The outer wood was then carved, and covered with pigment. Some traces of the original color can still be seen on the backs of the garments. These are masterful examples of Two Guardian Kings sculptures, with the musculature and dynamism characteristic of the *Kei* school works.

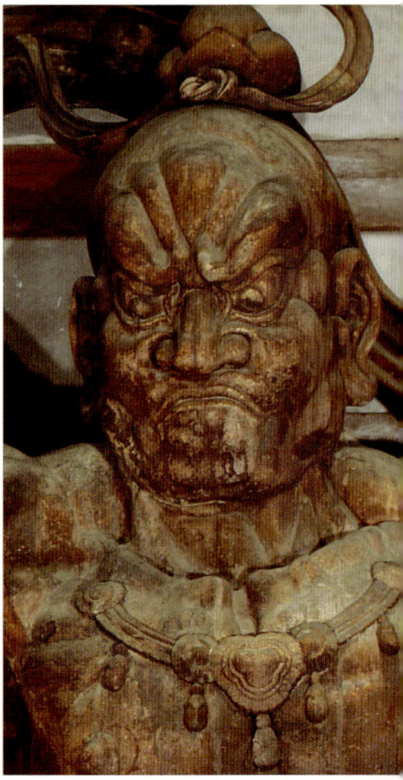

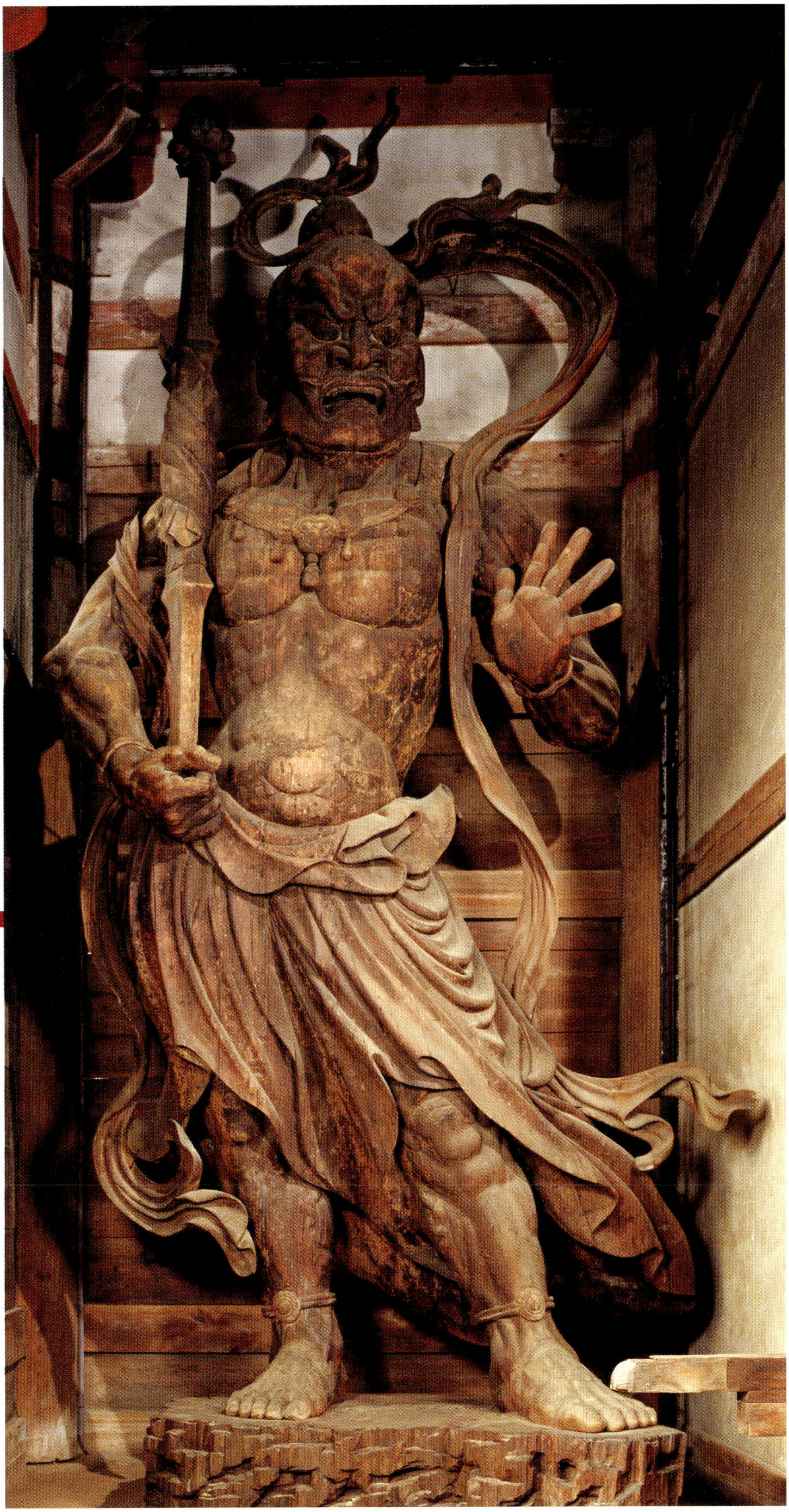

鎌倉時代
運慶・快慶等作金剛力士立像

Kamakura period
Kongō Rikishi Ryūzō
Unkei Kaikei nado saku

Data

金剛力士立像（阿形、吽形）
奈良 東大寺 南大門
建仁３年（1203）
像高　836.0cm（阿形）
　　　842.3cm（吽形）
運慶・快慶等作
国宝
木造 ヒノキ 彩色

Pair of Guardian Kings (Vajrapani)
Agyō and Ungyō
Nandai-mon, Tōdai-ji temple, Nara
AD 1203 (Kennin 3)
836.0 cm (Agyō)
842.3 cm (Ungyō)
Made by Unkei, Kaikei and their studio
National Treasure
Wood (Japanese cypress; hinoki), joined-block technique, with traces of pigments

盧舎那仏坐像
Seated Vairocana

光背に千仏を従える唐招提寺金堂の本尊
The principal image of the Main Hall at Tōshōdai-ji temple, accompanied by one thousand Buddhas

天平文化の雰囲気を色濃く残す金堂｜唐招提寺は、日本の仏教史で最も重要な人物の一人である鑑真和上が建てました。長い年月の間に奈良の多くの仏堂が失われましたが、この金堂は当初のまま守られてきた貴重な存在です。天平宝字3年（759）の唐招提寺創建の少し後に建立された金堂には、本尊の盧遮那仏（るしゃなぶつ）坐像が、その向かって右に薬師如来立像、左に千手観音立像を脇侍のように従え、梵天、帝釈天、四天王像に守られて安置されています。
仏教を体現する威風堂々たる仏｜脱活乾漆造の盧舎那仏坐像は、千仏をあらわした大光背を背にして、八重蓮華座の上に威風堂々と座っています。長く弧を描く眉とその下の切れ長の目、小ぶりながら形のはっきりした鼻と締まった口元、それに衣に包まれた足先などから、ほかの天平仏とは異なる独特な印象が漂います。経典によると、盧舎那仏は太陽神で、仏教の教えそのものを体現し全宇宙を照らす真の仏陀といわれます。釈迦如来もその化身（化仏）で、盧舎那仏の蓮華の千枚の花びらには釈迦が1人ずついるとされていて、この像の光背にあらわされた千仏はそのことを表現しています。

A Main Hall imbued with Tempyō culture atmosphere｜*Tōshōdai-ji* temple was built by *Ganjin* (Jianzhen, 689-763), a Chinese monk who was one of the most significant figures in Japanese Buddhism. Many temple buildings of ancient Nara have been lost, but Tōshōdai-ji's Main Hall (*Kondō*) still stands. The Main Hall was built shortly after the temple was founded in 759 enshrines as its main image (*honzon*) a seated Vairocana (*Rushana Butsu*), flanked by attendant figures of a standing *Yakushi Nyorai* on the viewer's right, and a *Senju Kannon* on the other side. Also arranged around the Vairocana are protecting sculptures of *Bon-ten* (Brahma), *Taishaku-ten* (Indra) and the Four Heavenly Kings.
The majestic Buddha who embodies Buddhism｜The *Rushana Butsu*, constructed in the hollow dry lacquer technique (*dakkatsu kanshitsu*), is seated majestically on an eight-fold lotus pedestal before a large halo embedded with one thousand small Buddha images (*kebutsu*). The features of this Rushana Buddha's face, with its arched eyebrows, wide slit eyes, small but sharply cut nose and firm lips, as well as the crossed legs beneath the robes, differentiate this sculpture from other Nara period statuary. According to the scriptures, Rushana Buddha is the sun deity and manifests himself as such, radiating light throughout the cosmos. The Shaka Buddha is another manifestation (*kebutsu*) and each of the thousand petals of his lotus dias carries a Shaka Buddha. Here, the one thousand small Buddhas in the halo represent this belief.

奈良時代
盧舎那仏坐像

Nara period
Rushana Butsu Zazō

Data

盧舎那仏坐像
奈良 唐招提寺 金堂
8世紀後半
像高　304.5cm
国宝
脱活乾漆造 漆箔

Seated Vairocana
Kondō, Tōshōdai-ji temple, Nara
Latter half of the eighth century
304.5cm
National Treasure
Hollow dry lacquer and gold foil applied with lacquer

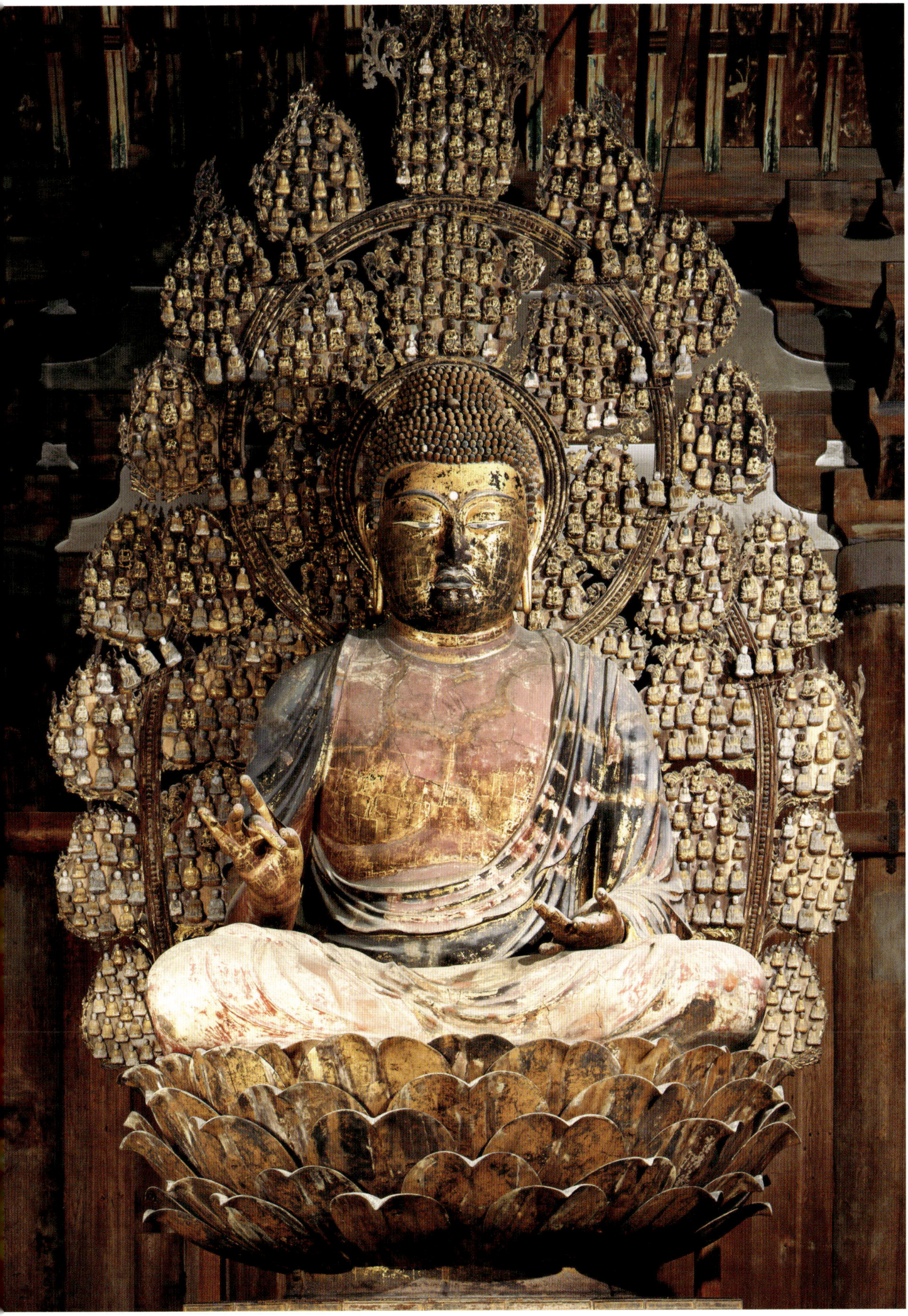

盧舎那仏坐像 | Seated Vairocana

千手観音立像
Standing Thousand-armed Kannon

千本の腕と眼が千の世界に救いをもたらす
One thousand arms and eyes bring salvation to a thousand worlds

本当に千本の腕を持つ千手観音像｜金堂本尊の盧舎那仏像の向かって左に安置される千手観音菩薩像は像高5メートルを超える巨大な仏像です。数本の木材を縦に寄せ合わせておよその形を作り、これに乾漆を盛り上げて作る木心乾漆といわれる技法で作られています。本尊に少し遅れた8世紀後半の作ですが、堂内の三尊の調和やバランスを考えると、当初からの構想で作られたと考えられています。日本の千手観音像としては最も初期のもので、千本の手を実際に持つ千手観音像は意外に少なく、唐招提寺像は貴重な存在です。

圧倒的な迫力の巨像の魅力｜像は頭上に仏面と9つの変化面をいただき、額にも縦に一眼が刻まれています。おおらかな面もちで、眉や目は盧舎那仏に少し似ているところがあり、堂々とした体つきには、巨像にふさわしい重量感がそなわっています。圧倒的なのは本体に取り付けられた千本の腕で、扇を広げるように群生する腕が迫力ある空間を作り、腕の合間からのぞく光背の透彫り文様が像の荘厳さをいっそう引き立てています。足下に立ってこの千手観音像を見上げると、大きな仏像を前にしたときならではの安心感に包み込まれるようです。

The Thousand-armed Kannon that actually has one thousand arms | The Thousand-armed Kannon (*Senju Kannon Bosatsu*) is a colossal statue over 5 meters in height. It stands to the viewer's left of the central image in the Main Hall, the seated Vairocana. The Thousand-armed Kannon is constructed in the wood-core dry lacquer technique (*mokushin kanshitsu*), which involves building up the image with layers of lacquer over a roughly carved wood core. The sculpture dates to the late eighth century, slightly later than the Vairocana, but judging from the balance and harmony among the three sculptures, they were probably made as a group. The *Tōshōdai-ji* Kannon is the earliest extant of any Japanese Thousand-armed Kannon sculptures, and is significant for the unusual feature of actually having one thousand arms.

The appeal of the colossal, intense image | This *Kannon* has "the third eye" (of wisdom) on its forehead, and a crown of nine small Buddha heads (*hengemen*) and a small image of *Amida* . The facial expression is serene, and the eyes and eyebrows resemble those of the Vairocana sculpture. The body has a solidity and dignity suited to its large size. Most striking are the thousand arms, spreading out like wings and invigorating the space. The fretwork halo visible through the arms makes the statue appear even more majestic. Looking up at this large image instills a feeling of spiritual peace.

奈良時代
千手観音立像

Nara period
Senju Kannon Ryūzō

Data

千手観音立像
奈良 唐招提寺 金堂
8世紀末
像高　535.7cm
国宝
木心乾漆造 漆箔

Standing Thousand-armed Kannon
Kondō, Tōshōdai-ji, Nara
Late eighth century
535.7 cm
National Treasure
Wood-core dry lacquer, Gold foil applied with lacquer

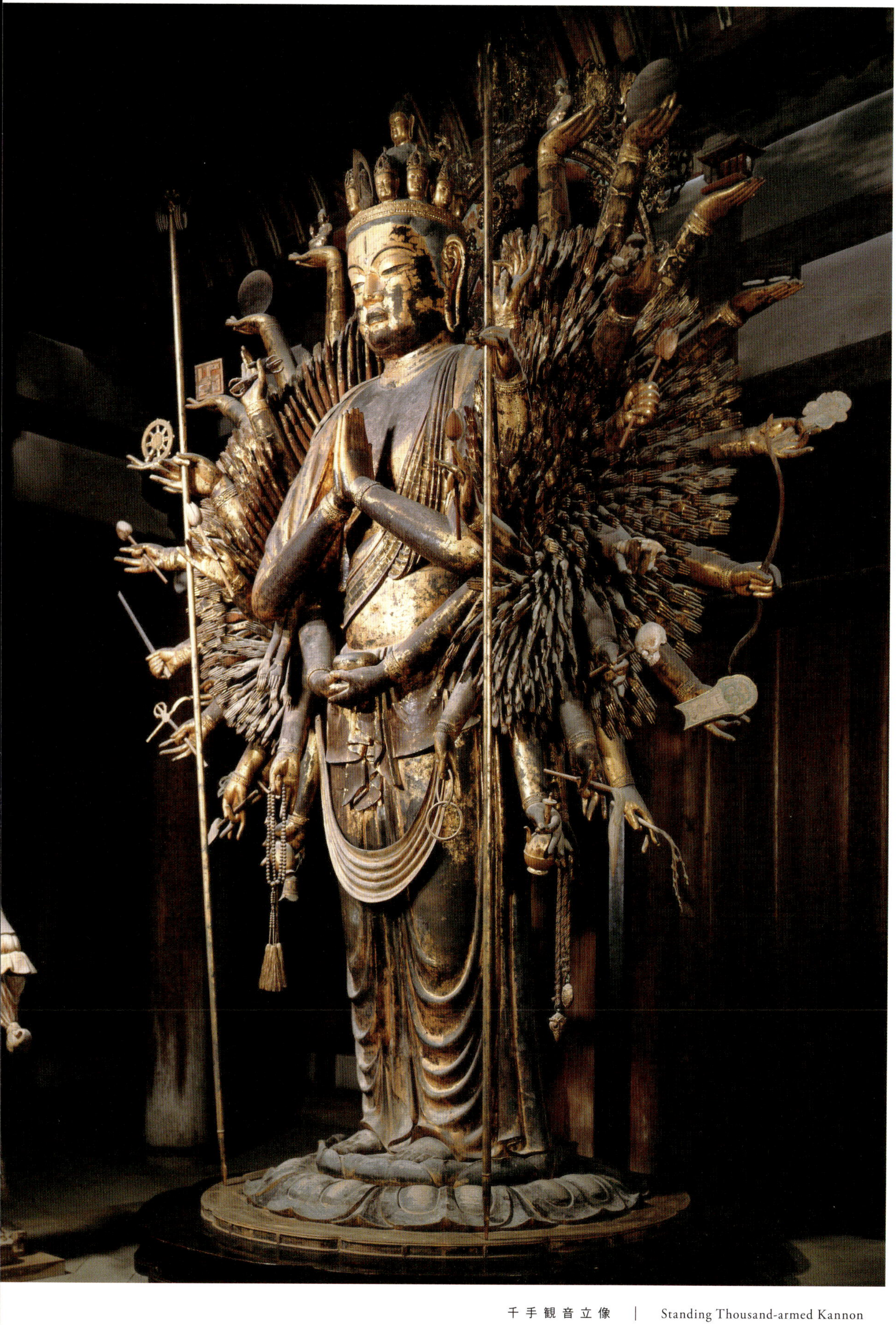

千手観音立像 ｜ Standing Thousand-armed Kannon

十一面観音立像
Standing Eleven-headed Kannon *Ekadasamukha*

木肌を生かした美しい木彫像
The beauty of natural wood grain

光明皇后をモデルにした観音像｜光明皇后は父藤原不比等の邸宅を相続して、のちに宮寺として法華寺を興したと伝えられ、この法華寺は日本の総国分尼寺にも位置づけられています。十一面観音立像は法華寺の本尊で、平安時代前期9世紀の代表的な仏像です。光明皇后をモデルに作られたという伝承もあり、当時の人々もこの像に女性的な魅力を感じていたことがうかがえます。総国分尼寺の本尊にふさわしい仏像といえるでしょう。

流行の先端を捉えた新しい作風｜この像はしなやかな体と長い手を持つ、スラリとしたスタイルが特徴の仏像です。それでいて胸や腹には膨らみがあり、やわらかさも感じられます。切れ長の眼の表情も個性的で、そのまなざしは一度見ると忘れられません。カヤ材を用いた一木造で、彩色や漆箔をほどこさずに、木肌を生かした素地のまま仕上げています。このような像は白檀製の檀像(だんぞう)に影響されたもので、9世紀に盛んに作られました。肩に垂れる髪や耳の上でなびく髪は薄い銅板製で、黒目にも銅板が貼り付けられています。このように木彫像に金属素材を使う手法は、当時の中国の仏像に影響されたものと考えられています。

A *Kannon* sculpture modeled on Empress Kōmyō | Empress Kōmyō inherited the mansion of her father *Fujiwara-no Fuhito* and subsequently established *Hokke-ji* temple there. *Hokke-ji* served as the chief temple of the government nunneries (*sōkokubunniji*) throughout Japan. Its principal icon is the Eleven-headed Kannon, an exemplary early Heian period sculpture, dating to the ninth century, said to have been modeled on Empress Kōmyō herself. One can imagine that this statue would have held a fascination for the worshippers of that time. It seems a most appropriate central icon to preside over the nation's nunneries.

A new style at the vanguard of artistic fashion | This statue is characterized by its slender, lithe body and long arms, while the swelling of the torso at the chest and belly lend it a certain softness. The expression of the wide slits of the eyes lends it a certain individuality, a gaze not soon forgotten once seen. It was carved from a single block of Japanese nutmeg (*kaya*), the natural wood grain left perfectly plain, without any pigments or gilding added. This type of statue was popular in the ninth century, probably under the influence of the earlier sandalwood sculptures. The locks of hair falling on the shoulders and waving over the ears are made of sheet copper and the pupils of the eyes are copper plated. This technique of applying metal to wood sculptures probably reflects the influence of contemporary Chinese Buddhist sculpture.

平安時代前期
十一面観音立像

Early Heian period
Jūichimen Kannon Ryūzō

Data

十一面観音立像
奈良 法華寺 本堂
9世紀半ば
像高 100.0cm
国宝
木造 カヤ 素地

Standing Eleven-headed Kannon
Hondō, Hokke-ji temple, Nara
Mid-ninth century
100.0 cm
National Treasure
Plain wood (Japanese nutmeg; kaya)

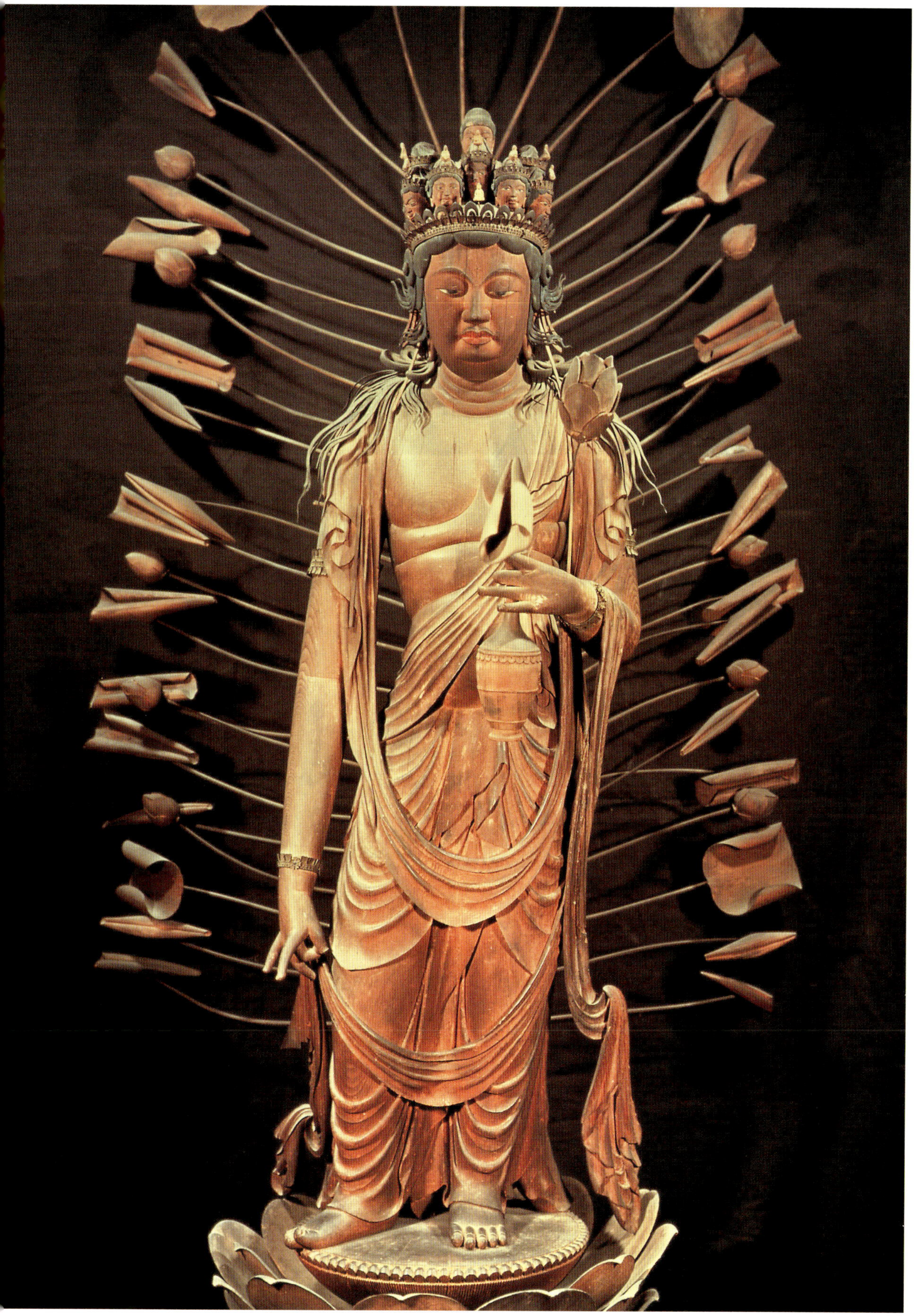

十一面観音立像 | Standing Eleven-headed Kannon

薬師如来坐像
Seated Yakushi Nyorai

新時代を象徴する表現力豊かな木彫像
Richly expressive carved wood sculpture symbolizing a new age

新たな時代の幕開けを告げる姿｜聖武天皇の病の治癒を祈り、光明皇后が天平19年（747）に建立したのが新薬師寺です。本堂は鎌倉時代に大規模な修復がされていますが、奈良時代の建築物の雰囲気を色濃く残しています。本堂の円形の土壇上に、奈良時代の塑造十二神将像に囲まれて安置される薬師如来坐像は、胸や腹が大きく盛り上がり、脚も太く、見るからに安定感があります。丸々とした顔には大きな目がはっきりと刻まれ、そこには強い意志が感じられます。両端を上げた唇には明るさが漂い、若々しく溌剌（はつらつ）とした印象を見る人に与えます。

平安前期の木彫技法、一木造｜この像は、天平時代までに多かった金銅仏や乾漆像、塑像ではなく、その後の日本の仏像の主流となる木彫像です。像高1.9メートルの大きな像ですが、両手の一部と両足をのぞき、頭から腰までが1本の太い材木から彫られます。これが平安時代前期に多い一木造（いちぼくづくり）という技法です。表現と技法のどちらを取っても、平安時代前期という新時代にふさわしい仏像といえましょう。像の背後の光背も同時に作られたもので、大ぶりの草花と化仏がにぎやかに絡みあう大胆な形が特徴です。

A figure that sets the stage for a new era｜*Shinyakushi-ji* temple was erected in 747 by the Empress Kōmyō as an offering of prayers for the recovery of the ill Emperor Shōmu. The Main Hall of the temple was refurbished on a major scale in the Kamakura period, but retains much of the architectural character of the Nara period. The image of *Yakushi Nyorai* sits on a circular pedestal, surrounded by a group of the Nara period Twelve Divine Generals (*Jūni Shinshō*) made of clay. The swelling chest and thick legs give the *Yakushi* a sense of stability. His broad face with crisply carved large eyes add gravity, whereas the mouth with its slightly upturned edges gives an impression of cheer and youthful vigor.

Early Heian period sculpting technique: single-block construction (*ichiboku-zukuri*)｜This sculpture differs from the Nara period images that were made of gilt bronze, dry lacquer or clay, in that it is carved from wood. This huge statue is 1.9 meters tall, and the head and torso (excluding parts of the hands and the legs) were made from one enormous tree trunk in the so-called single-block construction (*ichiboku-zukuri*). This technique became common during the early Heian period. In terms of both the creative expression and technique, this *Yakushi* image is worthy of the new era, the early Heain period (late eighth century). The halo, probably made at the same time as the *Yakushi Nyorai*, features intricate floral motifs and small seated Buddha images.

平安時代前期
薬師如来坐像

Early Heian period
Yakushi Nyorai Zazō

Data

薬師如来坐像
奈良 新薬師寺 本堂
8世紀末
像高　191.5cm
国宝
木造 カヤ 彩色

Bhaisajyaguru
Seated Yakushi Nyorai
Hondō, Shinyakushi-ji temple, Nara
Late eighth century
191.5 cm
National Treasure
Wood (Japanese nutmeg; kaya), Black pigment

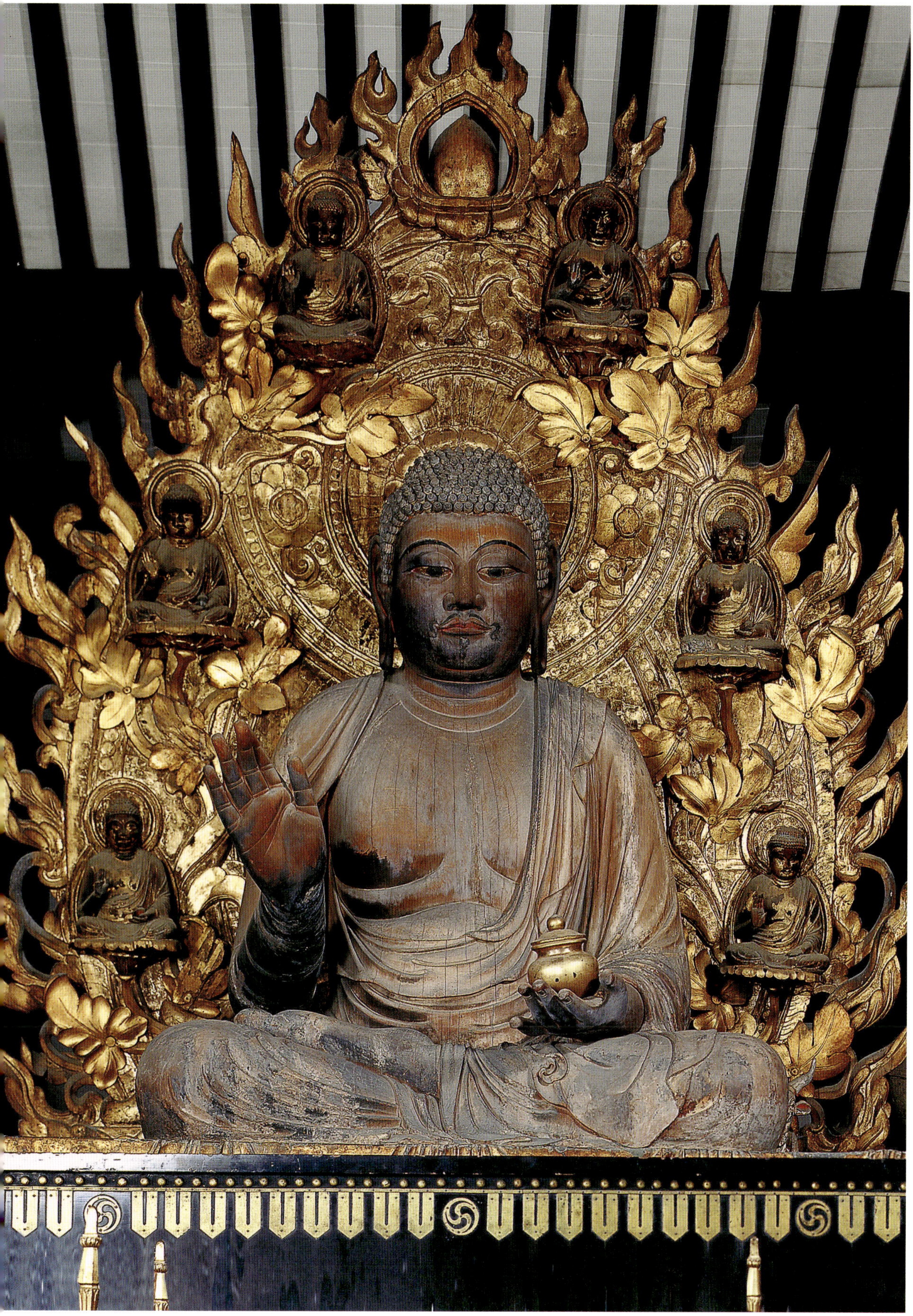

薬師如来坐像　|　Seated Yakushi Nyorai

運慶作大日如来坐像
Seated Dainichi Nyorai *Made by Unkei*

仏師運慶の才能が開花した大日如来像
Dainichi Nyorai, Unkei's talent revealed

仏師運慶のデビュー作｜奈良市街から柳生に向かう街道沿いに円成寺はあります。その多宝塔に安置される大日如来坐像は、鎌倉時代のみならず、日本の仏像の歴史上最も有名な仏師の一人である運慶が､安元2年(1176)に完成させた彼の最初の仏像です。台座の内側には運慶と、その父康慶の名や制作日などがくわしく記されています。運慶はこの仏像で、それまでの平安時代に流行したおだやかな作風とは違う、新しい鎌倉時代の仏像様式をはっきりと打ち出しました。

天才的な技術と美的感覚｜密教の中心尊である金剛界大日如来像は、如来でありながら、髪を結い上げて宝冠を戴き、智拳印(ちけんいん)を結ぶ菩薩のような特異な姿をしています。高い髻(もとどり)に、はっきりとした目鼻立ちを持つ張りのある若々しい顔つき、肉付きのよいたくましい体に自然な流れを持つ衣文、そして美しい髪の流れなど、各部にみずみずしい若さを感じる造形は、運慶ならではの才能の発露を感じさせます。ヒノキ材の寄木造(よせぎづくり)で作られていて、両眼にはこの時代から始まった水晶製の玉眼がはめられています。このような新技法も新しい時代のさきがけであるこの仏像の魅力です。

Unkei's talent revealed in his first work | *Enjō-ji* is a temple located northeast of the city of Nara. The seated *Dainich Nyorai* image that is enshrined in the *Tahō-tō* (Treasure Pagoda) was completed in 1176, the first known work by *Unkei* (1151-1223), the most famous sculptor not only of his time, but in the whole of Japanese history. The names of *Unkei* and his father *Kōkei*, details of the dedication and date of completion of the *Dainichi Nyorai* are inscribed inside the pedestal. With this image *Unkei* introduced a new style for the Kamakura period, distinct from the softer Heian mode.

Skilled technique and esthetic sensibility | This *Dainichi Nyorai*, the principal icon of Esoteric Buddhism, is here depicted in the unusual form of a bodhisattva, with the hand gesture of "supreme wisdom" (*chiken-in*), the hair arranged in a tall topknot, and adorned with a crown. Unkei's talent is manifested in every aspect of the vitality of the carving, the high topknot, the clarity and youthful vigor of the face, the powerfully built torso, the natural drapery of the robes, and the delineation of the hair. The sculpture is made of cypress in the joined-block (*yosegi-zukuri*) construction. A new method of inserting crystals for the eyes was also used for this image, which embodies the pioneering techniques of the new age.

鎌倉時代
運慶作大日如来坐像

Kamakura period
Dainichi Nyorai Zazō
Unkei saku

Data

大日如来坐像
奈良 円成寺 多宝塔
安元２年（1176）
像高　98.8cm
運慶作
国宝
木造 ヒノキ 漆箔 玉眼

Mahavairocana
Seated Dainichi Nyorai
Tahō-tō, Enjō-ji temple, Nara
AD 1176 (Angen 2)
98.8 cm
Made by Unkei
National Treasure
Wood (Japanese cypress; hinoki),
Gold foil applied with lacquer,
Crystal eyes

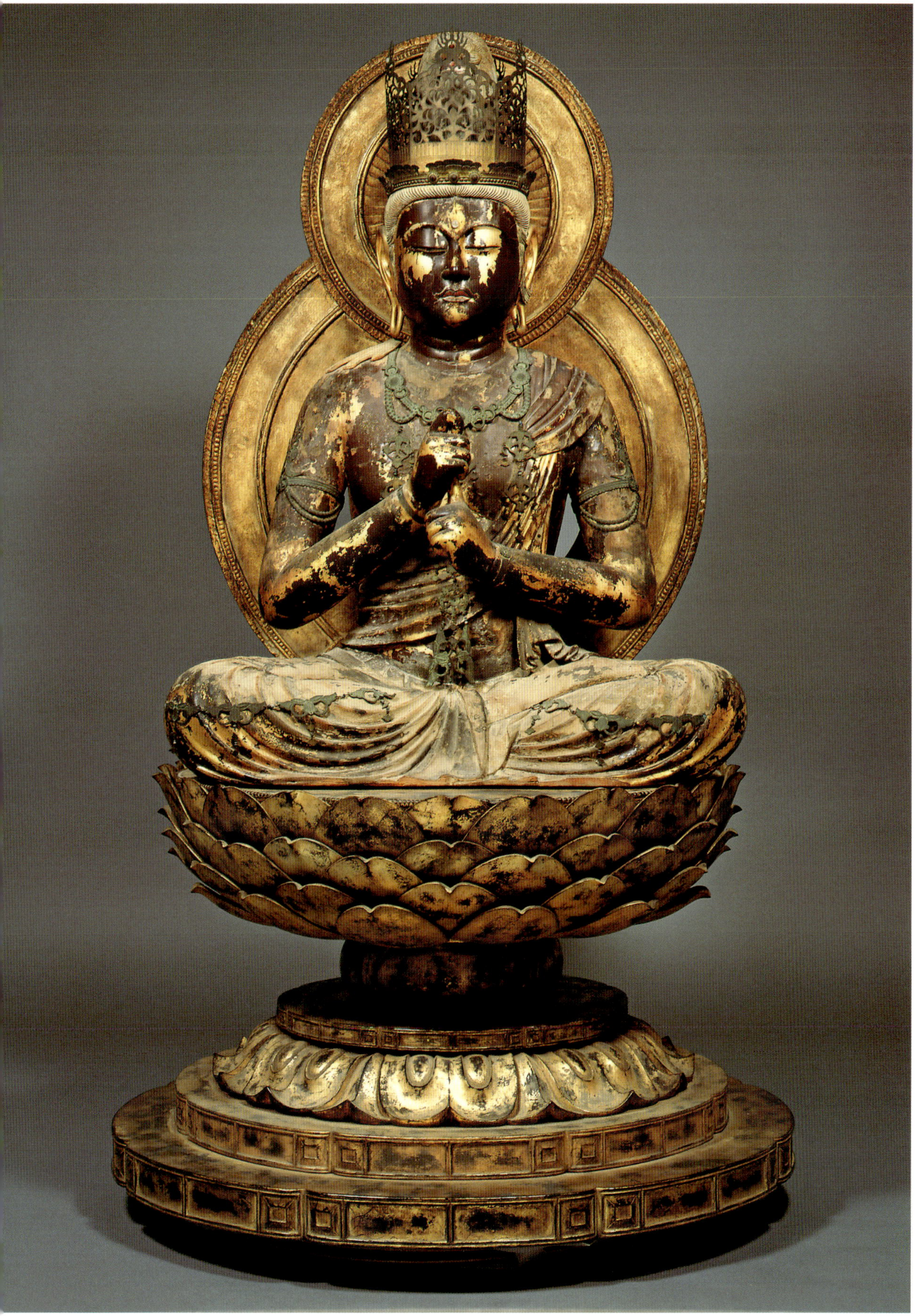

運慶作大日如来坐像 | Seated Dainichi Nyorai

十一面観音立像
Standing Eleven-headed Kannon *Ekadasamukha*

檀像彫刻の逸品
A masterpiece of sandalwood sculpture

仏教美術の殿堂、奈良国立博物館 | 明治28年（1895）に開館された帝国奈良博物館を前身とする奈良国立博物館は、仏教美術の殿堂として世界的にも有名です。明治時代に作られた本館には、寄託や所蔵品など多くの仏像が並びます。特別展も多く開催されています。その所蔵品の一つに、像高42センチながら、緻密に細工のほどこされた十一面観音立像があります。香り高い高価な白檀材の一木造の檀像彫刻で、はっきりした目鼻立ちを持つ、明るい表情が特徴です。

驚くほど緻密な変化面の彫刻 | この像は、檀像彫刻が流行した平安時代前期9世紀初め頃の仏像です。この十一面観音像の頭頂部に並ぶ変化面は緻密そのもので、まさに驚異的な技術というほかありません。細部の表現は十一面観音の姿を説いた経典に記された通りで、本面以外に十一面を持ち、頭頂に仏面、正面に慈悲面（菩薩面）が3つ、左には瞋怒面（しんぬめん）（目を見開いて怒った顔）が3つ、右には狗牙上出面（くげじょうしゅつめん）（牙を出した顔）が3つ、真後ろには暴悪大笑面（ぼうあくだいしょうめん）（大笑いの顔）が1つあります。香木である白檀が使われ、像高が約40センチであることも、経典通りになっています。

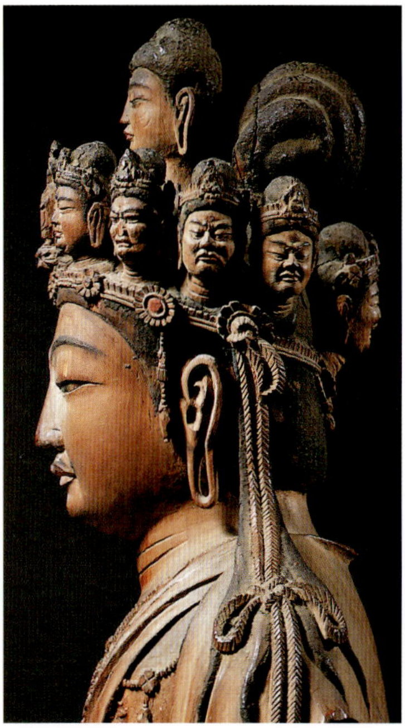

Nara National Museum, a treasure house of Buddhist art | The Nara National Museum, opened in 1895 as the Nara Imperial Museum, is world renowned as a treasure house of Buddhist art. The museum exhibits a large number of Buddhist sculptures, both from its own collection and loans, which are often featured in their special exhibitions. This image of a standing Eleven-headed Kannon from the museum's permanent collection, while only 42 centimeter tall, is executed in exquisite detail. Carved from fragrant sandalwood in the single-block technique, the image is distinguished by its features such as the sharply defined eyes and nose.

Astonishingly detailed carving of the small heads | This image was carved during the early Heian period in the beginning of ninth century, when the use of sandalwood was in vogue. The eleven heads that form the crown are precision itself, to a degree that is astonishing. The iconography of the features of the heads follows the scriptures closely, with a small standing *Amida* at center, flanked by three benevolent bodhisattva heads, three heads with angry expressions, and three heads with fangs protruding from their mouths, and one with a laughing countenance. The size of the image (approx. 40cm) also follows the textural prescription.

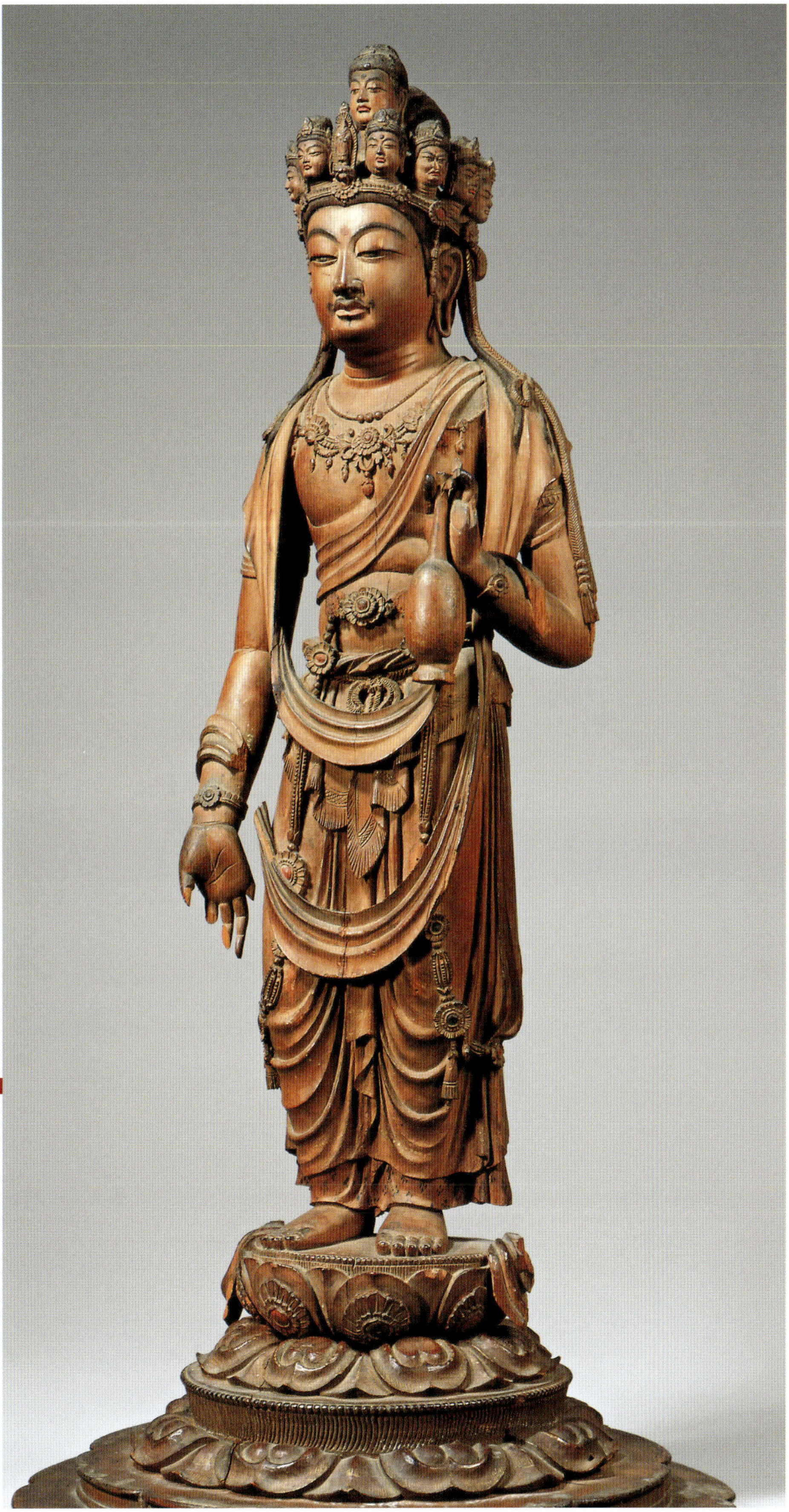

奈良時代
十一面観音立像

Nara period
Jūichimen Kannon Ryūzō

Data

十一面観音立像
奈良国立博物館
8 世紀～ 9 世紀
像高　42.8cm
重要文化財
木造 白檀 素地

Ekadasamukha
Standing Eleven-headed Kannon
Nara National Museum, Nara
Eighth or Ninth century
42.8 cm
Important Cultural Property
Plain wood (sandalwood; byakudan)

N
奈良
Nara

TEMPLE GUIDE

寺院ガイド
Temple Guide

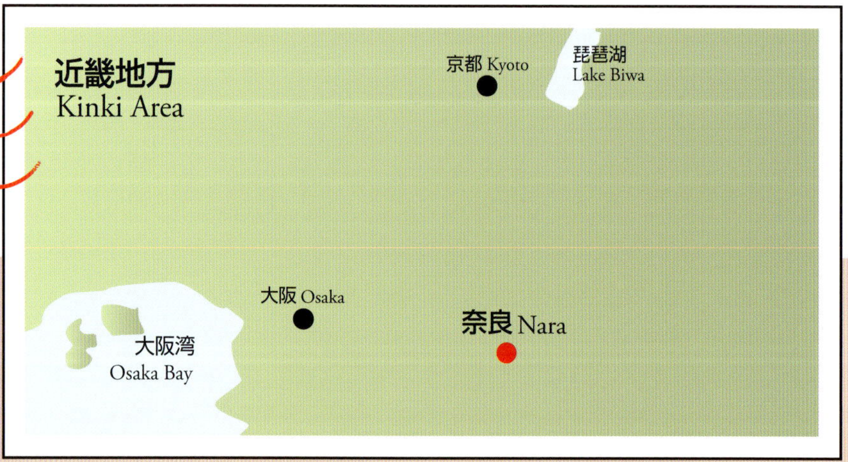

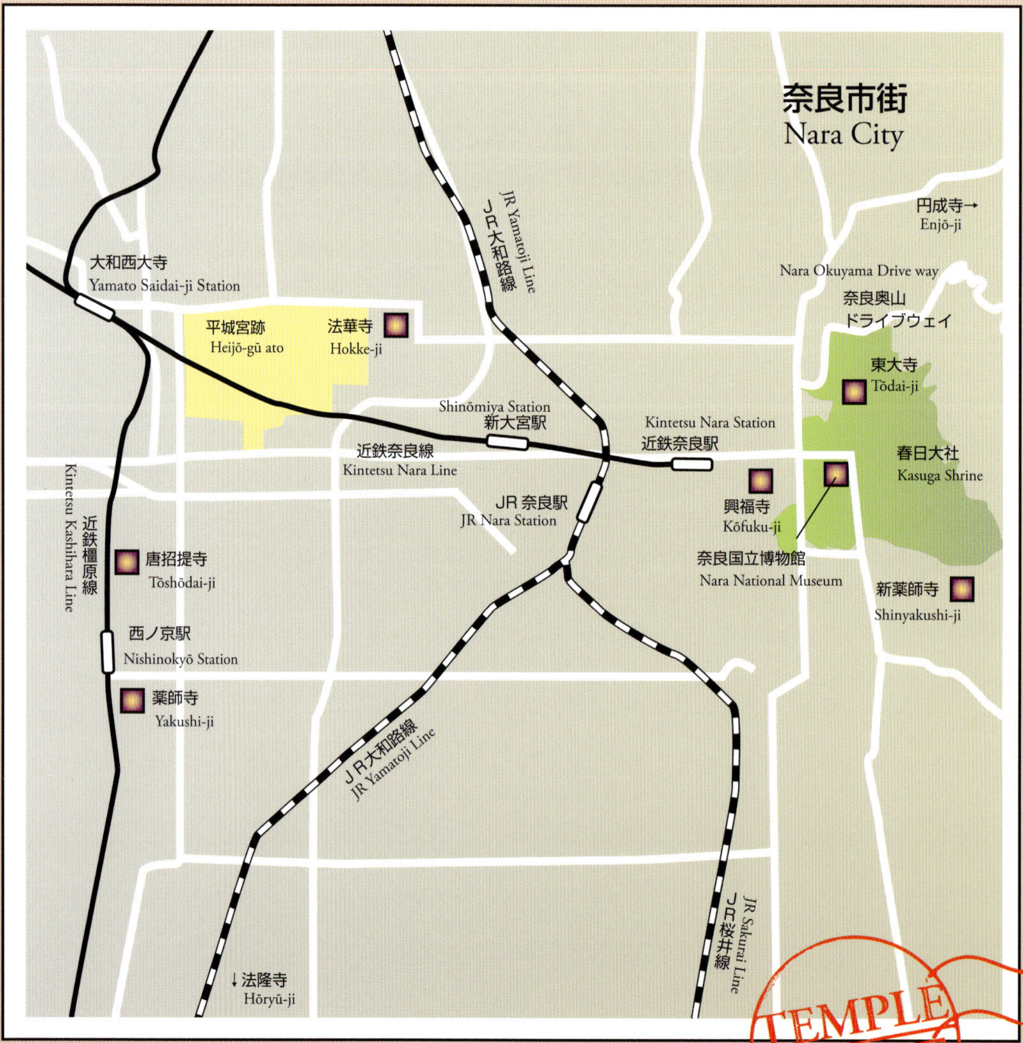

TEMPLE GUIDE

法隆寺

Hōryū-ji temple

奈良県生駒郡斑鳩町法隆寺山内 1-1
JR 大和路線 法隆寺駅 徒歩 20 分
Hōryū-ji sannai 1-1, Ikaruga-cho, Ikoma-gun, Nara-ken
JR Yamatoji Line, Hōryū-ji Station, 20 min on foot
OPEN 8:00 – CLOSE 17:00 (16:30)
http://www.horyuji.or.jp/

■止利作釈迦三尊像 Shaka Triad（→ p.40）
■観音菩薩立像（救世観音）Standing Guze Kannon （→ p.42）
■塔本四面具 Four Walls of a Pagoda （→ p.44）

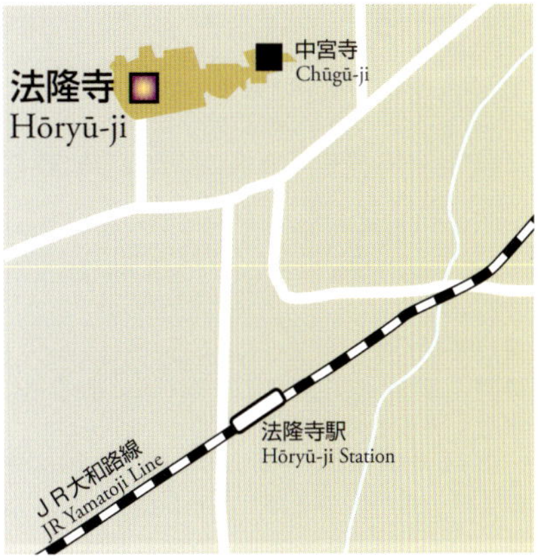

薬師寺

Yakushi-ji temple

奈良県奈良市西ノ京町 457
近鉄西ノ京駅 徒歩すぐ
Nishinokyō-chō 457, Nara-shi, Nara-ken
Kintetsu Line, Nishinokyō Station, 1 min on foot
OPEN 8:30 – CLOSE 17:00
http://www.nara-yakushiji.com/

■薬師三尊像 Yakushi Triad（→ p.46）
■日光菩薩立像 Standing Nikkō Bosatsu （→ p.14）
■観音菩薩立像（聖観音）
Standing Kannon (Shō Kannon) （→ p.7）

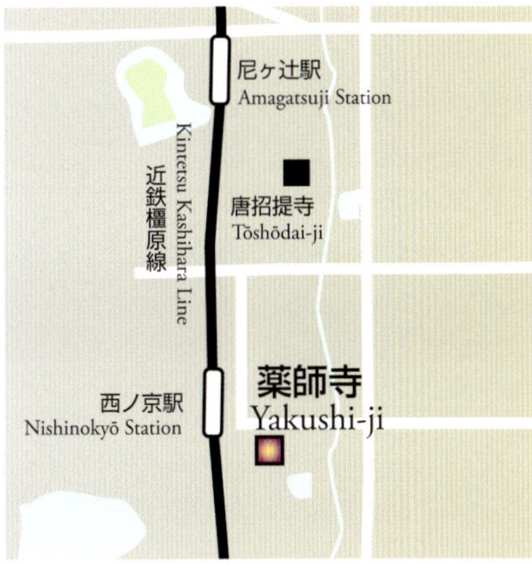

TEMPLE GUIDE

興福寺

Kōfuku-ji temple

奈良県奈良市登大路町 48
近鉄奈良駅 徒歩 3 分
Noboriōji-chō 48, Nara-shi, Nara-ken
Kintestsu Line, Nara Station, 3 min on foot
OPEN 9:00 – CLOSE 17:00
http://www.kohfukuji.com/

■阿修羅像（八部衆像）Ashura（→ p.48）
■康慶作不空羂索観音坐像
Seated Fukūkensaku Kannon （→ p.50）
■運慶等作無著菩薩立像、世親菩薩立像
Mujaku and Seshin（→ p.52）

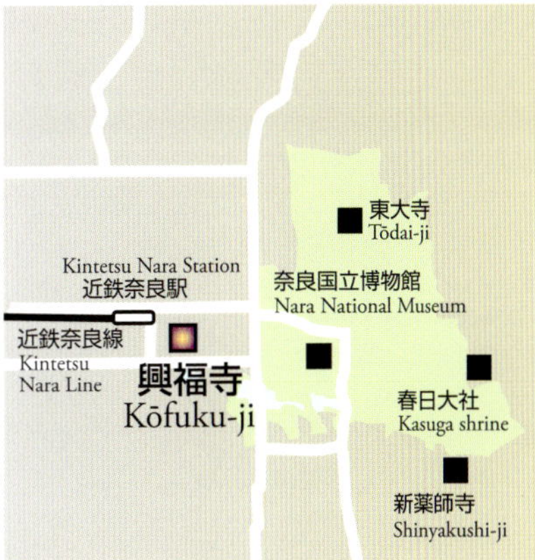

※拝観時間は変更になる場合があります。インターネットや観光案内所でご確認ください。
*Opening hours are subject to change. Please visit websites or tourist bureaus for the latest information.

TEMPLE GUIDE

東大寺

Tōdai-ji temple

奈良県奈良市雑司町 406-1 ／近鉄奈良駅 徒歩 10 分
Zōshi-chō 406-1, Nara-shi, Nara-ken
Kintetsu Line, Nara Station, 10 min on foot
OPEN 7:30 (8:00) – CLOSE 17:30 (17:00, 16:30)
http://www.todaiji.or.jp/

■不空羂索観音立像 Standing Fukūkensaku Kannon (→ p.54)
■四天王立像（広目天）Four Heavenly Kings (→ p.56)
■盧舎那仏坐像（奈良の大仏）
Seated Vairocana (the Great Buddha of Nara) (→ p.58)
■運慶・快慶等作金剛力士立像 Two Guardian Kings (Vajrapani) (→ p.60)
■伝日光菩薩立像 Standing Nikkō Bodhisattva (→ p.20)

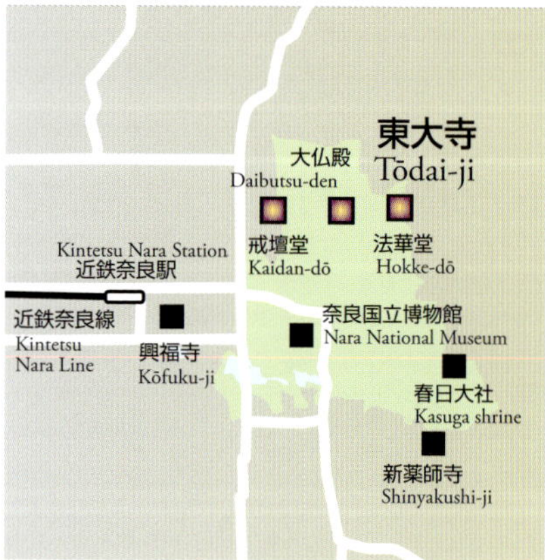

唐招提寺

Tōshōdai-ji temple

奈良県奈良市五条町 13-46
近鉄西ノ京駅　徒歩 8 分
Gojō-chō 13-46, Nara-shi, Nara-ken
Kintetsu Line, Nishinokyō Station, 8 min on foot
OPEN 8:30 – CLOSE 17:00
http://www.toshodaiji.jp/

■盧舎那仏坐像 Seated Vairocana（→ p.62）
■千手観音立像
Standing Thousand-armed Kannon （→ p.64）

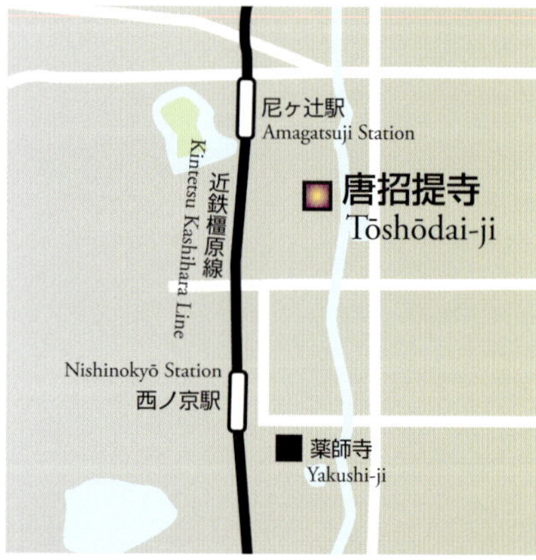

法華寺

Hokke-ji temple

奈良県奈良市法華寺町 882
近鉄大和西大寺駅　バス 10 分　徒歩 3 分
Hokke-ji-chō 882, Nara-shi, Nara-ken
Kintetsu Line, Yamato Saidai-ji Station,
10 min by bus, 3 min on foot
OPEN 9:00 – CLOSE 17:00
http://www.hokkeji-nara.jp/

■十一面観音立像
Standing Eleven-headed Kannon（→ p.66）

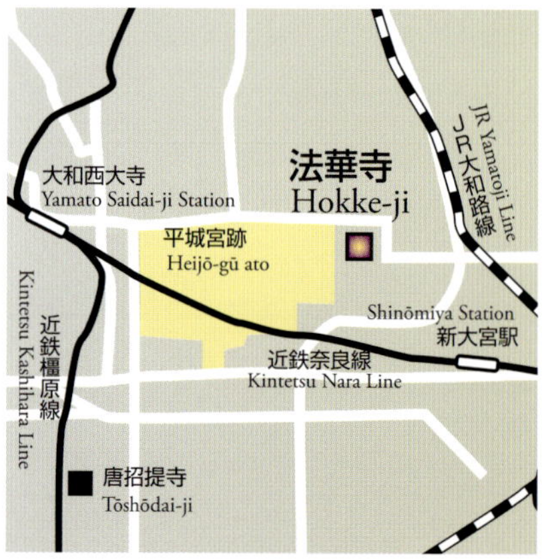

新薬師寺
Shinyakushi-ji temple

奈良県奈良市高畑町 1352
JR 大和路線奈良駅　バス 10 分　徒歩 10 分
Takahata-chō 1352, Nara-shi, Nara-ken
JR Yamatoji Line, Nara Station, 10 min by bus, 10 min on foot
OPEN 9:00 – CLOSE 17:00
http://www.shinyakushiji.or.jp/
■薬師如来坐像 Seated Yakushi Nyorai (→ p.68)

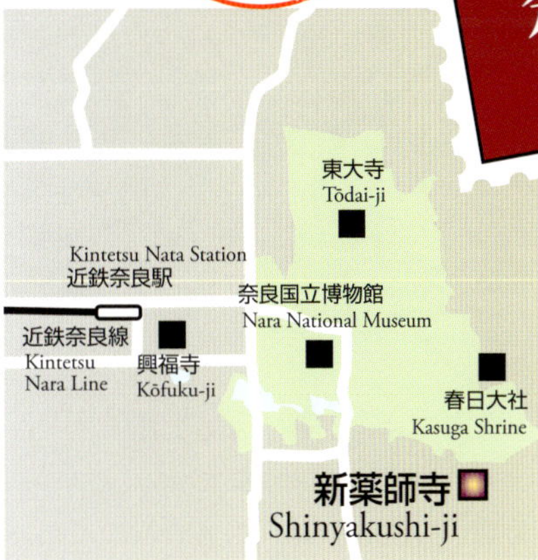

円成寺
Enjō-ji temple

奈良県奈良市忍辱山町 1273
JR 大和路線奈良駅 バス 36 分 徒歩 2 分
Ninnikusen-chō1273, Nara-shi, Nara-ken
JR Yamatoji Line, Nara Station, 36 min by bus, 2 min on foot
OPEN 9:00 – CLOSE 17:00
http://www.enjyoji.jp/
■運慶作大日如来坐像 Seated Dainichi Nyorai (→ p.70)

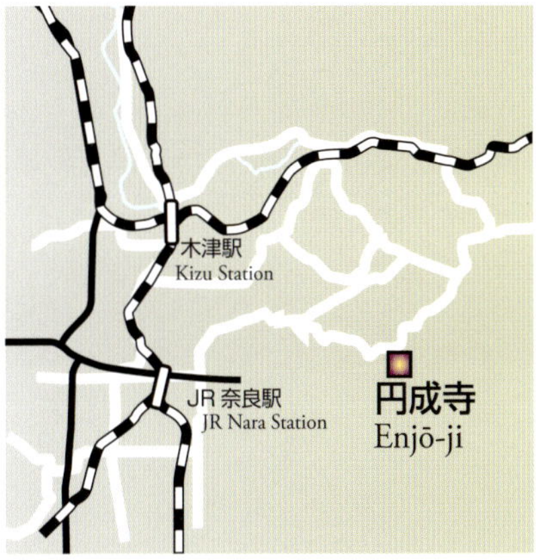

奈良国立博物館
Nara National Museum

奈良県奈良市登大路町 50
近鉄奈良駅　徒歩 15 分
Noboriōji-chō 50, Nara-shi, Nara-ken
Kintetsu Line, Nara Station, 15 min on foot
OPEN 9:30 – CLOSE 17:00 (19:00, 20:00)
http://www.narahaku.go.jp/
■十一面観音立像 Standing Eleven-headed Kannon (→ p.72)

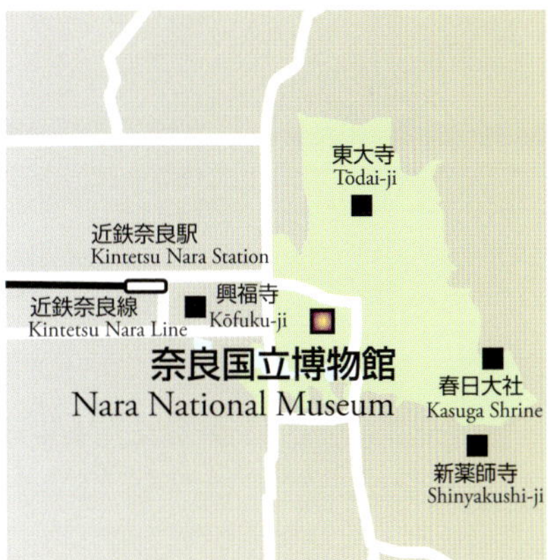

京都の仏像

Area2 Buddhist sculpture in Kyoto

平安京の都

京都は、8世紀末から明治時代に現在の東京に首都が移るまで、永きにわたり日本の都でした。千年の古都、といわれるゆえんです。とくに8世紀末から12世紀末までの平安時代には朝廷や貴族を中心とする華やかな文化が栄え、東寺をはじめ多くの伽藍が建てられました。

東寺は弘法大師空海が伝えた密教を広める寺院で、密教の思想を具現化した立体曼荼羅が圧巻です。現在の京都駅の東方にあたる地には、東福寺をはじめ、妙法院三十三間堂、六波羅蜜寺、京都国立博物館などが並び、さらに琵琶湖との境の比叡山には延暦寺があります。

京都の西方の嵐山周辺には清凉寺や広隆寺などが、また東南の山科の地には醍醐寺や法界寺などの名刹があり、その南の宇治市には一世を風靡した「定朝様」の代表作である定朝作阿弥陀如来坐像を安置する平等院があります。

京都は鉄道やバスなどの公共交通機関が充実しているために、比較的短い時間でいろいろな場所を訪ねることができます。

東寺（教王護国寺）講堂
The Lecture Hall (Kōdō), Tō-ji temple (Kyō-ō gokoku-ji temple)

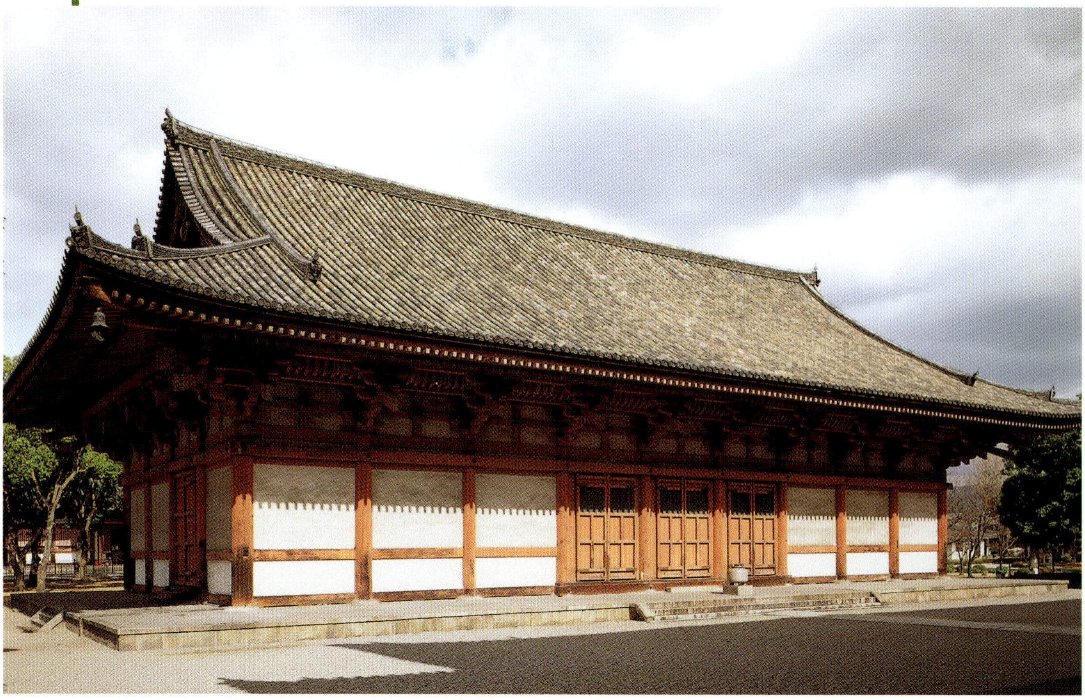

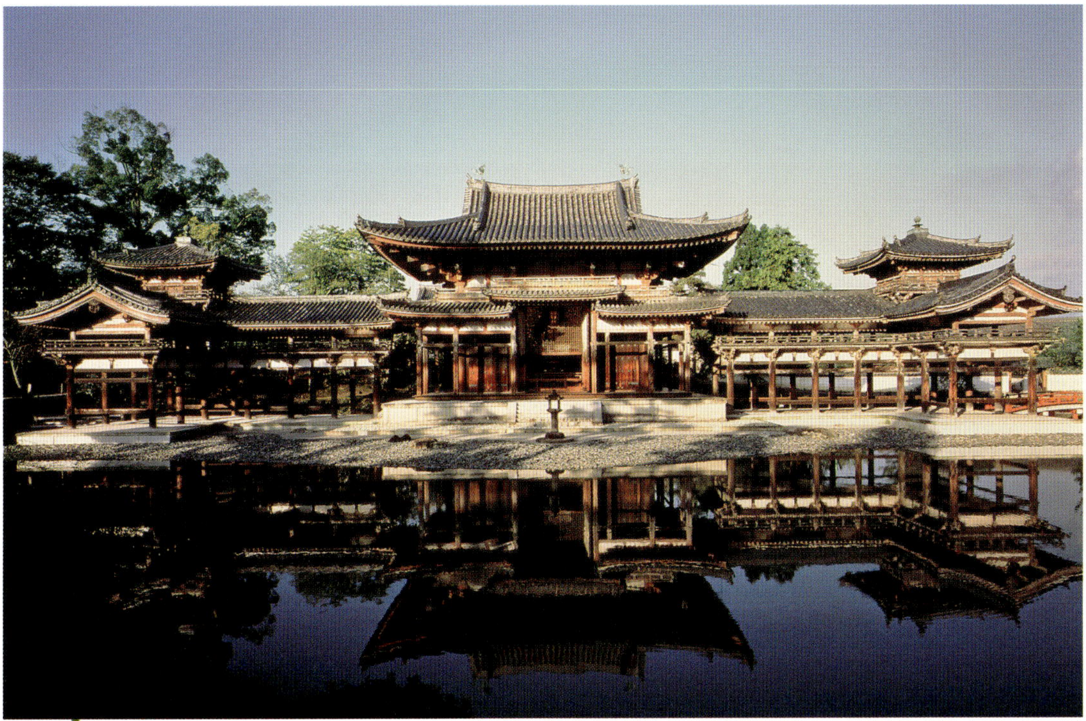

平等院 鳳凰堂
Hō-ō-dō, Byōdō-in temple

Kyo-no-miyako, the capital city of the Heian period

Kyoto was the capital city of Japan after Nara since the end of eighth century, until the nineteenth century, with the move of the capital to present-day Tokyo. Thus, Kyoto is highly admired as the 1000 year old city. From the end of eighth century to the end of twelfth century of the Heian period, the Japanese Emperor and aristocrats were at the center of the rich culture, and many temples were built, such as *Tō-ji*.

Tō-ji is the temple where the teachings of Esoteric Buddhism,or *Mikkyō*, was introduced by *Kōbō-daishi* (*Kūkai*). The three dimensional Mandala in *Tō-ji* has overwhelming power. It is said to embody the conception of the world according to the principles of *Mikkyo*. You can visit *Tōfuku-ji*, *Myōhō-in-sanjūsangen-dō*, *Rokuhara-mitsu-ji*, and Kyoto National Museum in the area east of Kyoto station. *Enryaku-ji* is located in *Hiei-zan* (Mt. Hiei) at the shores of Lake Biwa (*Biwa-ko*).

To the west of Kyoto, *Seiryō-ji* and *Kōryū-ji* are near the Arashiyama district. In the south-east area, you can see Buddhist sculptures that are national treasures in the great temples, such as *Daigo-ji* and *Hōkai-ji* in Yamashina district. Uji city is south of Yamashina district, and *Byōdō-in* is the "must see" place which houses the masterpiece of *Amida Nyorai* made by *Jōchō*, who set the artistic trend of his time.

Kyoto is a city with good transportation, and you can go anywhere by bus and train in a relatively short time.

弥勒菩薩半跏像（宝冠弥勒）
Seated Bodhisattva Maitreya *Crowned Maitreya*

時を超えて救済を思索する美しき救世主
Beautiful savior contemplating universal salvation through eternity

人々の救済に、静かに思いをめぐらせて | 片足を組んで腰かけ、ほほに指先を添えて思念にふける弥勒菩薩像。その表情は静かに微笑を浮かべています。弥勒は、釈迦入滅から56億7千万年後にこの世にあらわれて人々を救うと言われる未来仏。この像は、そのときまでずっと救済の方法を思案している姿をあらわしているといわれています。頭上の宝冠から台座までをアカマツの一材から彫りだした木彫仏で、大きな頭とスリムな体つきに、すがすがしい均整が感じられます。シンプルな目鼻だちと微笑みは気品があふれ、美しく、飛鳥時代を象徴する名品です。一見飾り気のない像に見えますが、かつては全体に漆箔がほどこされ、光背もあったことが、わずかに残る痕跡から推測されます。

国内の作か渡来仏か | この像に関するいくつかの史料には「献上仏」という記述があります。主な材質がアカマツである点から、朝鮮半島で作られて日本に贈られたものであるという説と、綬帯(じゅたい)や背板など一部にクスが使われている点から、渡来系の仏師が朝鮮半島から送られてきたアカマツを使って作り、材料の不足した分を国産のクスで補って作り、献上したのではないか、という2つの説が考えられています。

Serenely meditating on the salvation of all | The bodhisattva Maitreya (*Miroku Bosatsu*) is shown in a meditative pose, his right leg crossed over the pendent left one, with the tips of the fingers of the right hand touching his cheek, and a serene expression on his face. Maitreya is the Buddha of the future who will appear 5.67 billion years after the historical Buddha Shakamuni's death. This figure depicts Maitreya contemplating the forms of salvation until that future time when he reappears. This statue is carved of red pine, from the crown to the base, and the large head and slim torso are perfectly balanced. The refined features and smile are filled with grace, and this is one of the masterpieces of Asuka period sculpture. Although seemingly plain in appearance, the statue was originally covered in gold leaf, and judging from the traces on the back, there was also a halo (*kōhai*).

Made domestically or imported from Korea? | In the historic records, this sculpture is referred to as the "presentation Buddha" (*kenjō Butsu*). There are two theories about its production. One holds that because the primary material is red pine, the statue was carved in Korea and sent to Japan. The second theory is based on the fact that some parts (such as the ribbon at the side, and part of the back) are carved from camphor wood native to Japan, and therefore the sculpture was carved in Japan by an immigrant artisan who brought the red pine with him from Korea, and that the piece was then presented to the Japanese government.

飛鳥時代
弥勒菩薩半跏像（宝冠弥勒）

Asuka period
Miroku Bosatsu Hankazō (Hōkan Miroku)

Data

弥勒菩薩半跏像
京都 広隆寺 霊宝殿
7世紀前半
像高 123.0cm
国宝
木造 アカマツ 漆箔

Seated bodhisattva Maitreya
Crowned Maitreya
in the meditative pose (hanka)
Reihō-den, Kōryū-ji temple, Kyoto
First half of the seventh century
123.0 cm
National Treasure
Wood (red pine), traces of gold foil applied with lacquer

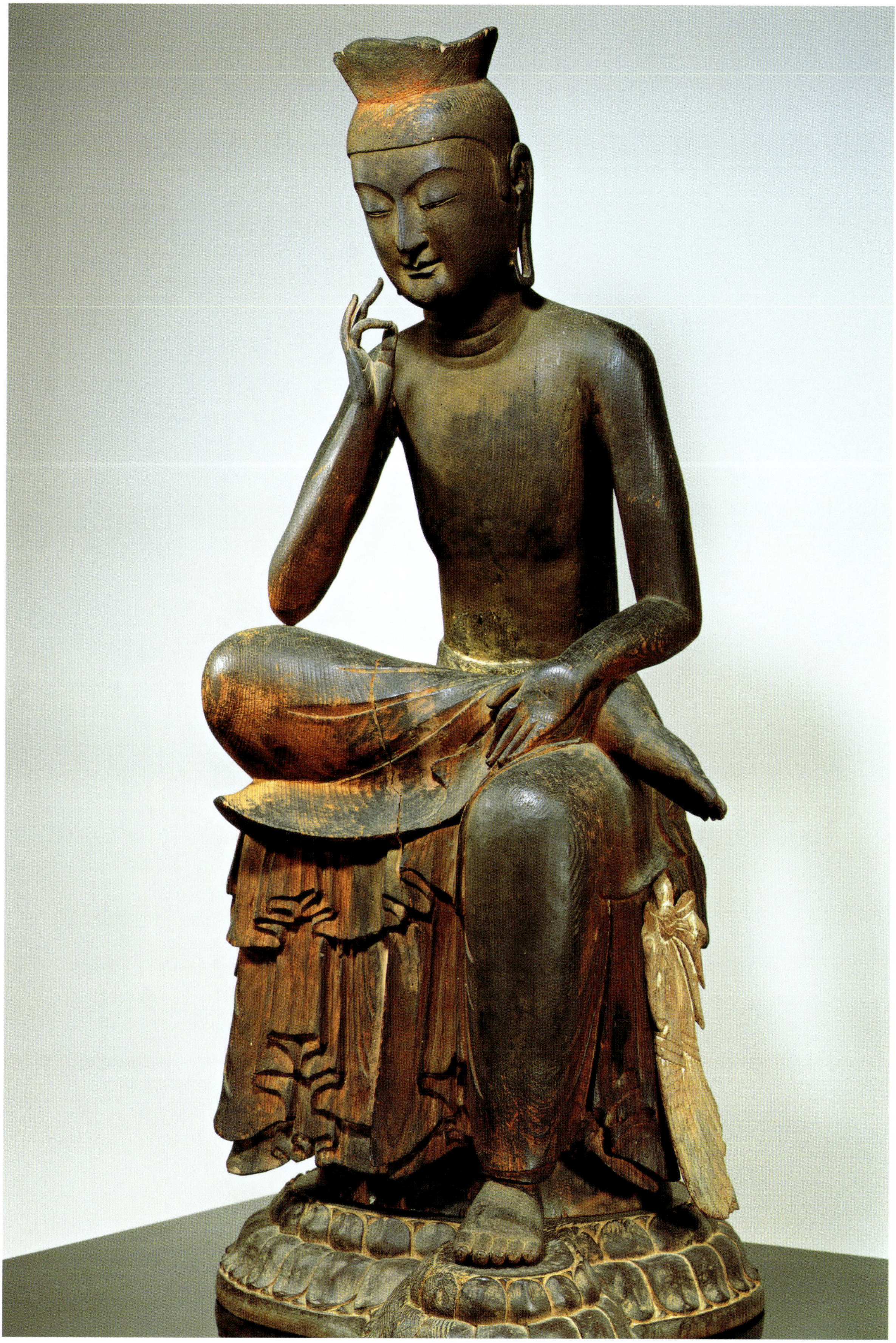

弥勒菩薩半跏像（宝冠弥勒）　|　Seated Bodhisattva Maitreya

降三世明王立像（五大明王像）
Standing Gōzanze Myō-ō *the Five Great Myō-ō in the Lecture Hall at Tō-ji temple*

空海が構想した立体曼荼羅
A three-dimensional mandala designed by Kūkai

講堂21体の像が織りなす密教の具現化｜東寺の境内に建つ講堂には、中央に五仏、右に五菩薩像、左に五大明王像が、そして東西両端に梵天像、帝釈天像、四隅に四天王像の合計21体が並びます。この群像は空海が構想した曼荼羅を表現したもので、承和6年（839）に開眼供養されました。五仏と五菩薩像の中尊像、多聞天像以外は当初のものが伝わっています。

仏の守護神としての降三世明王像｜五大明王像の中尊不動明王は両目を見開き下唇をぐっと噛み締めて、怒りを内に秘める様子をあらわします。一方、他の4体の明王像は憤怒の表情もすさまじく、多面多臂の怪奇な姿に作られます。なかでも降三世（ごうざんぜ）明王像は4つの顔に8本の腕を持ち、腰を落として身構えた様子は、今にも動きだしそうです。胸の前で、降三世印と呼ばれる仏敵を武力によって降伏させる独特な印相を結び、両足の下には大自在天（だいじざいてん）（シヴァ神）とその后を踏みつけています。このような複雑な姿を自然な造形として無理なくまとめあげている点に、制作した仏師の確かな手腕が知られます。諸像は一木造で作られ、背中から内刳（うちぐ）りされ、像にほどこされた彩色の多くは剥落（はくらく）していますが、四天王像などには造立時の文様が残っています。

Esoteric doctrine embodied in twenty-one statues | A grouping of twenty-one sculptures is enshrined in the Lecture Hall (*Kōdō*) of *Tō-ji* temple: at the center are images of five Buddhas, flanked by five bodhisattvas on the right and the Five Great Myō-ō on the left, with figures of *Bon-ten* and *Taishaku-ten* at the eastern and western ends, and the Four Heavenly Kings guarding the four corners. This layout was conceived by *Kūkai* as a three-dimensional mandala which was dedicated in 839. Most of the images are originals, except five Buddhas, the central image of five bodhisattvas and Tamon-ten (one of the Four Heavenly Kings).

Guardian of Buddhism, *Gōzanze Myō-ō* | The central figure of Five Great Myō-ō, *Fudō Myō-ō*, with his wide-open eyes and tightly closed mouth, seems to be containing his anger. In contrast, the remaining four Myō-ō have fierce expressions and are strangely multi-faced and multi-armed. The *Gōzanze Myō-ō* is depicted with four faces and eight arms, and his stance with one hip lower makes him seem ready for action at any moment. The hands in front are in a particular gesture called "subduing the three worlds" (*gōzanze-in*) symbolizing victory over the enemies of Buddhism, and under his feet he tramples on the Hindu deity Siva (*Daijizai-ten*) and his consort. The ability to carve such complex images in a seemingly naturalistic manner testifies to the exceptional skill of the sculptor. The images are all made in the single-block technique, with hollowed out backs. While most of the pigment has deteriorated, some traces of the original motifs can still be found on the statues of the Four Heavenly Kings.

平安時代前期
降三世明王立像（五大明王像）

Early Heian period
Gōzanze Myō-ō Ryūzō (Godai Myō-ō Zō)

Data

降三世明王立像
京都 東寺（教王護国寺）
講堂
承和６年（839）
像高　173.6cm
国宝
木造乾漆併用 彩色

Standing Gōzanze Myō-ō
Kōdō, Tō-ji temple (Kyō-ō gokoku-ji temple), Kyoto
AD 839 (Jōwa 6)
173.6 cm
National Treasure
Wood with lacquer and pigments

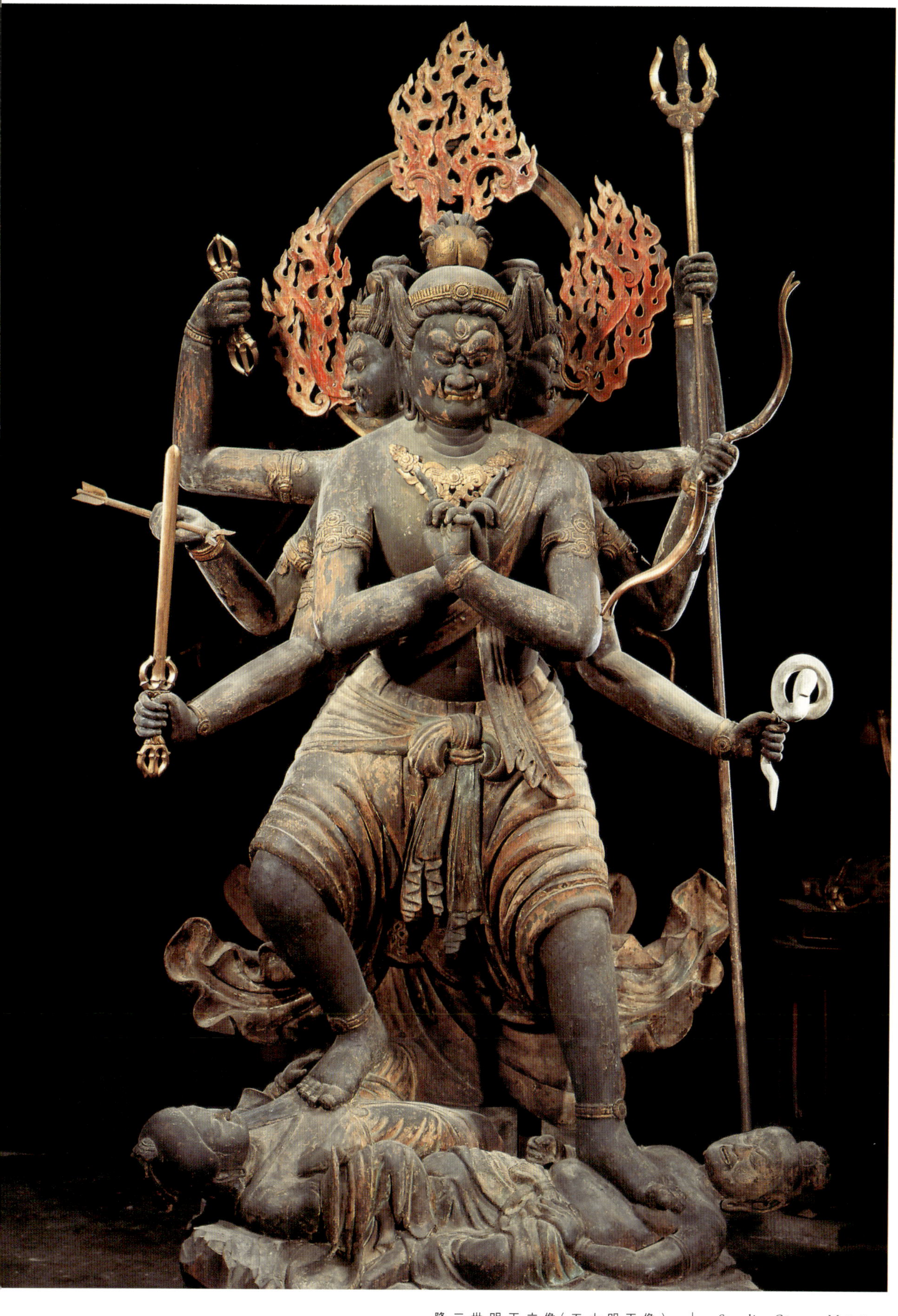

降三世明王立像（五大明王像）　|　Standing Gōzanze Myō-ō

薬師三尊像
Yakushi Triad *Daigo-ji temple*

平安前期の最後を飾る名品
A crowning jewel of the early Heian period

広大な境内を見守る厳かな本尊｜醍醐寺は、9世紀後半に高僧聖宝(しょうぼう)により山上の上醍醐寺が建てられ、後に麓に五重塔や金堂のある下醍醐寺が作られました。延喜13年（913）頃に造立されたこの薬師三尊像もかつては上醍醐の薬師堂に安置されていましたが、今は下醍醐の霊宝館に移され、春秋の開館時にはいつでも拝観できるようになりました。どっしりと座る薬師如来像は、太い腕と大きく張り出した両脚を持つ安定感のある姿で、大きな頭や太い首もボリュームにあふれています。一方､両脇侍像はひと回り小さく､おだやかな表情で立っていて､中尊像を引き立てるようなつつましさを表現しています。

伝統様式と新様式｜3体はいずれもカヤ材の一木造(いちぼくづくり)で作られています。中尊像の左すねにあらわされた舌状の衣のひだは、この像より100年ほど古い新薬師寺の薬師如来坐像にも見られる、古いデザインです。また、左足を衣で包み隠すのも、奈良時代の仏像によく見られる表現です。その一方で、大きな頭や堂々とした体型は、平安時代前期の仏像に多い様式です。新旧両様がまじりあった作風には、この時代の仏像の特徴がよくあらわれています。

The solemn principal statue watching over the precincts | The *Daigo-ji* temple complex consists of two separate precints: the *Kami-Daigo* (Upper Daigo), which was established in the late ninth century by the monk *Shōbō* (832-909) in a mountain setting, and subsequently the *Shimo-Daigo* (Lower Daigo) temple was built at the foot of the mountain, including a five-story pagoda and *Kondō*. The Yakushi Triad of 913 was originally installed in the Main Hall (also called *Yakushi-dō*) of the *Kami-Daigo* temple, but has been moved to the Reihō-kan Museum of the *Shimo-Daigo* temple, where it can be viewed during the spring and autumn exhibition periods. The imposing central figure of *Yakushi Nyorai* has a solidity emphasized by the round arms and the wide crossed legs, and that is also seen in the large head and thick neck. The two attendant figures, with their small size and calm expressions, stand modestly aside as supporting actors to the central image.

Traditional style and a new style | All three statues were carved from Japanese nutmeg (*kaya*) in the single-block construction (*ichiboku-zukuri*). The triangular section of drapery over the left shin of the central *Yakushi* reflects an older style, as seen in the *Yakushi Nyorai* sculpture at *Shinyakushi-ji* temple, which is about one hundred years earlier in date. The way in which the robe covers the left foot is also common in earlier Nara period Buddhist sculptures. On the other hand, the large head and solid torso are frequently found in the early Heian period images. This amalgamation of the old and new styles is characteristic of Buddhist statuary of this era.

平安時代前期
薬師三尊像

Early Heian period
Yakushi Sanzonzō

Data

薬師如来及び両脇侍像(中尊)
京都 醍醐寺 霊宝館
延喜 13 年（913）
像高　176.1cm
国宝
木造 カヤ 漆箔

Yakushi Nyorai and flanking attendants (Central image)
Reihō-kan, Daigo-ji temple, Kyoto
AD 913 (Engi 13)
176.1 cm
National Treasure
Wood (Japanese nutmeg; kaya), Gold foil applied with lacquer

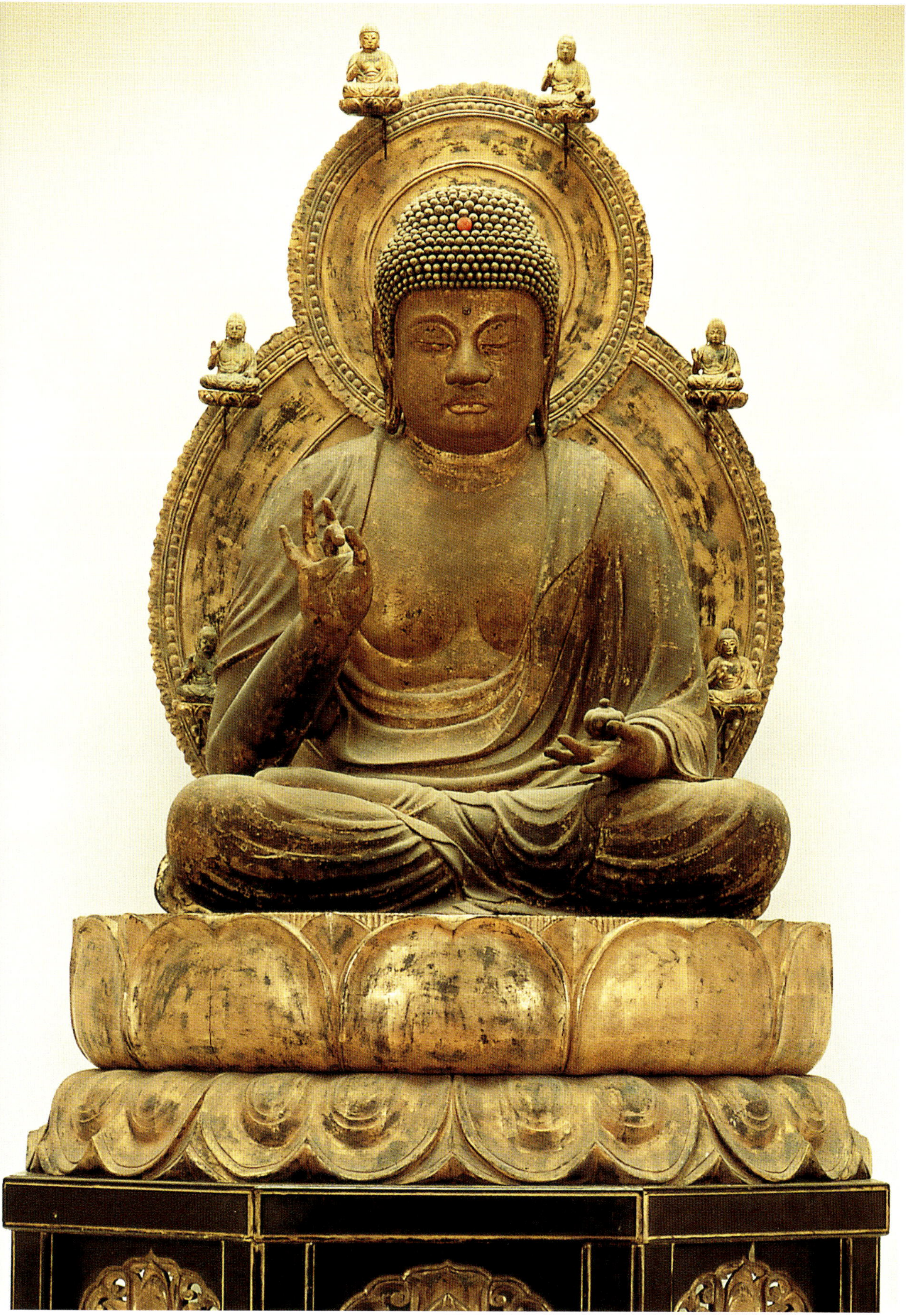

薬 師 三 尊 像 | Yakushi Triad

定朝作阿弥陀如来坐像
Seated Amida Nyorai *Amitabha, Made by Jōchō (d. 1057)*

仏師定朝の唯一の遺作
The only extant work by the sculptor Jōchō

宇治に建つこの世の極楽浄土 | 宇治は8世紀末の平安遷都以来、貴族の別荘地として親しまれ、当時の権力者藤原道長の別邸もここにありました。それを受け継いだ道長の子息、頼通は、永承7年（1052）の仏法の滅びる時代「末法（まっぽう）」の到来を受け、この別荘を寺院にし、名を平等院としました。翌年には本堂の阿弥陀堂（鳳凰堂）が完成し、定朝作の阿弥陀如来坐像が置かれました。定朝は平安時代随一の仏師ですが、現存する仏像で彼の作であることがわかっているものはこの像だけです。

和様彫刻の完成 | 鳳凰堂の内部には、円形と方形の華麗な二重の天蓋が吊られ、壁には雲中供養菩薩が舞い踊り、そこはまさに極楽浄土の再現というべき空間です。阿弥陀如来像は、なだらかな曲面を持つ均整のとれたプロポーションで、どこから見ても美しい姿です。このような姿の仏像は定朝様と呼ばれ、平安時代後期を通じて全国で流行しました。木彫でありながら薄く透き通るような衣はまるで塑像や乾漆像のように自然で、台座の上面に広がった波打つような衣のひだなど細部まで見事な仕上がりです。ヒノキの寄木造で、像内には美しく彩色された蓮台などが納められています。

An earthly Paradise built in Uji | Uji was a popular resort area for the aristocracy since the end of the eighth century move of the capital to Kyoto. The powerful *Fujiwara-no Michinaga* (966-1027) had built his villa there. In 1052 his son and successor *Yorimichi* (992-1074) converted the residence into a private temple, to prepare for the advent of the Buddhist "latter days of the Law" (*Mappō*). The temple is named as *Byōdō-in*. The main building, the Amida Hall, or the Phoenix Hall was completed the following year, with a sculpture of the seated *Amida Nyorai* by *Jōchō* enshrined there. *Jōchō* was the premier sculptor of his day, but this is his only extant work.

Creation of a Japanese sculptural style (*wayō*) | The interior of the Phoenix Hall features a double canopy, a circular one within a square one, and along the walls bodhisattvas on clouds play musical instruments and dance. It is a space meant to recreate Amida's Pure Land Western Paradise. The sculpture of *Amida* is beautiful from any angle, with its rounded form and harmonious proportions. This became characteristic of the *Jōchō* style as it spread throughout Japan in the late Heian period. Although carved from wood, the Amida's robe appears thin, almost transparent, as was previously only possible with sculptures made from clay or dry lacquer. The perfect finish of the drapery as it ripples down over the pedestal is equally impressive. *Jōchō* made this sculpture of Japanese cypress (*hinoki*) using the joined-block technique (*yosegi-zukuri*), and there are some objects such as the beautifully pigmented lotus pedestal inside the statue.

平安時代後期
定朝作阿弥陀如来坐像

Late Heian period
Amida Nyorai Zazō
Jōchō saku

Data

阿弥陀如来坐像
京都 平等院 鳳凰堂
天喜元年（1053）
像高　278.8cm
定朝作
国宝
木造 ヒノキ 漆箔

Seated Amida Nyorai
Hō-ō-dō (Phoenix Hall),
Byōdō-in temple, Kyoto
AD 1053 (Tengi 1)
278.8 cm
Made by Jōchō
National Treasure
Wood (Japanese cypress; hinoki),
Gold foil applied with lacquer

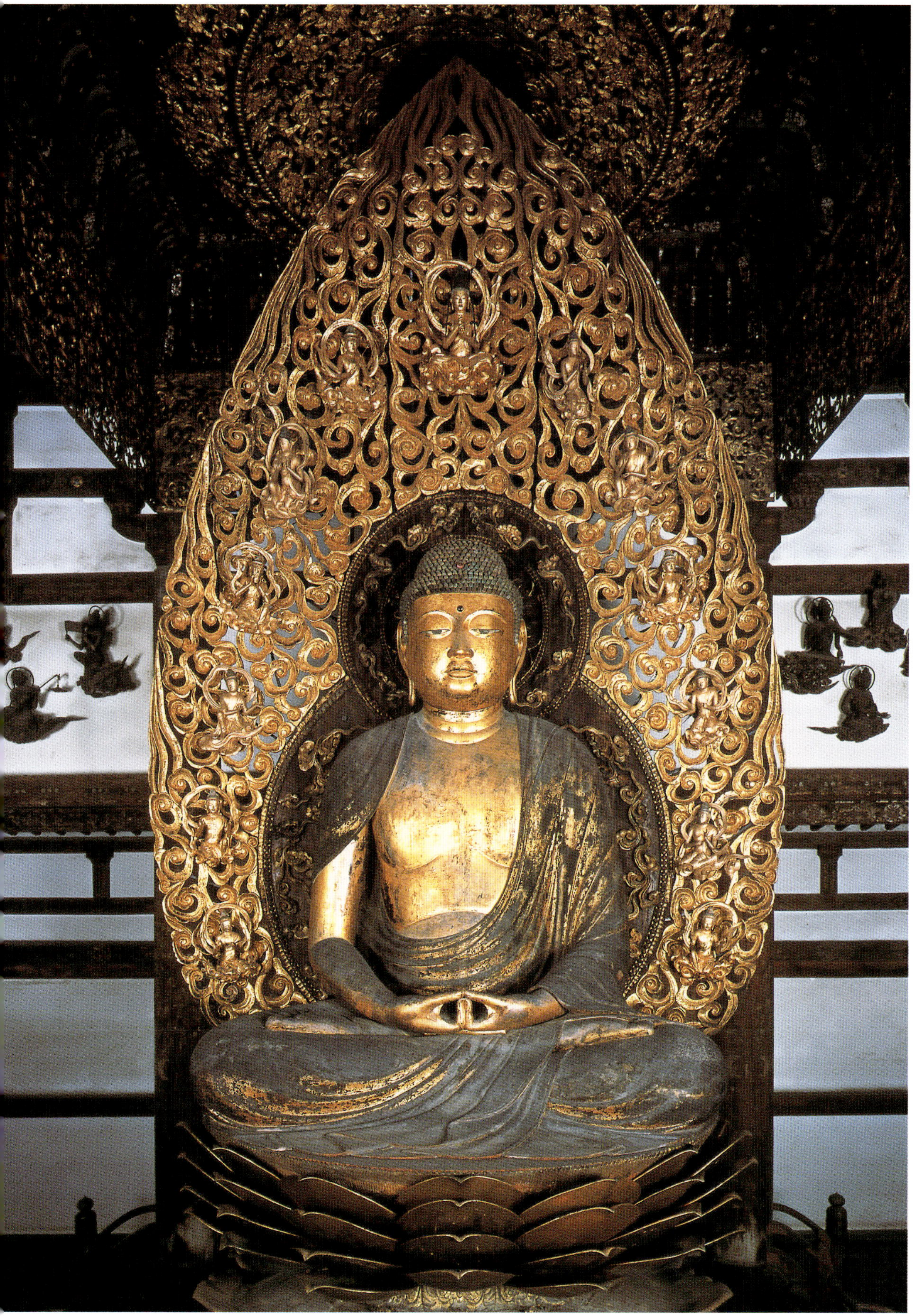

定朝作阿弥陀如来坐像　|　Seated Amida Nyorai

雲中供養菩薩像
Bodhisattva Riding on Clouds

阿弥陀如来の極楽浄土を華やかに飾る定朝工房の傑作
Masterpieces from Jōchō's atelier ornamenting Amida Buddha's Paradise

阿弥陀如来を讃嘆供養する菩薩たち｜平等院鳳凰堂の長押上の壁面には、阿弥陀如来の極楽浄土へと誘う、木造高肉彫りの雲中供養菩薩が飾られています。これらの52体の菩薩像はどれもが国宝に指定されていて、僧形の像が5体、舞い姿の像が6体あり、半数以上の30体はさまざまな楽器を手にとっています。いずれもヒノキ材で作られ、造像当初は切金文様も用いて美しく仕上げられていました。

華やかな北25号、若々しさの南20号｜52体の飛天は飾られている壁の位置によって、それぞれ北1号、南20号というように名付けられています。とくに造形が素晴らしい北25号や南20号などは、定朝工房の中の主だった仏師の手によるものです。南20号は、細おもての顔立ちに、若々しくバランスのよい立ち姿で、天衣をふってかかとで拍子をとるかのように舞っています。その姿は平安貴族たちの優雅な様子をあらわしているかのようです。そのほかに繊細で華やかな造形を見せる北25号も高い評価を得ています。平等院の境内に建つ展示施設の鳳翔館では、供養菩薩像の何体かを間近に拝観することができます。

Heavenly beings in adoration of *Amida Nyorai* | Along the walls above the horizontal timbers of the Phoenix Hall at *Byōdō-in*, images of bodhisattvas riding on clouds, carved in wooden relief, are arrayed in welcome to Amida Buddha's Paradise. Surrounding the bodhisattvas a host of heavenly beings float on clouds. There are a total of fifty-two figures, all designated National Treasures. There are a variety of types, five of them are in priestly attire, six of them are dancing, and thirty of them are playing musical instruments. All are made from Japanese cypress (*hinoki*), and they were finished with beautiful cut gold patterns.

Florid North 25 and youthful South 20 | The fifty-two figures bear numbers such as North 1 or South 20, according to their location within the hall. These images are attributed to the atelier of *Jōchō*, and the sculptors of particularly beautiful pieces such as North 25 and South 20 must have been the best in the workshop. South 20 has a slender face, and a youthful figure balanced in a rhythmic dance pose, with fluttering scarves. The figure seems to embody the elegance associated with the Heian aristocracy. Another highly admired sculpture is North 25, in delicate and radiant modeling. These bodhisattvas are placed high above eye level, but some can be viewed at closer range in the temple's *Hōshōkan* building, a visit that is highly recommended.

平安時代後期
雲中供養菩薩像

Late Heian period
Unchū Kuyō Bosatsu Zō

Data

雲中供養菩薩像
京都 平等院 鳳凰堂
天喜元年（1053）
像高 62.0cm（南 20 号）
国宝
木造 ヒノキ

Bodhisattva riding on clouds
Hō-ō-dō (Phoenix Hall),
Byōdō-in temple, Kyoto
AD 1053 (Tengi 1)
62.0 cm (South 20)
National Treasure
Wood (Japanese cypress; hinoki)

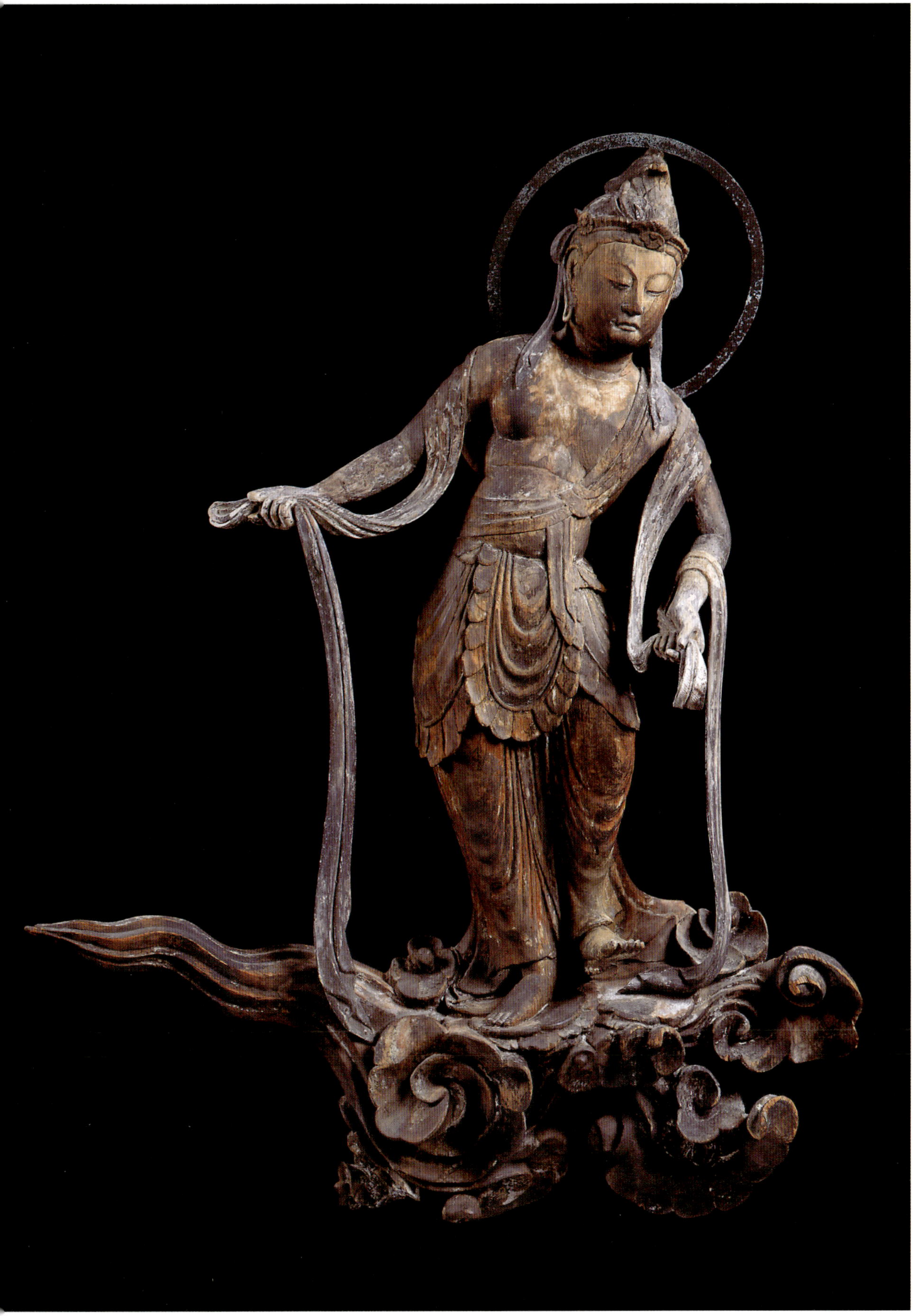

雲中供養菩薩像 | Bodhisattva Riding on Clouds

九体阿弥陀如来坐像
Nine Seated Amida Nyorai

九品の極楽往生と九体の阿弥陀如来像
Nine Amida Nyorai sculptures symbolizing the nine levels of the Western Paradise

平安時代から残る唯一の九体阿弥陀堂 | 京都府南部、奈良県境も近い南山城の静かな山中に浄瑠璃寺はあります。末法の時代に当時の人々は怯え、極楽浄土への往生を願って阿弥陀如来にすがる思想が、貴族から民衆にまで広まっていました。経典の一つ観無量寿経によれば、往生のあり方は生前に積んだ功徳によって9通りがあるとされ、そのすべてを救済するという願いを込めて、平安時代後期には九体阿弥陀如来像を作ることが流行しました。しかし今日、そのほとんどは戦火や災害で失われ、現在残っているのはこの浄瑠璃寺の九体阿弥陀如来像だけになっています。

統一された群像のなかの個性 | 丈六の中尊を中心に、木造漆箔の9体の阿弥陀如来像が一列に並ぶ様は荘厳そのもので、阿弥陀如来の救済への強い願いを感じさせます。中尊は右手を上げ左手を下げ、半丈六の大きさの脇仏はいずれも定印を結んでいます。いずれも定朝様の穏やかな相好ですが、中尊は張りのある顔と堂々とした体躯に特色があり、脇仏も少しずつ違った顔だちや体つきをしています。そこには、群像としての統一されたできばえとともに、一体一体を担当した仏師たちの個性もあらわれています。

The only Nine Amida Hall extant from the Heian period | *Jōruri-ji* temple is located in a quiet mountain setting in *Minami-Yamashiro* in southern Kyoto close to Nara. The late Heian period was a time when the idea of the "latter days of the [Buddhist] Law" (*Mappō*) became current among both the aristocracy and the general populace, leading to rise in the worship of Amida Buddha in hopes of attaining entry to his Western Paradise. According to one of the Buddhist scriptures, there are nine levels of birth in the Western Paradise, depending on good deeds accumulated during one's life. The iconography of nine *Amida Nyorai* images represented the nine levels of salvation. Most such sets of statuary have been lost or destroyed over time, however, leaving this as the sole surviving complete group of nine *Amida Nyorai*.

Individuality expressed within the unified group of nine sculptures | The array of nine *Amida Nyorai* lacquered wood images, with the central

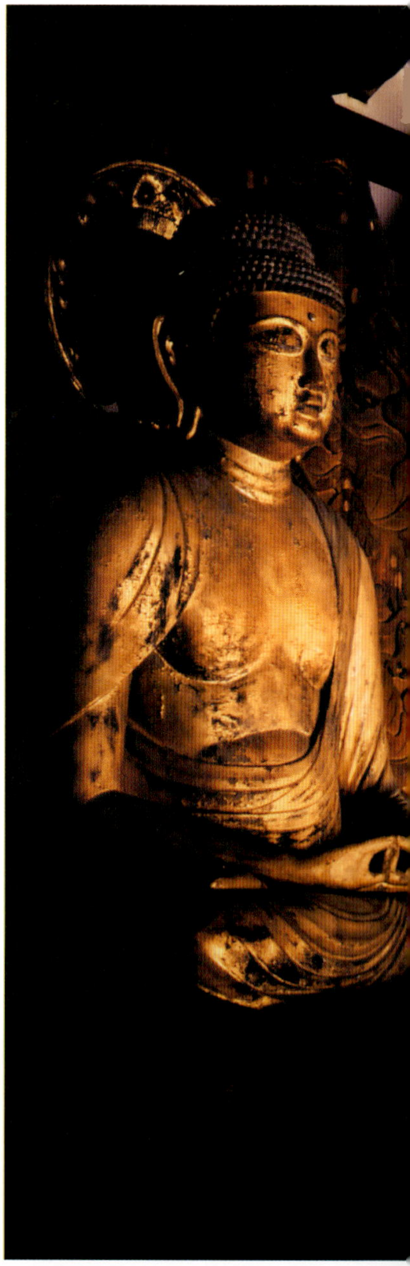

平安時代後期 **九体阿弥陀如来坐像**
Late Heinan period
Kutai Amida Nyorai Zazō

Amida of 4.84 meters tall is magnificent and communicates the belief in salvation granted by *Amida*. These statues are made in the *shippaku* technique, or gold leaf applied with lacquer, over wood. The central *Amida* raises his right hand and lowers the left, while the eight accompanying *Amida* have their hands in the meditation gesture (*jō-in*). Their elegant features reflect the *Jōchō* sculptural style. The central *Amida* is characterized by his firm face and dignified posture, and there are slight variations in the facial features and bodies of the attending eight Buddhas. While retaining unity as a group, each image reveals some sense of the individual sculptor's hands.

Data

阿弥陀如来坐像
京都 浄瑠璃寺 本堂
11 ～ 12 世紀
像高 224.0cm （中尊）
国宝
木造 ヒノキ 漆箔

Nine Seated Amida Nyorai
Hondō, Jōruri-ji temple, Kyoto
Eleventh or Twelfth century
224.0 cm (central sculpture)
National Treasure
Wood (Japanese cypress; hinoki) ,
Gold foil applied with lacquer

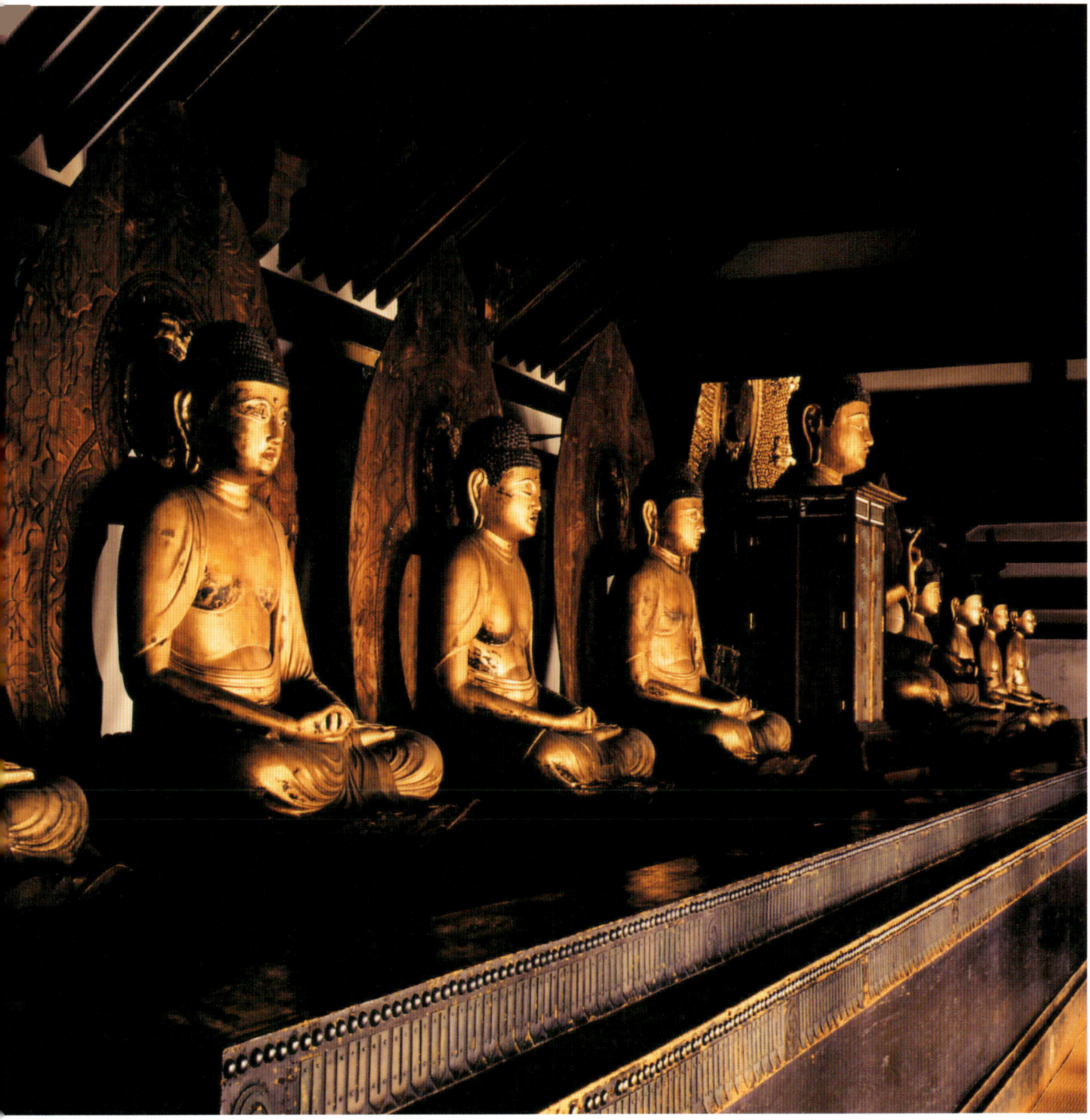

K TEMPLE GUIDE

京都
Kyoto

寺院ガイド
Temple Guide

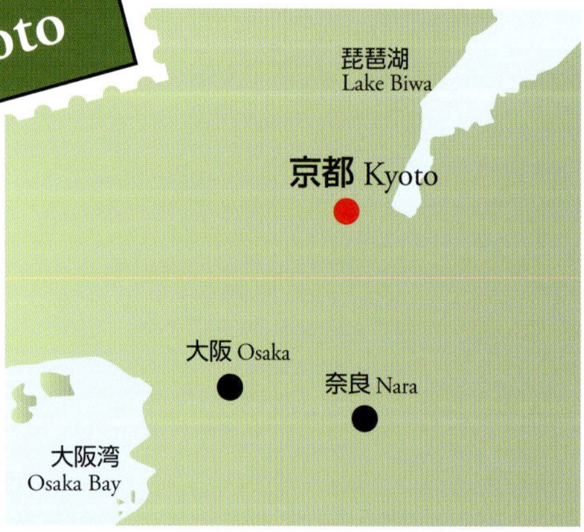

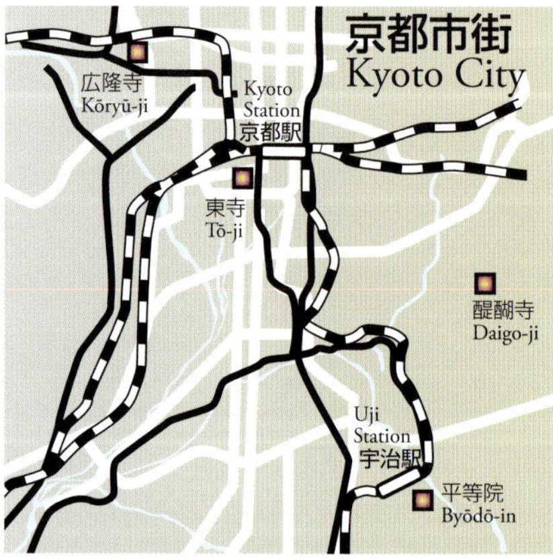

広隆寺
Kōryū-ji temple

京都府京都市右京区太秦蜂岡町 32
京福嵐山線太秦広隆寺駅 徒歩すぐ
Uzumasa-hachioka-chō 32, Ukyō-ku, Kyoto-shi, Kyoto-fu
Keifuku Arashiyama Line, Uzumasa Kōryū-ji Station,
1 min on foot
OPEN 9:00 – CLOSE 17:00 (16:30)
■弥勒菩薩半跏像（宝冠弥勒）
Seated Bodhisattva Maitreya（→ p.80）

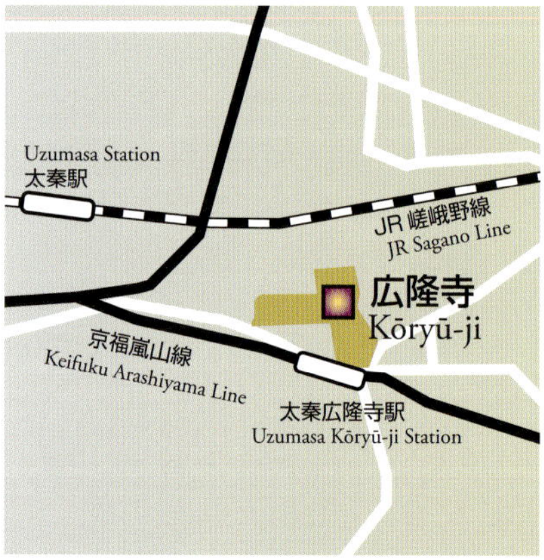

東寺（教王護国寺）
Tō-ji temple (Kyō-ō gokoku-ji temple)

京都府京都市南区九条町 1
近鉄京都線 東寺駅 徒歩 10 分
Kujō-cho 1, Minami-ku, Kyoto-shi, Kyoto-fu
Kintestsu Kyoto Line, Tō-ji Station, 10 min on foot
OPEN 8:30 – CLOSE 17:00
http://www.toji.or.jp/
■降三世明王立像（五大明王像）
Standing Gōzanze Myō-ō（→ p.82）
■四天王立像（持国天）
Four Heavenly Kings (Jikoku-ten)（→ p.15）

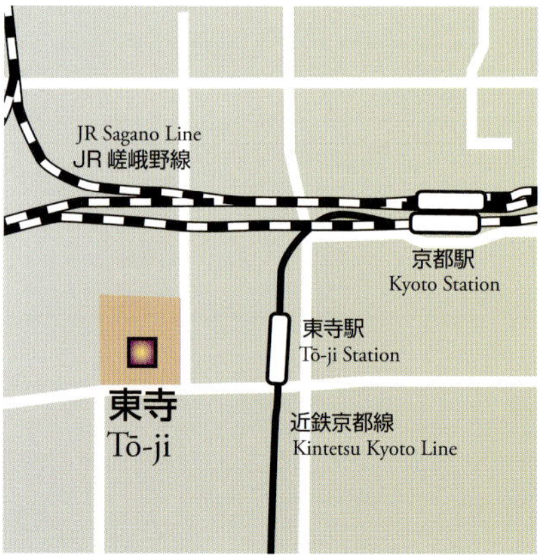

醍醐寺

Daigo-ji temple

京都府京都市伏見区醍醐東大路町 22
地下鉄東西線醍醐駅 徒歩 10 分
Daigo Higashiōji-chō 22, Fushimi-ku, Kyoto-shi, Kyoto-fu
Kyoto City Subway Tōzai Line, Daigo Station, 10 min on foot
OPEN 9:00 – CLOSE 17:00 (16:30)
http://www.daigoji.or.jp/
■薬師三尊像 Yakushi Triad (→ p.84)

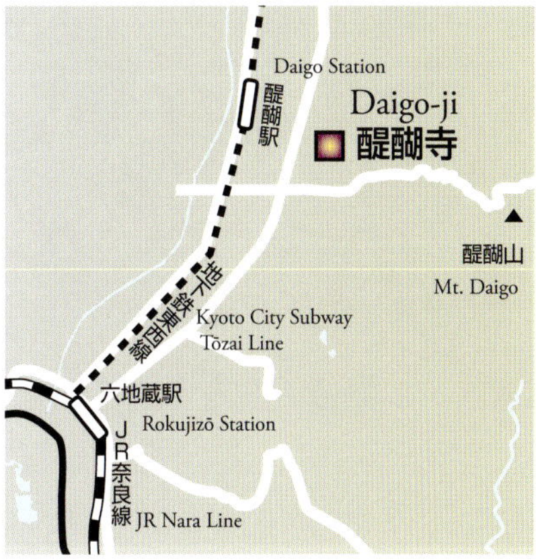

TEMPLE GUIDE

平等院

Byōdō-in temple

京都府宇治市宇治蓮華 116
JR 奈良線宇治駅 徒歩 10 分
Uji Renge 116, Uji-shi, Kyoto-fu
JR Nara Line, Uji Station, 10 min on foot
OPEN 8:30 – CLOSE 17:30
http://www.byodoin.or.jp/
■定朝作阿弥陀如来坐像 Seated Amida Nyorai (→ p.86)
■雲中供養菩薩像 Bodhisattva Riding on Clouds (→ p.88)

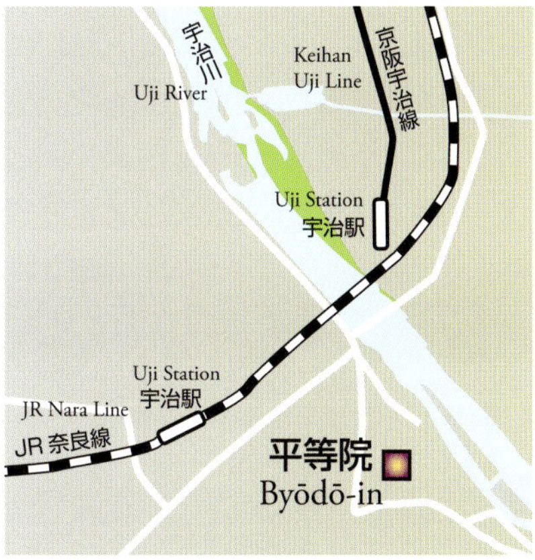

浄瑠璃寺

Jōruri-ji temple

京都府木津川市加茂町西小札場 40
JR 大和路線奈良駅 バス約 28 分 徒歩 3 分
Kamo-chō Nishiofutaba 40, Kizugawa-shi, Kyoto-fu
JR Yamatoji Line, Nara Station, 28 min by bus, 3 min on foot
OPEN 9:00 (10:00) – CLOSE 17:00 (16:00)
■九体阿弥陀如来坐像 Nine Seated Amida Nyorai (→ p.90)

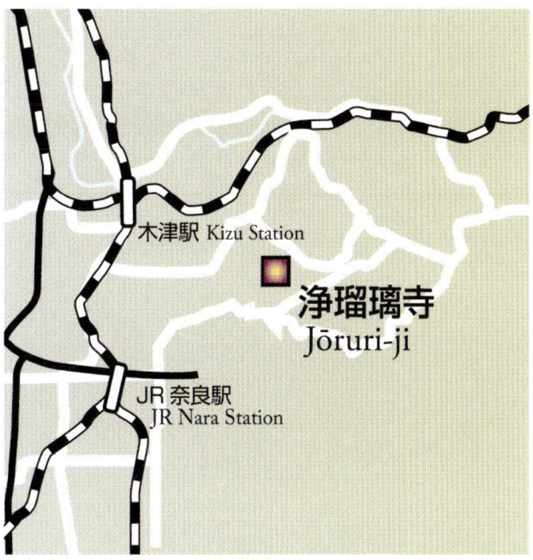

※拝観時間は変更になる場合があります。インターネットや観光案内所でご確認ください。
*Opening hours are subject to change. Please visit websites or tourist bureaus for the latest information.

Area 3

関東その他の仏像

Buddhist sculpture in Kanto and other areas

見どころは奈良、京都だけではない

鎌倉は、12世紀末から約150年の間、武士によって幕府が置かれた土地です。今でも鎌倉にはその時代の名残を伝える古寺が多く、有名な鎌倉大仏もその時代の遺品です。また、鎌倉近くの三浦半島の浄楽寺や伊豆半島の願成就院には、鎌倉時代の代表的仏師運慶の遺品が伝わっています。日本の歴史をひもとくと、歴史上重要な土地には寺院が建てられ、仏像が作られてきたことがわかります。仏像を訪ねることは日本の歴史を訪ねることにも通じます。

兵庫県浄土寺も、平安時代末から鎌倉時代に東大寺復興を主導した重源上人によって建てられた寺で、東北地方の平泉の中尊寺や、九州の太宰府に建つ観世音寺も、中央の文化とはまた違った、趣を感じさせる寺院です。

また、今日、東京には日本最大の博物館である東京国立博物館や、わが国最初の私立美術館の大倉集古館など多くの美術館があり、そこでも多彩な仏像に会うことができます。

法隆寺宝物館 東京 東京国立博物館
The Gallery of Hōryū-ji Treasures, Tokyo National Museum, Tokyo

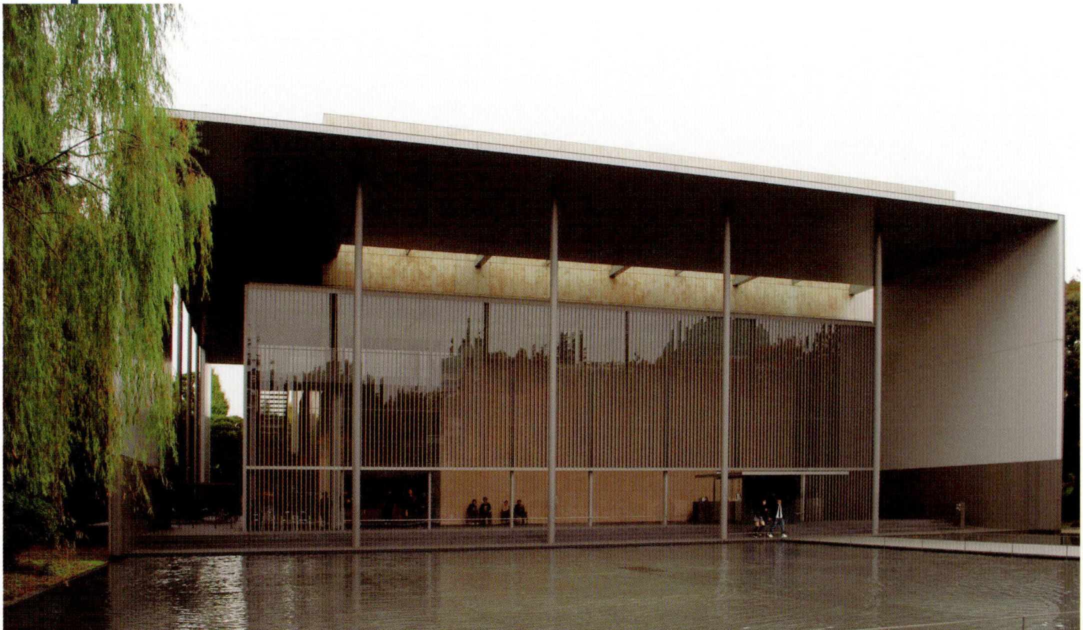

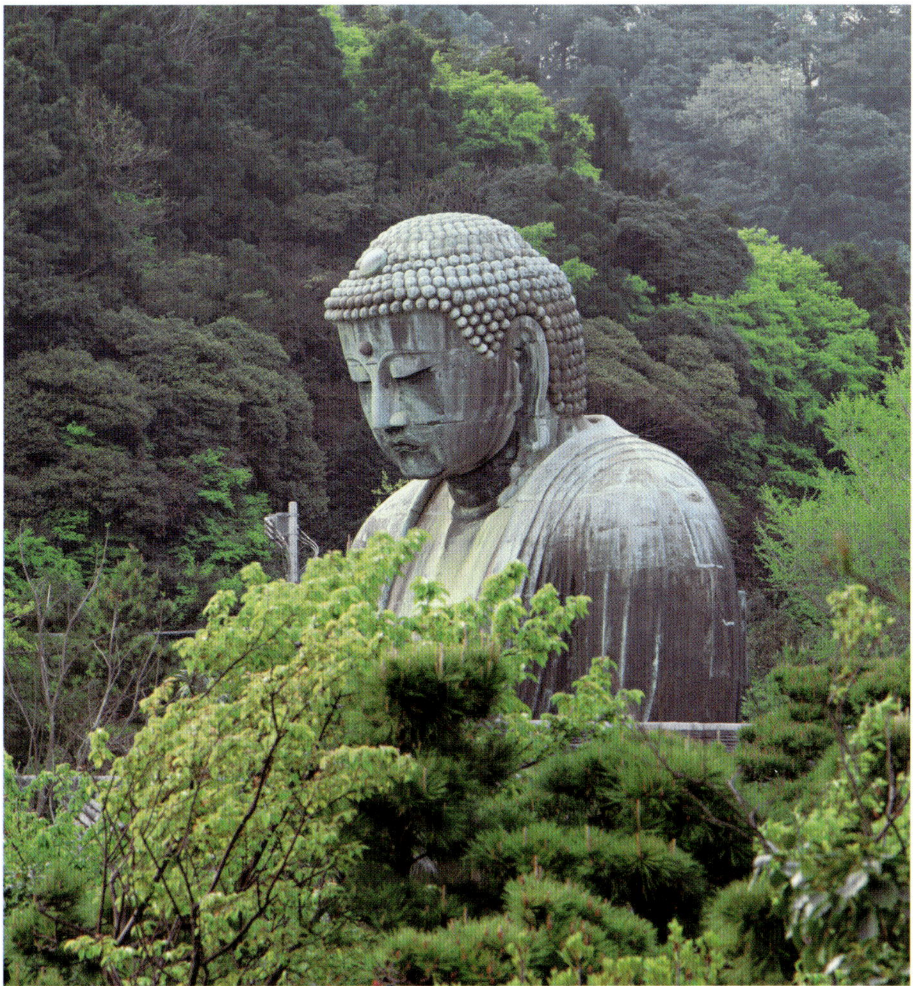

鎌倉大仏 神奈川 高徳院
Great Buddha of Kamakura, Kōtoku-in temple, Kanagawa

The masterpieces are not only in the Nara and Kyoto area

Kamakura was the seat of the military rulers of Japan for 150 years, since the end of twelfth century. Even now, there are many temples and sculptures dating from the Kamakura period, one of which is the famous Great Buddha of Kamakura (*Kamakura Daibutsu*). You can visit *Jōraku-ji* on Miura peninsula, near Kamakura, and *Ganjōju-in* on Izu peninsula, to see the works by *Unkei*, the leading sculptor of the Kamakura period. When you read about Japanese history, it becomes apparent that those great temples and Buddhist images were created in the important cities of the time. To visit the Buddhist statues means to visit Japanese history itself.

Temples in other areas include *Jōdo-ji* in Hyogo prefecture, which is one of the temples built by *Chōgen-shōnin* (master *Chōgen*), who had been the leading figure in the *Tōdai-ji* reconstruction in Nara during the late twelfth century. *Chūson-ji* in Hiraizumi in the Tohoku area, and *Kanzeon-ji* at Dazaifu in the Kyushu area have their own styles different from the central culture.

In Tokyo, you can visit many museums such as the Tokyo National Museum, the largest museum in Japan, and Ōkura Museum of Art (*Ōkura-Shūkokan*), the first private museum which exhibited Buddhist sculpture.

摩耶夫人及び天人像
Lady Maya and Attendants *Forty-eight Buddhist statues*

飛鳥時代より伝わる四十八体の秘宝
Fourty-eight treasures of the Asuka period

日本最大の博物館｜明治5年（1872）に創立された東京国立博物館は、日本最古にして最大の博物館です。絵画から彫刻、文化遺産などさまざまな収集品が約9万点も所蔵されています。館内に建つ法隆寺宝物館には、明治11年（1878）に法隆寺から皇室に献上された法隆寺献納宝物が収蔵、展示されていますが、そのなかに、四十八体仏と呼ばれる飛鳥時代から白鳳時代を中心に作られた多数の小金銅仏があります。
釈迦生誕の瞬間をあらわした小金銅仏｜この四十八体仏のなかの銅造摩耶夫人(まやぶにん)及び天人像は、釈迦の母親である摩耶夫人（マーヤー）が、その右脇から釈迦を産むという仏典に記された情景を再現した像です。像高16.6センチの摩耶夫人像は小さい像ですが、釈迦の物語の発端を躍動感のある生き生きとした表現であらわしています。摩耶夫人を取り囲む3体の天人も、生気ある姿で表現されていますが、鍍金がない1体だけは後の時代に補われたものです。四十八体仏にはこの像の他にも、菩薩半跏像や如来坐像、観音菩薩立像など、飛鳥時代の貴重な仏像が多数あります。

The largest museum in Japan | Built in 1872, the Tokyo National Museum is the oldest and largest in Japan, with a collection of over 90,000 paintings, sculptures and other cultural assets. The *Hōryū-ji* Treasury gallery within the museum houses and exhibits the valuable objects from the temple donated to the Imperial Household in 1878. Among the objects is a group of gilt bronze statuettes called the "Forty-eight Buddhist statues" dating to the Asuka period.
The gilt bronze image depicting the Buddha's birth | Among the forty-eight statues are images of Lady Maya and three attendants at the moment related in the scriptures that the historic Buddha, *Shaka*, was born, emerging from her right sleeve. Although only 16.6 cm in height, the image of Lady Maya vividly depicts the prologue of the story of *Shaka*. The attendant figures also seem alive, although one of them, without gilding, is a later replacement. Other sculptures in this group of forty-eight include images of the seated Bodhisattva, the seated *Nyorai* and the standing bodhisattva Kannon, among others.

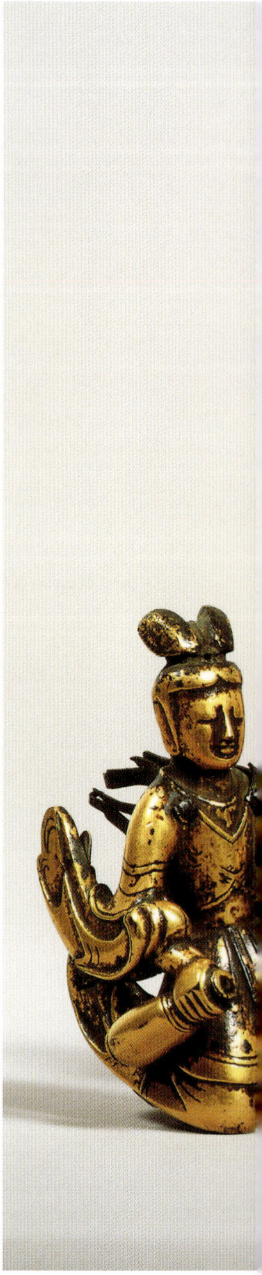

飛鳥時代 **摩耶夫人及び天人像**
Asuka period
Maya Bunin oyobi Tennin Zō

Data

摩耶夫人及び天人像
東京国立博物館 法隆寺宝物館
飛鳥時代
像高　16.6cm（摩耶夫人）
重要文化財
銅造 鍍金

Lady Maya and attendants
(from Forty-eight Buddhist statues)
Tokyo National Museum, Tokyo
Asuka period
16.6 cm (Maya)
Important Cultural Property
Gilt bronze

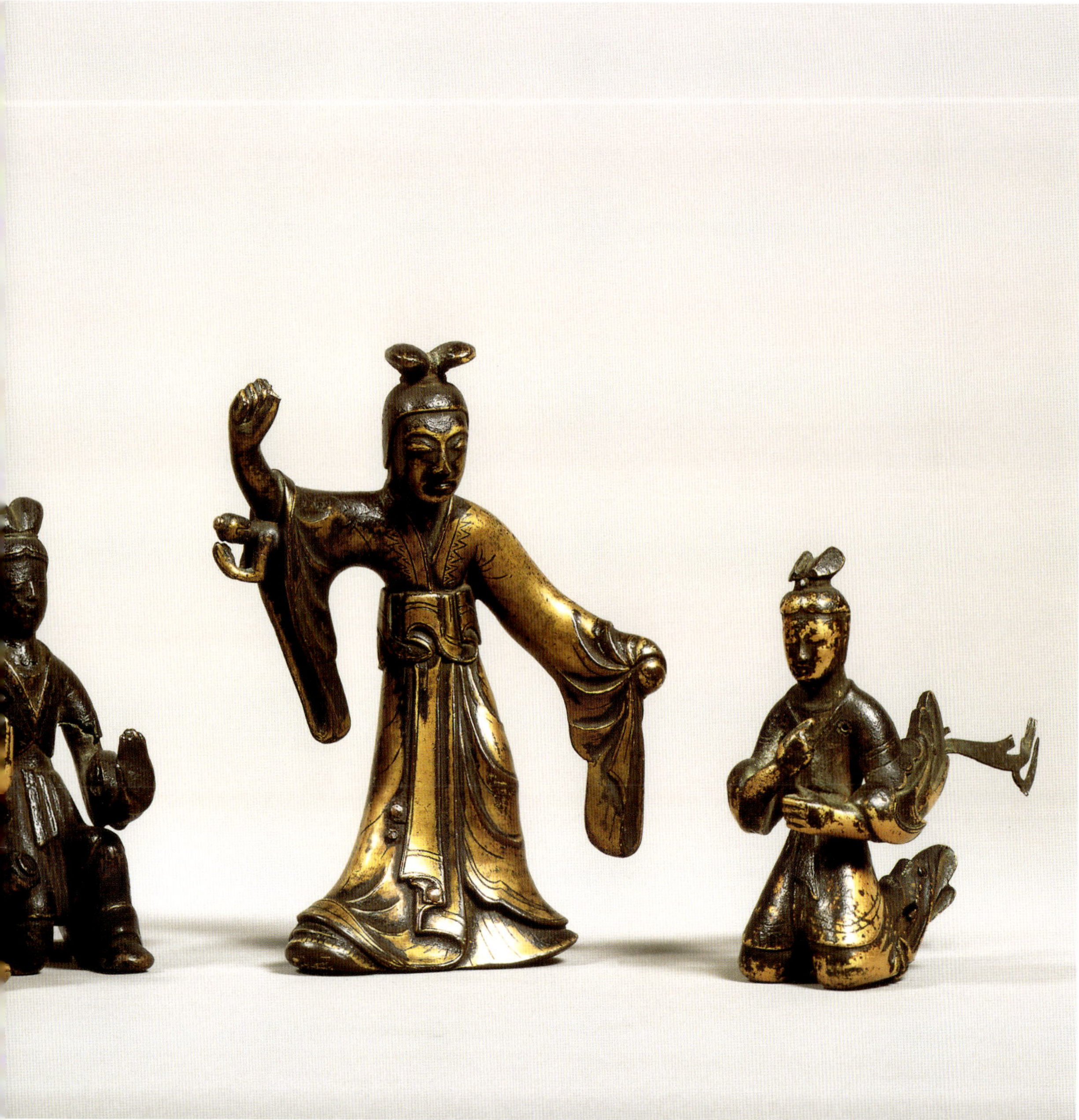

普賢菩薩騎象像
The Bodhisattva Fugen Riding on an Elephant

象に乗った慈悲の仏
The Buddha of mercy riding on the elephant

日本で初めての私立美術館「大倉集古館」｜明治維新以降、貿易や建設で財を成した実業家・大倉喜八郎は自らの美術品コレクションを公開し、大正6年（1917）に日本で初めての私立美術館として、大倉集古館をオープンしました。明治時代の海外への文化財流出を嘆いていた喜八郎は、水際でそれを阻止すべく私財を投じて50年以上文化財の蒐集を続けていましたが、その美術品の多くと建物、基金を寄付して大倉集古館を開設したのです。

平安時代に作られた美しい像｜大倉集古館には、平安時代や鎌倉時代の絵巻物や、陶器、絵画などが数多く展示されていますが、その中でも注目されるのは、平安後期の12世紀前半に作られたとされる国宝普賢菩薩騎象像です。合掌して蓮台ごと象の上に乗っているスタイルはあまりなじみがないかもしれませんが、普賢菩薩はこのような姿にあらわされることが多い仏です。普賢菩薩は釈迦如来の脇侍として、智慧を司る文殊菩薩と対をなす、慈悲の仏です。日本特産のヒノキ材で作られ、彩色が施されている美しい仏像です。もとは京都などの由緒ある寺院の像だったと思われますが、記録がないために詳しい伝来については不明です。

The first private museum in Japan, *Ōkura Shūkokan* | *Ōkura Kihachirō* was a successful entrepreneur in trade and construction, who began collecting Japanese art in the early Meiji period. In 1917 he opened the first private museum in Japan, the *Ōkura Shūkokan* (Ōkura Museum of Art), to exhibit his collection to the public. *Ōkura* lamented the transfer of Japanese art treasures overseas, and to stem the flow, he spent his private resources over the next fifty years collecting works of art. He donated most of the artworks, buildings and funds to the *Ōkura Shūkokan*.

A beautiful sculpture from the Heian period | The *Ōkura Shūkokan* collection includes Heian and Kamakura period scrolls, ceramics, paintings, and the like, but one exceptional piece is the late Heian period early twelfth century sculpture of the bodhisattva Fugen seated on an elephant, a designated National Treasure. *Fugen*, hands clasped in prayer is seated in a lotus pedestal on an elephant. This image may seem unusual, but there are many similar depictions of this bodhisattva, *Fugen*. *Fugen* symbolizes benevolence, and is an attendant figure to the Shaka Buddha, and often paired with the bodhisattva Monju, who embodies wisdom. The *Fugen* is a beautiful sculpture made of Japanese cypress (*hinoki*) and was covered with colorful pigments. Although no documentation is extant, this sculpture most likely came from one of the temples in the Kyoto area.

平安時代後期
普賢菩薩騎象像

Late Heian period
Fugen Bosatsu Kizōzō

Data

普賢菩薩騎象像
東京 大倉集古館
12 世紀前半
像高　87.0cm
国宝
木造 ヒノキ 彩色

Samantabhadra
The bodhisattva Fugen riding on an elephant
Ōkura Museum of Art, Tokyo
Early twelfth century
87. 0 cm
National Treasure
Wood (Japanese cypress; hinoki), Pigments

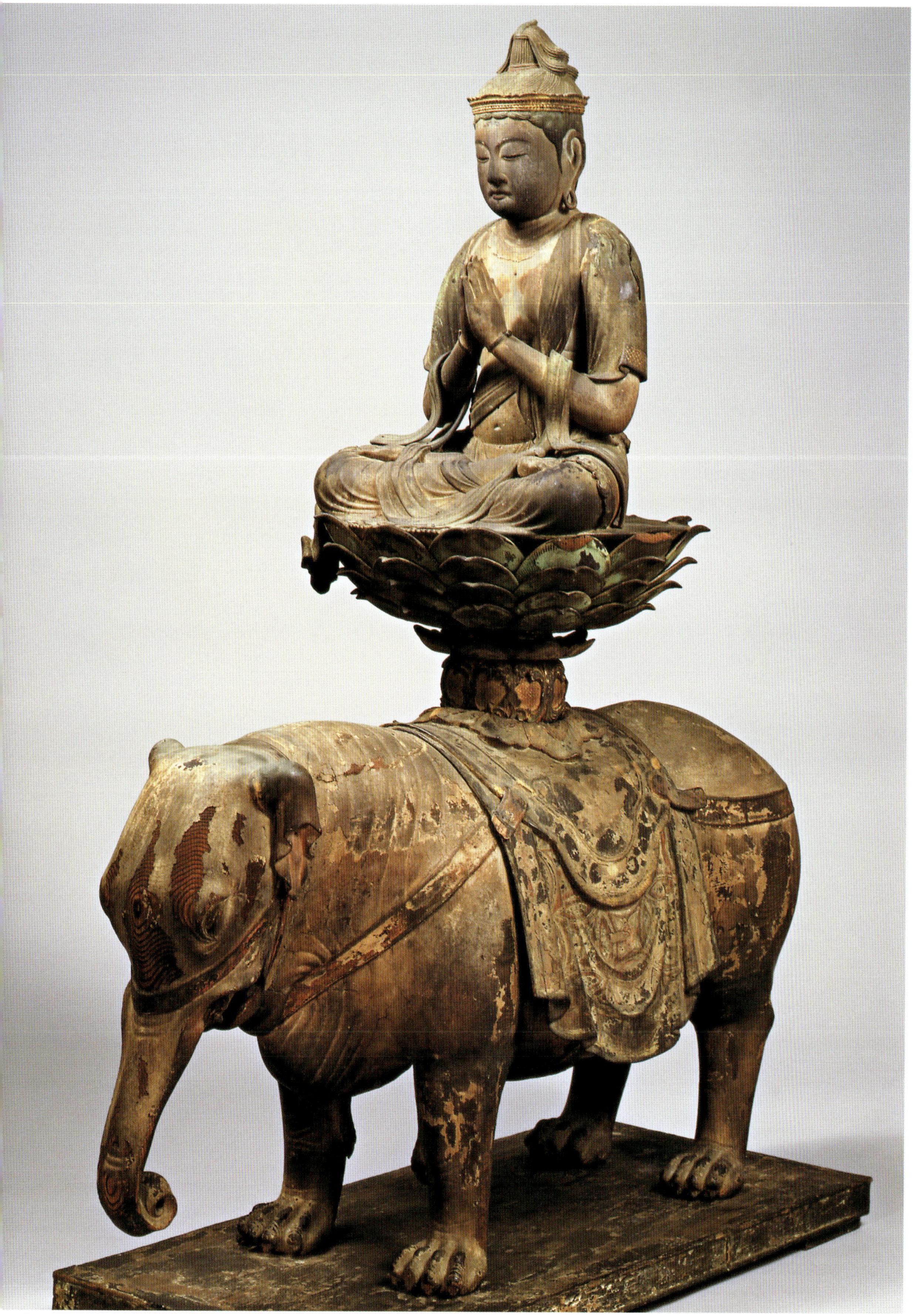

普賢菩薩騎象像 ｜ The Bodhisattva Fugen Riding on an Elephant

阿弥陀如来坐像（鎌倉大仏）
Seated Amida Nyorai (the Great Buddha of Kamakura)

鎌倉のシンボル的存在
Symbolic essence of Kamakura

造立の経緯は謎のまま | 江ノ島電鉄の長谷駅から徒歩で7分ほどゆるやかな坂を上ると、緑豊かな谷戸に囲まれた巨大な像が見えて来ます。これが「鎌倉大仏」あるいは「長谷大仏」と呼ばれる高徳院の銅造阿弥陀如来坐像です。大仏は建長4年（1252）に作られ始めましたが、どのような経緯で造立され、いつ完成したのかなどはっきりとしたことはわかっていません。
慶派の作風に宋の影響をプラス | 大仏は肩幅の広いがっしりとした体つきに鎌倉時代に流行した運慶ら慶派仏師の作風を感じさせますが、平面的な顔つきや頭が大きく猫背気味の姿勢などには、当時の中国宋王朝の仏像との共通性も見られます。このような作風は鎌倉時代の関東地方の仏像にしばしば見られ、大仏はその代表的存在です。鋳銅製の像で表面には金箔が押されていましたが、現在はほとんどなくなり、緑色に錆びた銅の地肌が目立ちます。右のほほをよく見ると一部金箔が残っているのがわかります。初めは木造の大仏殿に安置されていましたが、15世紀末に襲った地震と津波で建物を失って以来、今見るような露座となりました。

Process of construction still a mystery | Climbing up a gentle slope after a seven-minute or so walk from Hase station on the Enoshima railway line, one is confronted by a colossal statue surrounded by green valleys. This is the so-called the Great Buddha of Kamakura (*Kamakura Daibutsu,* or *Hase Daibutsu*), the seated bronze *Amida Nyora*i of *Kōtoku-in* temple. The construction of the *Daibutsu* was begun in 1252, but little is known of its background or completion date.
A style fusing the *Kei* school and Chinese Song dynasty modes | Although the broad shoulders and massive body of the *Daibutsu* express the style of *Kei* school artists such as *Unkei*, that was popular in the Kamakura period, the flattened face, large head and hunched shoulders have more in common with contemporary Chinese Buddhist sculpture of the Song dynasty. These features are frequently seen in Kamakura period sculpture made in Eastern Japan, as typified by the *Kamakura Daibutsu*. The bronze cast *Daibutsu* was once covered in gold leaf, most of which has disappeared and the surface has a green patina at the front now. Careful examination reveals remnants of gold foil on the right cheek. Originally the sculpture was enshrined in a wooden building, which was destroyed by an earthquake and tsunami at the end of the fifteenth century. Since then, the *Daibutsu* has been exposed to the open air as it is today.

鎌倉時代
阿弥陀如来坐像（鎌倉大仏）

Kamakura period
Amida Nyorai Zazō
(Kamakura Daibutsu)

Data

阿弥陀如来坐像
神奈川 高徳院
13 世紀半ば
像高　1138.7cm
国宝
銅造 箔押し

Amitabha
Seated Amida Buddha
The Great Buddha of Kamakura
Kōtoku-in temple, Kamakura, Kanagawa
Mid-thirteenth century
1138.7 cm
National Treasure
Bronze, Gold foil

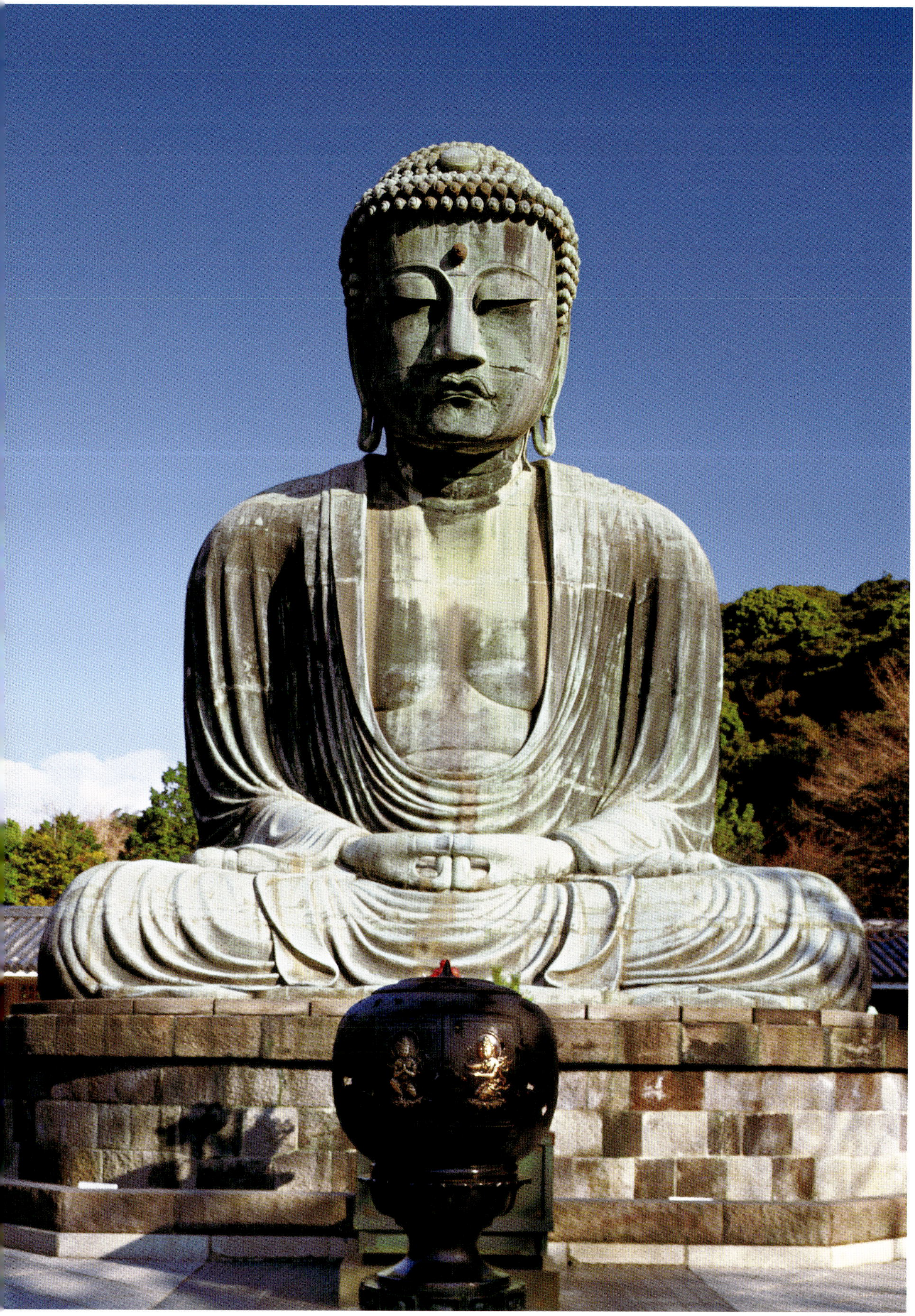

阿弥陀如来坐像（鎌倉大仏）　|　Seated Amida Nyorai (the Great Buddha of Kamakura)

金色堂諸尊像
Golden Hall and Buddhist Sculpture

平泉に燦然と輝く金色の諸尊像
Golden Buddhist statuary glittering at Hiraizumi

奥州藤原三代の遺骸を納める金色堂 | 岩手県中央を流れる北上川を望む高台に、中尊寺の大伽藍はあります。中尊寺は藤原清衡により建立された寺で、造営に際して多宝塔や二階大堂など数多くの堂塔が建てられましたが、なかでも現存する「金色堂」と呼ばれる阿弥陀堂は、全面に金をあしらい、螺鈿（貝殻を用いた）細工や金具で飾りたてた華麗きわまる建物です。堂内には、中央壇と左壇（向かって右方）、右壇の3つの須弥壇が置かれ、中央の下の木棺には藤原清衡の遺骸が、左右の各壇の下には二代基衡と三代秀衡の遺骸がそれぞれ安置されています。

3組の阿弥陀三尊、六地蔵、二天像 | それぞれの須弥壇には阿弥陀如来像を中尊とし、両脇侍に観音菩薩像と勢至菩薩像を、その左右に3体ずつ計6体の地蔵菩薩像と、前方に持国天像と増長天像を配します。中央壇の阿弥陀三尊像は、清衡による金色堂上棟の天治元年（1124）頃の作とされ、やわらかな雰囲気を持つ平安時代後期ならではの仏像です。いずれも木造漆箔の金色堂の仏像は時を経るうちに移動されたらしく、中央壇の二天と六地蔵像は、もとは二代基衡が没した保元2年（1157）頃に作られた左壇の像だったと考えられています。

A Gold Colored Hall for the remains of three generations of *Fujiwara* | The large temple complex of *Chūson-ji* temple stands high on a hill with a view of the Kitakami River which flows through central Iwate Prefecture. The *Chūson-ji* temple was built by *Fujiwara-no Kiyohira*, and encompassed numerous halls such as the Nikai Great Hall and several pagodas such as the *Tahō-tō*. Among the halls is the Amida Hall, called the *Konjiki-dō* (Gold Colored Hall) because of its luxuriant decoration. Its interior is completely covered in gold leaf, with encrusted nacre (inlaid shells, *raden*), and gold ornamentation. There are three sets of *Amida* daises (*Shumi-dan*), under which the remains of *Fujiwara-no Kiyohira*, the second-generation *Motohira*, and the third-generation *Hidehira* are installed in coffins, at center, left and right, respectively.

Three sets of Amida triads, six bodhisattva Jizō, and two Guardian Kings | Each of the three daises holds a central Amida Buddha, flanked on either side by the bodhisattva Kannon and Seishi, three images of the bodhisattva Jizō on either side (for a total of six), and two Guardian Kings, *Jikoku-ten* and *Zōchō-ten* at front. The Amida Triad, with serene expressions typical of the Heian period, placed on the center platform was dedicated by *Kiyohara* in 1124 when the *Konjiki-dō* was completed. The gold lacquered images of the *Konjiki-dō* seem to have been displaced over time. For example, the two Guardian Kings and six Jizō sculptures now on the middle dais date to 1157, when the second-generation *Motohira* died, and were probably originally part of the group on the left-hand dais.

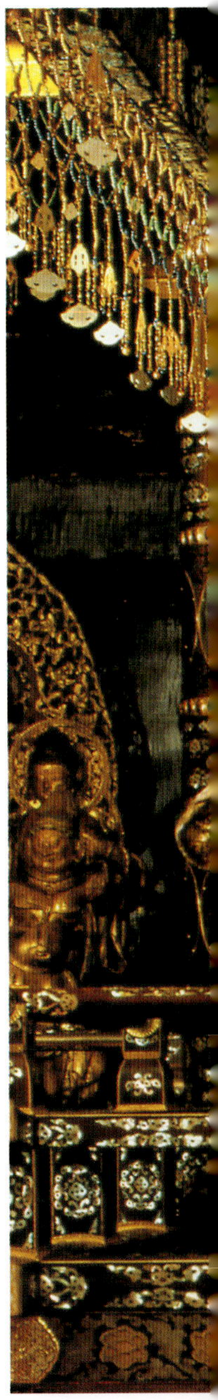

平安時代後期 **金色堂諸尊像**

Late Heian period
Konjiki-dō Shosonzō

Data

金色堂諸尊像
岩手 平泉 中尊寺 金色堂
天治元年〜文治３年（1124 〜 1187）
像高　62.3cm（中央壇阿弥陀如来）
国宝
木造 漆箔

Golden Hall and Buddhist sculpture
Konjiki-dō, Chūson-ji temple, Hiraizumi, Iwate
AD 1124-1187 (Tenji 1-Bunji 3)
62.3 cm (central sculpture, central dais)
National Treasure
Wood, Gold foil applied with lacquer

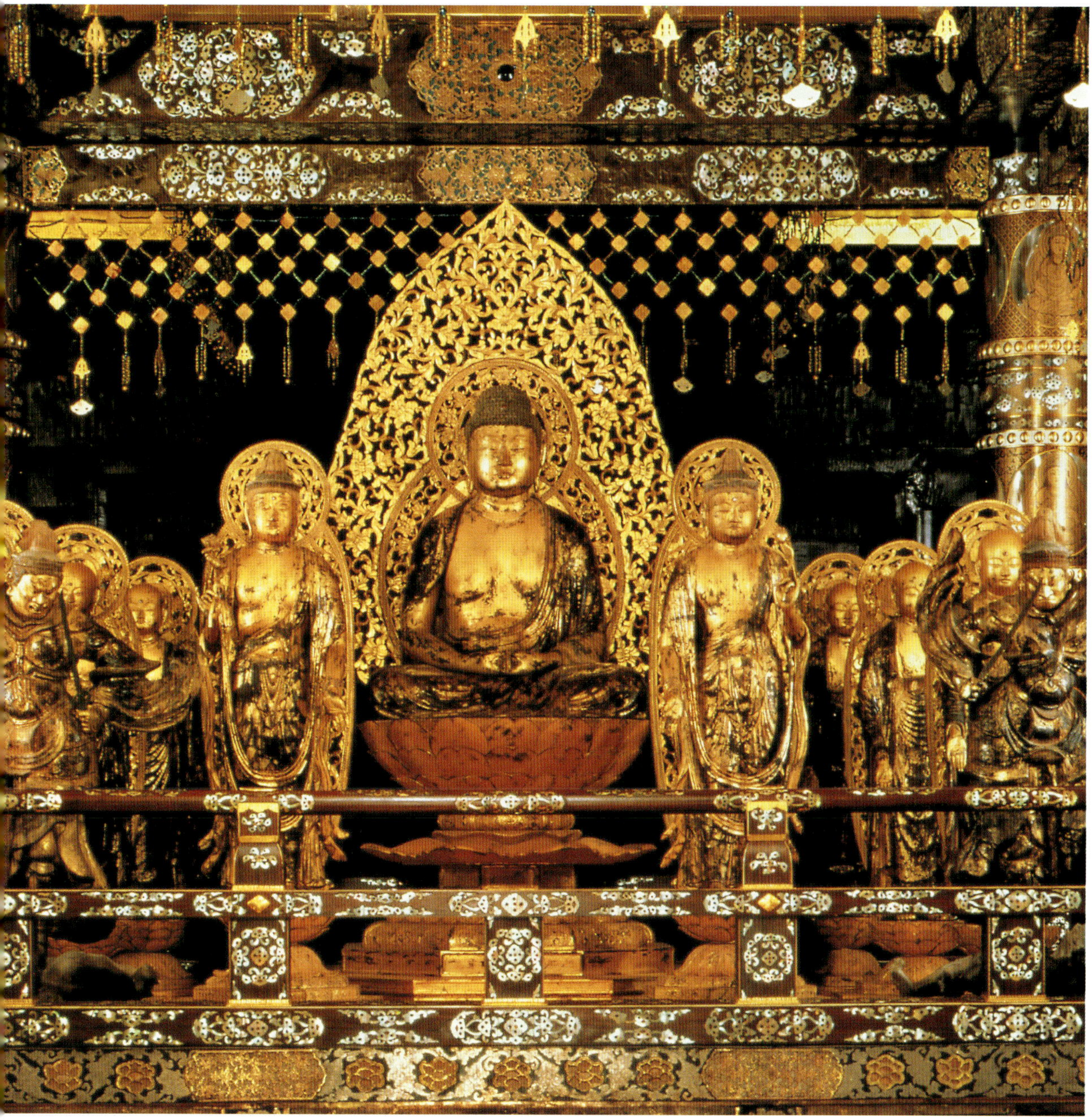

運慶作毘沙門天立像
Bishamon-ten (Vaisravana) *Made by Unkei*

東国武士を彷彿させる新様式の天部像
A new style of guardian sculpture reminiscent of samurai warriors

北条時政発願の願成就院｜時は平安時代から鎌倉時代へ。貴族の支配する時代から武士の支配する時代へ移り変わろうとしていたその頃、仏像もそれまでの和様彫刻から鎌倉時代の新様式へと、大きく様変わりをしようとしていました。鎌倉幕府を開いた源頼朝の妻北条政子の父であり、支援者でもあった北条時政は、頼朝の奥州征伐の戦勝を祈願して、北条氏の本拠地である伊豆韮山(にらやま)の地に願成就院を建てました。今、願成就院大御堂に安置されている本尊阿弥陀如来像と、不動明王二童子像、そしてここに紹介する毘沙門天像は、文治2年（1186）、仏師運慶によって作られたことが、像内に納められた五重塔形の銘札から知られます。

運慶が導き出した新たな潮流｜毘沙門天像の腰高で颯爽としたスタイルは、重厚で威圧感のあるそれまでの四天王像とはずいぶんと雰囲気が異なります。運慶がめざしたのは、新時代の人々が求めた生気に富む活動的な姿の仏像でした。この像には、そうした鎌倉時代の新しい仏像様式がはっきりと示されています。ヒノキ材の寄木造(よせぎづくり)で、目には水晶製の玉眼がはめ込まれています。当初は彩色仕上げでしたが、今は漆塗りの地肌があらわれています。

Ganjōjū-in* temple sponsored by *Hōjō Tokimasa | With the change from the Heian period to the Kamakura, came a shift in power, from the dominance of the court aristocracy to that of the warrior class, or samurai. The style of Buddhist sculpture too changed radically, from the serene Heian mode to one suited to the new Kamakura period. *Ganjōjū-in* temple was built by *Hōjō Tokimasa* at Izu Nirayama, the home territory of his family. *Tokimasa* was the father of *Hōjō Masako*, wife of the founder of the Kamakura shogunate, *Minamoto-no Yoritomo*, and dedicated the temple to pray for *Yoritomo's* victory in battle in northeastern Japan. An inscription found in the five-story pagoda indicates that the principal *Amida Nyorai* image, as well as a *Fūdō Myō-ō* with two attendants, and this *Bishamon-ten* were made by the Buddhist sculptor *Unkei* in 1186.

New vogue initiated by *Unkei* | *Unkei's Bishamon-ten* exhibits a rakish stance with one hip raised that is unlike anything seen in earlier images of the Four Heavenly Kings with gravity and forcefulness. *Unkei's* aim here was to create Buddhist sculpture filled with vitality and energy that would appeal to worshippers in this new age. This *Bishamon-ten* clearly demonstrates the new Kamakura period Buddhist sculptural style. It is made of Japanese cypress (*hinoki*) in the joined-block technique, and crystals are inserted at the eyes. Originally covered with pigments, the sculpture now reveals the lacquer surface beneath.

鎌倉時代
運慶作毘沙門天立像

Kamakura period
Bishamon-ten Ryūzō
Unkei saku

Data

毘沙門天立像
静岡 願成就院 大御堂
文治２年（1186）
像高 147.0cm
運慶作
国宝
木造 ヒノキ 漆塗り 玉眼

Vaisravana
Standing Bishamon-ten
Ōmi-dō, Ganjōju-in temple, Shizuoka
AD 1186 (Bunji 2)
147.0 cm
Made by Unkei
National Treasure
Wood (Japanese cypress; hinoki), Lacquer, Crystal eyes

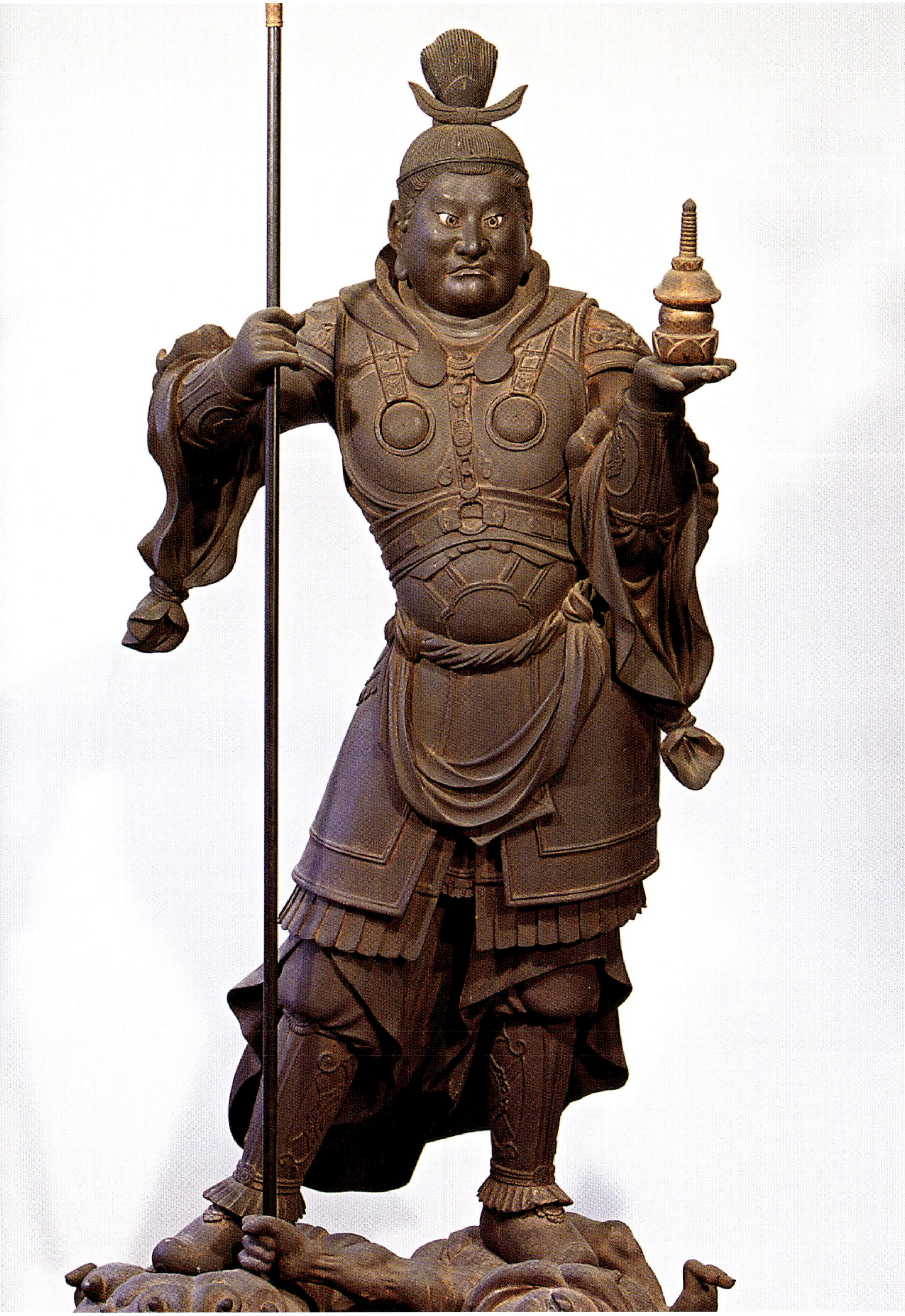

運慶作毘沙門天立像 | Bishamon-ten (Vaisravana)

快慶作阿弥陀三尊立像
Standing Amida Triad *Made by Kaikei*

快慶の美意識と技術
Kaikei's esthetics and technique

けたはずれの数の遺品を残す仏師快慶 | 東大寺の復興を行った勧進上人重源（かんじんしょうにんちょうげん）は、全国7カ所に東大寺の別所を置きました。播磨（はりま）別所である浄土寺もその1つです。浄土寺浄土堂は鎌倉初期の大仏様建築の遺構で、その本尊阿弥陀如来三尊立像は、仏師快慶によって建久6年（1195）に作られました。浄土堂の堂内には朱塗りの四天柱がそびえ立ち、阿弥陀三尊像の背後から夕日が差すと堂内は茜色に染められて、まさに阿弥陀如来が来迎する光景が堂内に出現します。快慶の仏像は現存のものだけでも約40件にのぼり、当時の絶大な人気のほどが知られます。
快慶らしさあふれる阿弥陀三尊像 | 丈六の阿弥陀如来立像は像高5メートルを超え、両脇侍もそれぞれ4メートル近い現存する日本の仏像では最大級の像です。中尊は通常の来迎阿弥陀像とは左右の手の形が逆で、脇侍像の姿も独特ですが、これらは宋仏画に着想を得たものといわれます。他の慶派仏師とは一線を画す豊かな表現力を持つ、快慶の代表作の一つです。各像とも巨像制作には欠かせない寄木造の手法が駆使され、また、主要部材は建物の床下から立てて通し、床下で各材をたがいにしっかりと固定しているなど、巨像ならではの工夫が随所にこらされています。

Unusually large number of extant sculptures by the master *Kaikei* | The monk *Chōgen* who undertook the reconstruction of *Tōdai-ji* temple, also established satellite temples (*bessho*) in seven provinces throughout Japan. One of these was *Jōdo-ji*, also known as *Harima bessho* from its location. The Jōdo Hall of the temple reflects the heritage of early Kamakura period Buddhist architecture, and its main image, the standing Amida Triad, was made by the master sculptor *Kaikei* in 1195. The Jōdo Hall is fitted with four vermillion-lacquered pillars (*shiten-bashira*), which lend a red glow to the hall when the rays of the setting sun come in from behind the central Amida Triad, almost an embodiment of the scene of the *Amida* coming to welcome believers to the Western Paradise. There are approximately forty extant sculptures by *Kaikei*, an indication of his enormous popularity at that time.
Kaikei's style fully evident in the Amida Triad | The total height of the central *Amida* figure is over 5 meters, and the attendant are pair almost 4 meters tall, making them among the largest sculptures extant in Japan. The hand gestures of the central *Amida* are reversed, and the two attendant figures also have some unusual features, which may have been influenced by Chinese Song dynasty painting style. These characteristics are what distinguish *Kaikei's* work from others of the *Kei* school artisans. Each of the triad sculptures are constructed in the joint-block technique, for which the large wood elements had to be brought into the hall from underneath the floor, and then firmly secured in place, all of which necessitated great skill to be accomplished successfully.

鎌倉時代
快慶作阿弥陀三尊立像

Kamakura period
Amida Sanzon Ryūzō
Kaikei saku

Data

阿弥陀如来及び両脇侍立像
兵庫 浄土寺 浄土堂
建久6年（1195）
像高 530.0cm（中尊）
快慶作
国宝
木造 ヒノキ 漆箔

Standing Amida Nyorai and flanking attendants
Jōdo Hall, Jōdo-ji temple, Hyogo
AD 1195 (Kenkyū 6)
530.0 cm (central sculpture)
Made by Kaikei
National Treasure
Wood (Japanese cypress; hinoki), Gold foil applied with lacquer

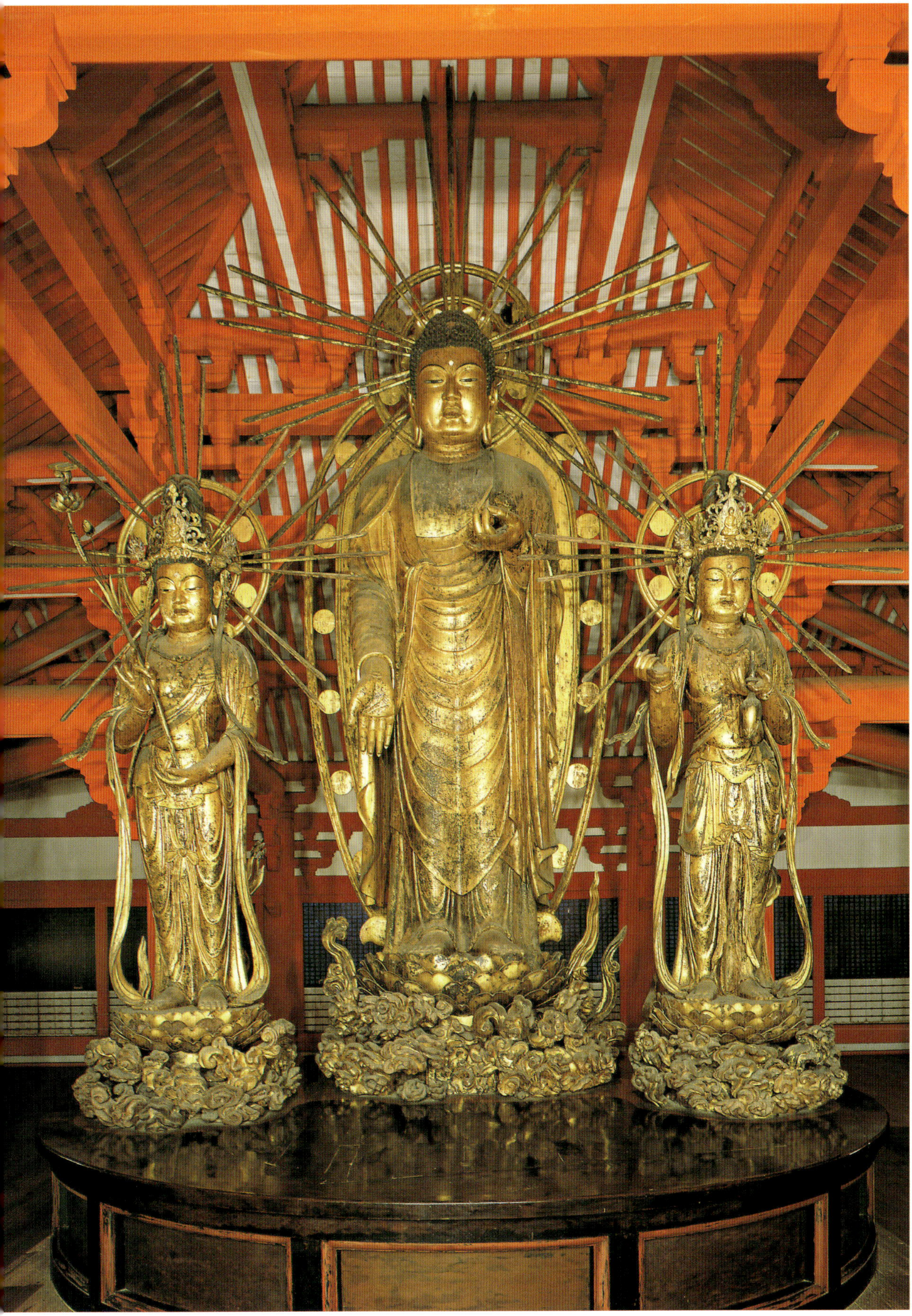

快慶作阿弥陀三尊立像 | Standing Amida Triad

馬頭観音立像
Standing Horse-headed Kannon *Hayagriva*

遥か九州まで広まった和様彫刻
Japanese style sculpture in distant Kyushu

九州を代表する古寺・観世音寺｜日本でも屈指の歴史を誇る福岡県太宰府市の観世音寺は、天智天皇が発願し、完成は天平18年（746）のこととされます。その後の火災などで創建当初の建物の多くを失ったものの、平安時代などの優れた仏像が今日も多く残されており、馬頭観音立像はそのうちの1体です。この像は像内に書かれた銘文から仏師真快（しんかい）・明春（めいしゅん）をはじめとした多くの仏師によって大治年間（1126〜1130）頃に作られたことがわかります。
各地に広がる都の美意識｜馬頭観音像は頭上に文字通り馬の頭を載せ、顔は4面で、各面に3つの目を持ち、8本の手をあらわしています。控えめな怒りの表情で、抑揚の少ない体の線と起伏を強調しない衣文の彫りが相まって、憤怒像でありながらどこか穏やかさを漂わせています。優しげでおっとりとした表現が好まれた平安時代後期の特徴がよくあらわれた仏像です。都から遠く離れた太宰府にも当時の都の流行が伝わっていたのです。5メートルを超える大きな像はヒノキ材の寄木造で、頭部と体部は別に作られ、首の部分で接合されています。体部も複数の材をはぎ、各腕、手首などをはいでいます。

***Kanzeon-ji*, one of Kyushu's ancient temples** | One of a handful of temples with a long history is the *Kanzeon-ji* at Dazaifu in Kyushu, sponsored by Emperor Tenchi and completed in 746. Although many of the original buildings were destroyed by fire, numerous outstanding examples of Heian period sculpture are extant, including an image of a Horse-headed Kannon. An inscription inside the statue gives the names of sculptors *Shinkai* and *Meishun*, among others, who completed it in 1126-1130.
Esthetic standards of the capital spread to the rest of Japan | This eight-armed image of Horse-headed Kannon is literally crowned with a horse head, and has four faces, each of which has three eyes. Its facial expression is one of moderation, combined with the fairly straight torso and flattened folds of the robes lend this normally angry deity a sense of reserve and calm. The image reflects the characteristics of the gentle, sweet expression favored in the late Heian period, and reveals that the influence of the imperial capital at Kyoto made its way even to distant locales such as the Dazaifu. The over 5 meter image is made in the joined-block technique of Japanese cypress (*hinoki*). The head and torso were made separately and joined at the neck. The torso itself is made from several blocks, including both arms which have joints at the wrists where the hands are attached.

平安時代後期
馬頭観音立像

Late Heian period
Batō Kannon Ryūzō

Data

馬頭観音立像
福岡 観世音寺 宝蔵
大治年間（1126〜1130）
像高 500.0cm
真快等作
重要文化財
木造 ヒノキ 漆箔 古色

Hayagriva
Standing Horse-headed Kannon
Hōzō, Kanzeon-ji, Fukuoka, Kyushu
1126-1130 (Daiji era)
500.0 cm
Made by Shinkai and others
Important Cultural Property
Wood (Japanese cypress; hinoki),
Gold foil applied with lacquer,
Traces of color

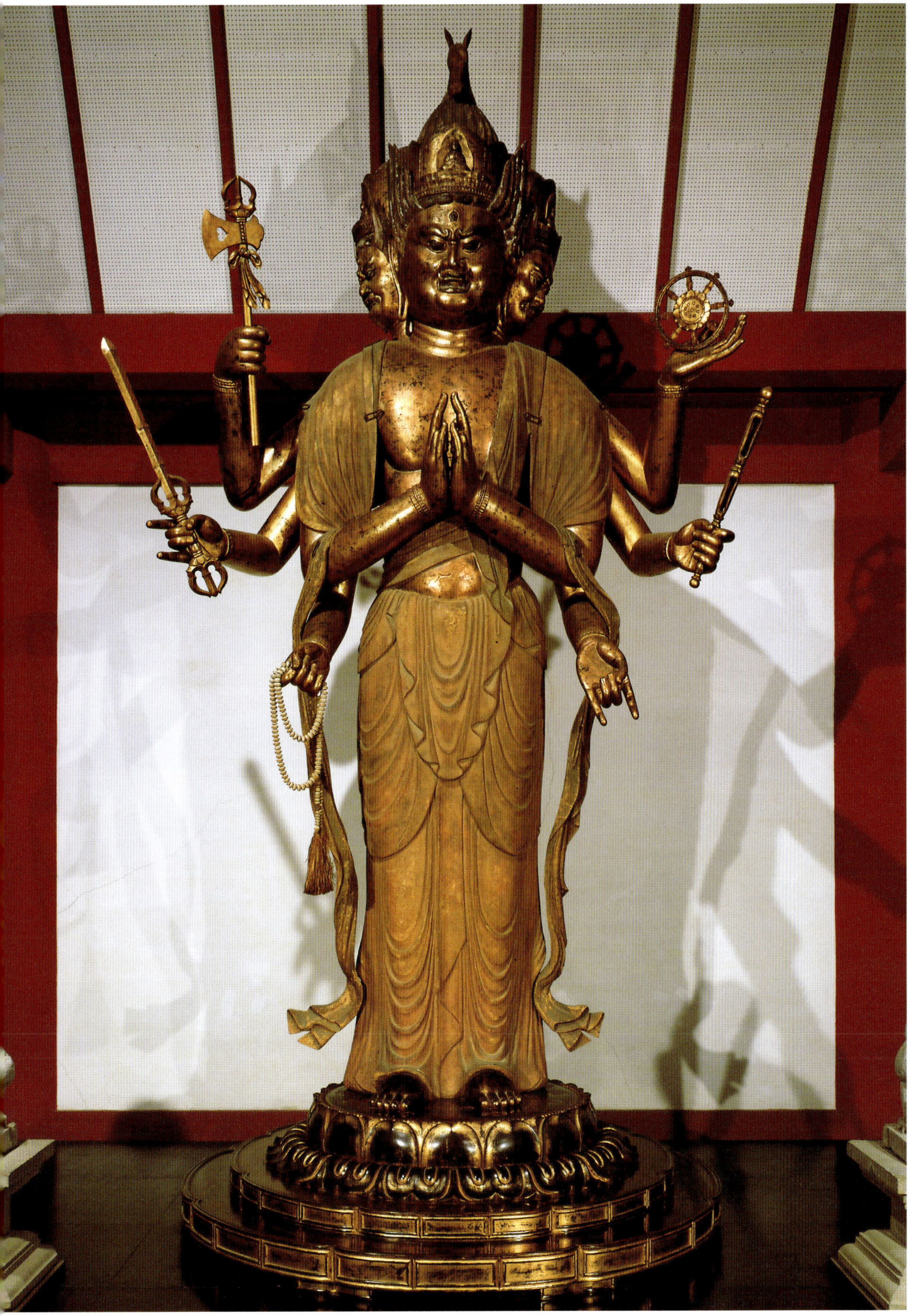

馬頭観音立像　|　Standing Horse-headed Kannon

寺院ガイド

Temple Guide

中尊寺

Chūson-ji temple

岩手県西磐井郡平泉町平泉衣関 202
JR 東北本線平泉駅 徒歩 25 分
Hiraizumi Koromonoseki 202, Hiraizumi-chō, Nishiiwai-gun, Iwate-ken
JR Tohoku Line, Hiraizumi Station, 25 min on foot
OPEN 8:30– CLOSE 17:00 (16:30)
http://www.chusonji.or.jp/
■金色堂諸尊像
Golden Hall and Buddhist Sculpture (→ p.102)

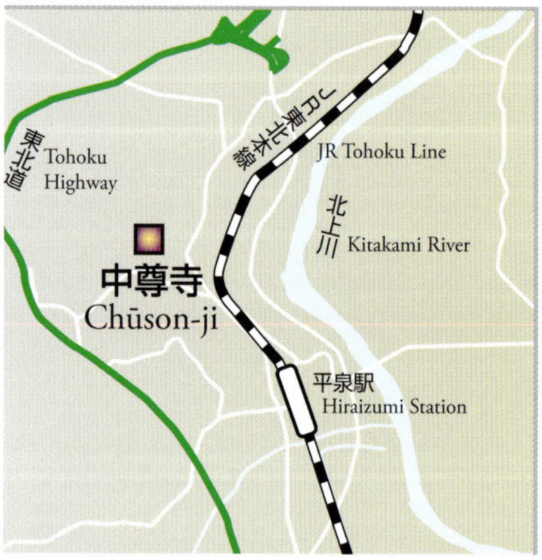

高徳院

Kōtoku-in temple

神奈川県鎌倉市長谷 4-2-28
江ノ島電鉄長谷駅 徒歩 10 分
Hase 4-2-28, Kamakura-shi, Kanagawa-ken
Enoshima Dentetsu Line, Hase Station, 10 min on foot
OPEN 8:00 – CLOSE 17:30 (17:00)
http://www.kotoku-in.jp/
■阿弥陀如来坐像（鎌倉大仏）
Seated Amida Nyorai (the Great Buddha of Kamakura) (→ p.100)

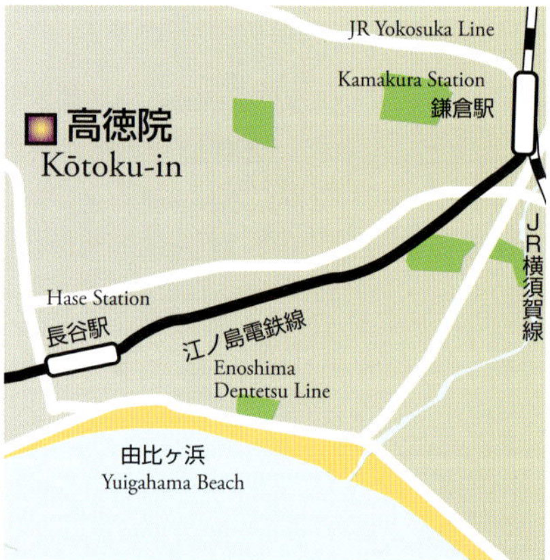

願成就院

Ganjōju-in temple

静岡県伊豆の国市寺家 83-1
伊豆箱根鉄道駿豆線韮山駅 徒歩 15 分
Jike 83-1, Izunokuni-shi, Shizuoka-ken
Izu-hakone Railway Sunzu Line, Nirayama Station, 15 min on foot
OPEN 10:00 – CLOSE 16:00
http://ganjoujuin.jp/
■運慶作毘沙門天立像 Bishamon-ten (Vaisravana) (→ p.104)

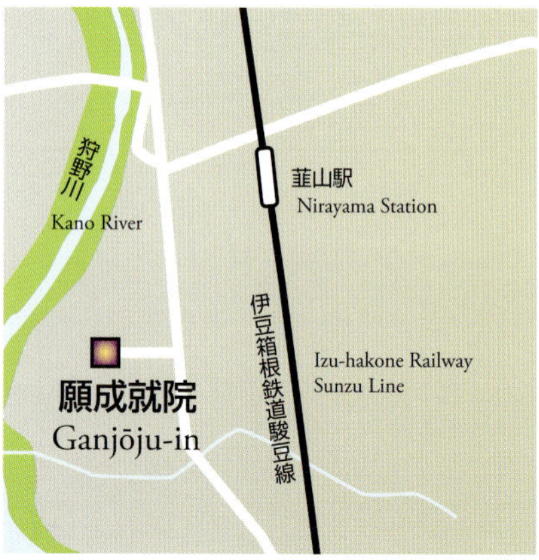

浄土寺

Jōdo-ji temple

兵庫県小野市浄谷町 2094
神戸電鉄粟生線小野駅 バス 30 分 下車すぐ
Kiyotani-chō 2094, Ono-shi, Hyogo-ken
Kobe Dentetsu Ao Line, Ono Station, 30 min by bus, 1 min on foot
OPEN 9:00–12:00, 13:00 – CLOSE 17:00 (16:00)
■快慶作阿弥陀三尊立像 Standing Amida Triad (→ p.106)

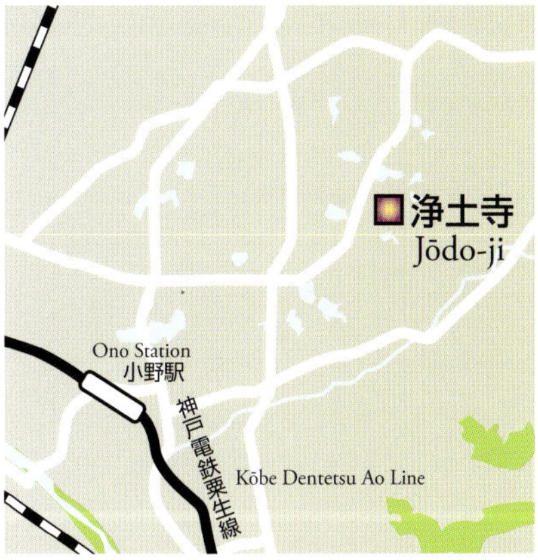

観世音寺

Kanzeon-ji temple

福岡県太宰府市観世音寺 5-6-1
西鉄太宰府線西鉄五条駅 徒歩 10 分
Kanzeon-ji 5-6-1, Dazaifu-shi, Fukuoka-ken
Nishitetsu Dazaifu Line, Nishitetsu Gojō Station, 10 min on foot
OPEN 9:00 – CLOSE 17:00
■馬頭観音立像 Standing Horse-headed Kannon (→ p.108)

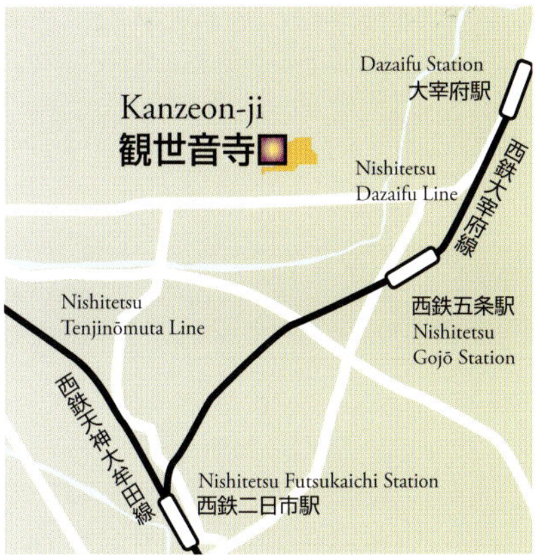

TEMPLE GUIDE

東京国立博物館 Tokyo National Museum

東京都台東区上野公園 13-9 ／ JR 上野駅 徒歩 10 分
Ueno Kōen 13-9, Taitō-ku, Tokyo-to
JR Line and Tokyo Metro, Ueno Station, 10 min on foot
OPEN 9:30 – CLOSE 17:00 http://www.tnm.jp/
■摩耶夫人及び天人像 Lady Maya and Attendants (→ p.96)

大倉集古館 Ōkura Museum of Art

東京都港区虎ノ門 2-10-3 ／東京メトロ日比谷線神谷町駅 徒歩 8 分
Toranomon 2-10-3, Minato-ku, Tokyo-to
Tokyo Metro Hibiya Line, Kamiya-chō Station, 8 min on foot
※ 2019 年まで休館 Closed until 2019. http://www.shukokan.org/
■普賢菩薩騎象像 The Bodhisattva Fugen Riding on an Elephant (→p.98)

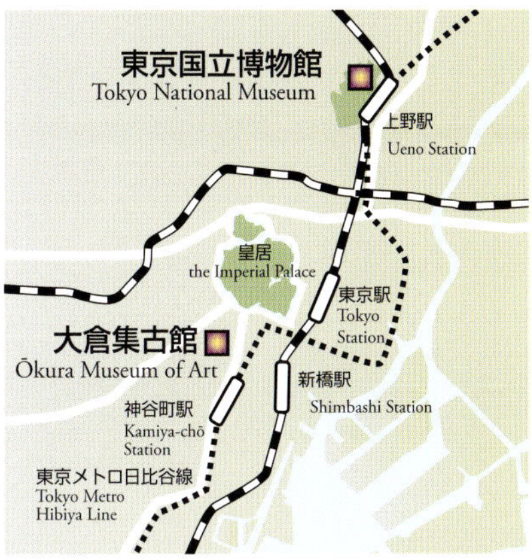

※拝観時間は変更になる場合があります。インターネットや観光案内所でご確認ください。
*Opening hours are subject to change. Please visit websites or tourist bureaus for the latest information.

監修者　副島弘道（そえじま ひろみち）

文化庁・東京国立博物館に勤務した後、跡見学園女子大学教授を経て、現在は大正大学文学部教授。専攻は日本彫刻史・文化財学。『運慶　その人と芸術』（吉川弘文館）、『仏像に会いに行こう　美術の見かた感じかた』（東京美術）、『十一面観音像・千手観音像』（至文堂）などの著書のほか、『日本彫刻史基礎資料集成鎌倉時代造像銘記篇』（中央公論美術出版、既刊1〜13巻）の編集、『仏像の楽しみ方完全ガイド』（池田書店）の監修に携わる。

Supervisor　Hiromichi Soejima

Professor, Faculty of Literature, Taisho University. Specialist in the history of Japanese sculpture and research of cultural properties, he worked with the Agency for Cultural Affairs and Tokyo National Museum. Among his many publications are books about Unkei and his art, Eleven-headed Kannon/Thousand-armed Kannon sculptures, and he is co-editor of a series on Japanese Buddhist sculpture and the supervisor in guidebook of Japanese Buddhist sculpture for beginners.

監訳者　フェリス・フィッシャー

フィラデルフィア美術館東洋美術部部長。専攻は日本文学・日本美術。アメリカで初めて、本阿弥光悦（2000年）、池大雅・徳山玉瀾（2007年）、日本工芸美術（2008年）の展覧会を主催した。2013年旭日双光章受章。

English language editorial supervisor　Felice Fischer

Curator of East Asian Art, Philadelphia Museum of Art. Specialist in Japanese literature and art, who organized the first exhibitions in America of the Arts of Hon'ami Kōetsu (2000), Ike Taiga and Tokuyama Gyokuran (2007), and the Arts of Japanese Crafts (2008). Recipient of the Order of the Rising Sun, Gold and Silver Rays (2013).

編集協力	株式会社オメガ社
執筆協力	宮下真　青木一平　原田晶文
翻訳	森高人　ジェイ・サイバー
本文デザイン	ヤマシタツトム
本文イラスト	スタジオ杉
DTP	株式会社明昌堂

※本書の英文は、英語話者にとってわかりやすい、より自然な英語表現を採用しているため、日本語文と必ずしも一致しないことがあります。

First published in Japan in 2008 by Ikeda Publishing Co., Ltd.

英訳付　仏像鑑賞ガイド

A Guide to Japanese Buddhist Sculpture

監修者　副島弘道
発行者　池田士文
印刷所　図書印刷株式会社
製本所　図書印刷株式会社
発行所　株式会社池田書店
〒162-0851　東京都新宿区弁天町43番地
電話 03-3267-6821（代）／振替 00120-9-60072

落丁・乱丁はおとりかえいたします。

ISBN978-4-262-14533-4

23011510